Best Wishes,

Bill Gildea

THE FUTURE IS NOW

William
Gildea
& Kenneth
Turan

THE FUTURE IS NOW

GEORGE ALLEN
Pro Football's
Most Controversial
Coach

1972 HOUGHTON MIFFLIN COMPANY BOSTON

First Printing c

ISBN: 0-395-14000-5
Library of Congress Catalog Card Number: 72-2051
Printed in the United States of America

To the patience of women

I am betting on the Redskins for the championship in 1971 or 1972.

Richard Nixon
January 29, 1971

Contents

I The Second Coming 1
II The Future Is Now 19
III The Ice Cream Man 37
IV Sounds Like You've Got Yourself a Hell of a Coach 60
V The People's Choice 83
VI Exhibitionism 111
VII The Over the Hill Gang 130
VIII True Believers 149
IX How He Does It 163
X Hail to the Redskins 209
XI Crisis and Controversy 230
XII Presidential Pardon 259
XIII The George Allen Bowl 276
XIV An End and a Beginning 296

Illustrations

following page 154

George Allen — The Future is Now
Allen at Alma College, 1943
Coach Allen with the 1948 Morningside varsity
Allen at his last college job, Whittier College, 1956
Allen at his first professional job, Los Angeles Rams, 1957
Allen and George Halas, Sr.
Allen and George Halas, Jr.
Allen as Rams head coach
A watchful Allen
Allen with Roman Gabriel
Allen: Explaining
Exhorting
Beseeching
Tony Guillory blocks Donny Anderson's punt in Rams' 27-24 victory over Green Bay, 1967
Claude Crabb and Jeff Jordan carry Allen off the field
Dan Reeves hires Allen as Rams Coach, 1966
Lamar Lundy protests Allen's firing, 1968
Edward Bennett Williams introduces new Redskins coach and general manager Allen
Sonny Jurgensen breaks a shoulder bone
Jurgensen applauds his team from the sidelines
A defensive strategy review
Allen congratulates Chris Hanburger
Allen surrounded by fans at Dulles Airport

Allen, with his play books, holds onto his hat
Allen leads the cheers after victory over Houston . . .
and after St. Louis
Charley Taylor scores against Kansas City . . .
and breaks his ankle as he falls into the end zone
Kansas City's Otis Tayor scores despite a clinging Pat Fischer
Diron Talbert after the Redskins first loss
Billy Kilmer and Allen after a 24-14 victory over New Orleans
Allen's final handwritten instructions before meeting the Eagles
An unhappy Baughan, Allen, and Jurgensen in the 7-7 tie with Philadelphia
Chicago's Dick Butkus scores in a 16-15 loss to the Bears
President Richard M. Nixon visits the Redskins . . .
and poses with the team
Allen runs, even in the snow
Allen runs alone
The Ramskins before the Los Angeles game
Allen and football commissioner Pete Rozelle
Allen instructs Kilmer before the George Allen Bowl
We win, Part I
We win, Part II
The beginning of the end. Gene Washington scores a 49er touchdown in the play-off game
Paradise lost. Happy 49ers and a dejected Mike Bragg after a bad center snap in the play-off game
Manny Sistrunk and Myron Pottios in the closing minutes of the game
The end, for now

THE FUTURE IS NOW

CHAPTER I

The Second Coming

SQUINTING INTO A BATTERY of television lights, George Allen stepped into a second-floor conference room at the Washington Redskins downtown office to meet the massed media for the first time in his capacity as the team's coach and general manager.

When the lights were turned down, Allen continued to squint. He squints constantly, as if he has spent too much time in dark rooms watching football films and never really come to terms with daylight. His normal expression is that of a coach who loses most of his games.

In fact, he wins most of them. In five years as coach of the Los Angeles Rams, Allen compiled a 49-17-4 record for a .742 percentage and led his team to two divisional titles while gaining the reputation of a relentless enemy of the status quo by making fifty-one trades.

His 1967 record was 11-1-2 during the regular season and 18-2-2 including preseason and postseason games, an accomplishment, he could rightfully boast, that would stand as the hallmark for future Ram teams. In turning around a seemingly hopeless situation in Los Angeles, seven straight losing seasons, Allen established an unparalleled record of road-game successes, including twenty-three victories in four years.

Fresh from the Chicago Bears, where as George Halas' principal assistant he had forged reputations as defensive architect nonpareil and astute judge of young talent, Allen immediately rebuilt the Rams with a lightning series of successful trades and maintained the winning momentum with still more trades.

So known were his coaching skills by the end of the 1970 season when he was fired by Rams owner Dan Reeves in a personality conflict that Allen remained unemployed only a week. Green Bay wanted him and so did Houston and Philadelphia. Washington begged him to name his own terms. And he did.

Standing there that evening, January 6, 1971, in the Redskins downtown office, which he would soon shut down in his passion for seclusion in suburbia, Allen had reached his almost lifelong dream: a professional coaching job with unlimited authority.

Yet he didn't look like the typical football coach. Though in excellent physical condition, he was pale and sunken-chested and seemed more like a cheerleader or an academic dean. His stooped shoulders gave the impression that he carried the burden of more problems than any man should. He spoke in whispers, not like Lombardi, rather like one of his players. He looked like a guy who had written six books. His favorite drink is milk, his strongest language "Gol dang." And his middle name is Herbert.

Taking control of a $15 million football franchise, he looked more like an absent-minded fellow who had just discovered melted chocolate in his pocket. Fidgeting uncomfortably, he seemed to reinforce one of the countless mottoes he preaches, "Is what I am doing, or about to do, getting us closer to our objective — winning?"

It being a press conference, the answer obviously was no. "We'll have a team that Washington can be proud of," he was saying, but he would rather have been talking long-distance with some other team, plotting one of those multiplayer deals that had become his trademark.

While other coaches believed raw youth was the key to the

future and hoarded draft choices like life itself, Allen surrounded himself with mature veterans who could be counted on to make fewer mistakes and hence win more ball games. Only in such a timid, hidebound organization as the National Football League could such a simplistic philosophy of trading pieces of paper for proven pros be considered revolutionary.

Given a system where winning is everything, Allen functions within it to the utmost, believing nothing is impossible and no price in time or money too much to pay. To him, the first exhibition game is the same as the Super Bowl. A player he once coached in the postseason Pro Bowl, considered a nuisance by many, said, "I couldn't believe that any man could be that intense about a game that really didn't mean anything."

For Allen, who neither eats nor sleeps when he could be making another trade, hunger and fatigue are small discomforts compared to losing. As for money, George Allen had not coached his first league game for the Redskins when their president, Edward Bennett Williams, remarked, "When Coach Allen came to Washington, we agreed he had an unlimited budget. He's already exceeded it."

Knowing a good player when he saw one and knowing what to do with him when he got him, Allen aroused the envy of the have-not franchises around the league and catapulted to the top of the list of most-wanted coaches. One such beleaguered club anxious to romance him was the Redskins. Here was a team with a proud but entirely ancient history, one winning season in the previous fifteen years, and an absence from the play-offs for twenty-five years.

Clearly, he was just what the Redskins needed. Scant of material and mired in morale problems, they offered the perfect allure for Allen. Asked one time why he took his first job at tiny Morningside College in Iowa, he replied, "Because they hadn't won a conference game in two years." Likewise, the Redskins provided a fitting disaster to improve upon.

Then, too, there was the matter of money. An unprecedented contract that would make him the highest-paid coach in NFL history, perhaps in all of sports, included a raft of benefits, in all a $1 million package. The $125,000-a-year salary for seven years was just for openers.

Among the fourteen points of his contract were a $25,000 bonus simply for signing, the home of his choice up to $150,000, incentive bonuses, a limousine and chauffeur, an unlimited expense account, and something Allen's craving for work will never permit him to accept, six weeks' annual vacation. There also was the understanding that Allen could purchase stock in the club.

There were bonuses each year of $5000 for reaching the divisional play-off, $10,000 more for getting to the conference championship game, and $15,000 more for making it to the Super Bowl. There were travel expenses for visiting his family on the West Coast until they moved to Washington, hotel expenses until he got a house in Washington, permission to keep all revenue from television and radio appearances and personal endorsements.

Avoiding the subject of money that night he was introduced to the press by Edward Bennett Williams, Allen listed three reasons that influenced his decision to choose Washington:

"Complete authority to run the football program. I don't think Paul Brown could have had the success he has had at Cincinnati without calling all the shots.

"A situation where you can show improvement. The Washington situation is parallel to that of the Rams in 1966. When we went there, they had seven straight years of losing football.

"The opportunity to bring my family to a great area, the nation's capital, a fine area for education."

Shortly, the extent of Allen's power became dramatically clear when a seven-acre wooded site far out in the Virginia countryside near Dulles Airport was staked out and a $500,000 office building and practice complex took shape in less than four months. Complete with exercise rooms and sauna bath, carpeted locker room and half basketball court, this was to become Allen's sylvan paradise, one of those impossibilities he considered essential to winning.

Surveying the green expanse from his office one quiet morning after his first season, Allen said, "I can remember coming out here and walking around and I had on a new pair of knit pants — I've always just worn regular trousers — and I got caught out in these prickers and bushes and, holy cripes, I ruined the pants. They just ran like stockings.

"But I said, 'Hey, we're going to build two football fields and office facilities and training facilities right here.' Well, gee, everybody thought this guy is nuts. You know, 'How are we going to do it? At least why don't we take one of those clearings over there?' I said, 'No, we want it surrounded by woods on three sides with the building on the fourth side.' I wanted it that way for privacy, for concentration. I think when the players come out here it helps them understand that we're here for one thing, to prepare to win. I think it's more aesthetic. You're out in the country, not surrounded by a wall. The worst thing we could have done would have been to keep the same team and the same facilities because I don't think we would have won.

"But it took a selling job. First, I had to convince Ed Williams, then we in turn had to convince the board of directors. I told them it was something that had to be done, that we'd been in last place so gad-darned long that it was time we do something positive for a change.

"And what's more, I said we could get it done this year. Well, nobody believed we could get it done this year."

The Redskins directors just didn't know George Allen. Neither did the Washington fans, really. Despite the coach's promise of a winning team immediately, the Redskin faithful greeted his arrival with skepticism. Ed Williams' ebullient recommendation of his new man as "the best football coach in the world" did nothing to stir excitement. Washingtonians had had their momentary saviors only to be inevitably filled with disappointment. The city was in no mood to celebrate.

For just two years before, it had witnessed a similar transfer of power when Williams turned over the Redskins to Vince Lombardi. At news of the coming of that untempered autocrat and Green Bay legend, the town went bananas. "I've just asked Vince if I could have my same season tickets," Williams said in jest the day Lombardi came to Washington. His status was that of demigod and the community was grateful.

But the Vince Lombardi story never got past act one. Cut down by cancer, Lombardi had given Washington the hint of what winning football would be like with a 7-5 record in his only season as Redskins coach, but following his death on the eve of the 1970 season, the Redskins immediately lapsed into their traditionally chaotic ways. Many came to view the town itself as a jinx.

Compounding the depression was a deterioration of the entire Washington sports scene. The baseball Senators were plotting their move to Texas. The basketball Caps had shifted their franchise to Virginia the year before. The city's soccer team, the Darts, were moving to Florida. The world's light-heavyweight boxing champion, Bob Foster, left to become a deputy sheriff in Albuquerque, New Mexico.

Washington had witnessed the end of too many eras. All the fun had gone out of the city. Even the weekly wrestling shows folded. No more Killer Kowalski and Bobo Brazil. The 625-pound Haystacks Calhoun was just a memory.

Into this sports desert stepped Allen, who vowed to win now by attacking the Redskins' most urgent problem, their porous defense, which ranked last in its conference against the rush the year before and twelfth out of thirteen teams in overall performance.

"I intend to concentrate on defense where I will spend a

majority of my time," Allen said in his first meeting with the Washington press. "Our whole thinking is to get the defense riled up. That will be my main goal. If there's the opportunity to get a solid football player, we'll trade." Whatever had to be done — obtaining players, increasing the number of coaches and scouts, buying land and building the training complex — Allen wanted to do it in one swoop and knew how to.

"I'm impatient," he reflected, after the 1971 season. "I don't want to have to say we're going to win next year or the next year. Everything we do is designed to help us win now. I believe in the first year you take over a job, whether it's insurance or banking or whatever, you have to make the changes that are necessary. I think if you wait a year and don't make the changes you lose something with your employees in the organization.

"There was some talk among the Redskins board of directors, 'Well, let's make them next year or the year after,' because it costs so much to do all this. I told them things had to be done, whether it was this year or next year or the year after, and we should make the changes the first year. If you change the first year, you have a chance to win, you see."

Holding the traditional NFL theory that a winning team is built painstakingly through the college draft, many Washington fans grew alarmed at Allen's references to trading, charging that he would ruin the long-range future of the team. A few went so far as to sell their season tickets to friends.

Bending enough to concede that Allen's preference for tested players might not be such a radical idea, Oakland's moving force Al Davis allowed, "With twenty-six teams selecting, it may be impossible to build a champion through the draft." But not even such a forward thinker as Davis could feel comfortable with the Allen technique in its purest form, which is not simply trading draft choices but all the draft choices. "I don't think," Davis added, "you have to go as far as he does."

On the draft day shortly after he took over the Redskins, the day Allen proved to Washington he was a shaker and trader the likes of which had not been seen, the Allen philosophy was manifested by his determination to trade more draft choices still. Having already unloaded seven that day, Allen, the story goes, sought desperately to deal the Redskins' second-round pick, which somehow still remained in his possession.

As the club's turn to choose came up in the New York meeting room, Allen frantically worked the phones in the Redskins office trying to make a deal. At the last minute, St. Louis offered a receiver, Dave Williams, but former Cardinal coach Charley Winner, now an Allen aide, talked Allen out of it.

Desperate for guidance with the time allotted to draft a collegian expired, the Redskins representative in New York, unable to raise anyone on the open line to Washington, blurted, "Washington takes Cotton Speyrer." Just then Allen picked up the phone to inquire what had happened. Told that Cotton Speyrer, the receiver from Texas, belonged to the Redskins, a frustrated Allen sputtered, "Look, I don't want Sprayer, Spryer, or whatever his name is."

But Allen had him just the same, a real, live draft choice, and he made the best of it. Midway through training camp, he did what came naturally, trading him to Baltimore in a deal for a veteran receiver, Roy Jefferson.

"The theory that I don't like draft choices is incorrect," Allen explained after his first Washington season. "We like certain draft choices, like firsts. I'm interested in firsts.

"The building procedure can work both ways. When I was an assistant with the Bears and when I was in Los Angeles, both times, we traded for draft choices and had three first-round picks in one year. We got Dick Butkus, Gale Sayers, and Steve DeLong with the Bears and Bob Klein, Larry Smith, and Jim Seymour for the Rams.

"It all depends on what you have available and the timing of the situation. The Bears had a pretty good team so we didn't have to do some of the things we had to do with the Redskins. So I feel that while we're trading choices now, when the situation is right, we'll come up to a period where we'll get some extra-high draft choices in trade. The important thing is getting on top quickly and dealing from strength.

"Now if a coach doesn't have the authority to do this, then he's always going to be frustrated. Yet there are some cases where I think if you give a coach the authority and he isn't ready for it, if he hasn't had the background and experience, he's going to hurt the organization. He's going to make decisions that are unsound, you see. That's happened many times throughout the league. All you have to do is look around and you'll see it.

"The break I got was that George Halas gave me a lot of leeway, a lot of authority, with the Bears and so even though I was an assistant coach I was doing nearly all the trading. I was doing all the drafting and I did a lot of the signing. So when I took over the Rams job, it wasn't just another assistant coach coming in. I had been doing the same thing in the background in Chicago."

His Los Angeles record notwithstanding, Washington could not be blamed for its cautious appraisal, for this was radical doctrine, indeed, promising to get something done, and quick, in a town where from Capitol Hill on down things happened in a painfully metered way and often not at all.

In addition, the city had been let down badly, even before Lombardi's coming. Hired away from the Coast Guard Academy in a coach-naping as trumpeted in Washington as Lombardi's and Allen's, Otto Graham arrived to buoy expectation beyond all reality. Those who remembered Graham as the arm around which Paul Brown built his Cleveland Browns rationalized that anyone who could throw a football as well as he did could coach a team with equal facility. When Ed Williams told Earl Warren confidentially that he had hired Graham, the former Chief Justice replied incredulously, "No shit!"

Hailing him as a messiah, the Redskins gave Graham $60,-000 for five years, but Graham, naive in the ways of the pro league, failed to last the duration. From 1966 through 1968, he coached, if that is the word, the Redskins to a 17-22-3 record while failing to maintain much discipline and abdicating much of his authority to Williams, who made locker-room pep talks on Graham's behalf. When Graham went on vacation after his third season, Williams made it permanent by charming Lombardi out of Green Bay.

Secure again in the tranquillity of the Coast Guard Academy, Graham told a reporter, "Coaching the Redskins proved to be quite an education for me, most of it an unpleasant initiation into the way life really is in professional sports.

"You're living a life where you're dealing with selfish people day in and day out. I just don't like to associate with that. Nothing is worth it. I talked to Lombardi about it. He said, 'Otto, this is a dog-eat-dog business and you have to be an s.o.b. one hundred per cent of the time.' That's what he told me."

When Allen arrived, the fourth coach in four years, it was the fans who were disillusioned. Lombardi's successor, Bill Austin, had watched his chances for more than a one-year term evaporate along with a nineteen-point lead in a midseason game in New York.

"We have had a losing syndrome for fifteen seasons with one exception," Williams said in his introduction of Allen. "The fans are impatient. I think we are obliged to get the best possible coach and personnel. I think we have taken a dramatic step in signing George Allen."

Then Williams added, "I am saying unequivocally, unqualifiedly, and unambiguously that this is the last coach I will ever hire."

Superfan that he is, Williams had little taste for firing Austin, Graham, and Graham's predecessor, Bill McPeak. Far more trying for Williams was Lombardi's death. All the expectations suddenly vanished when it became known that Lombardi was gravely ill.

For the Redskins, all hope seemed gone. This was the nadir of the highly successful trial lawyer's club presidency, which began in 1965. As a young man, Williams had played only sandlot football and failed to make the college baseball team at Holy Cross, but he brought to the Redskins a passionate desire to win, which he did consistently in the courtroom.

With the Redskins, he had to adjust to losing, a difficult transition for him. He listened to players' gripes during the McPeak regime, he tried to restore order under Graham, stormed into the coaches' quarters at half time under Austin. Only under Lombardi could Williams enjoy football.

The burden of worrying about winning on his shoulders once more with Lombardi gone, Williams had to find someone who could make Sunday afternoons fun again. Once before he had talked with Allen about the Redskin job, when Reeves fired Allen for the first time, the morning after Christmas 1968, but couldn't make it stick in the face of a possible player revolt. That same day Allen heard from Jack Kent Cooke, owner of the Los Angeles Lakers and Kings hockey team as well as a Redskins minority stockholder.

"I got a hand-delivered message from Jack," Allen recalled, "saying that it was urgent that I call him. He had tried to call me but the phone was so busy he couldn't get through. Two days later Ed Williams flew out to Jack's home in Bel Air and we met for approximately three hours.

"I told them then that I was interested in the Redskins job but I wanted to finish my job in Los Angeles. I thought we had a chance to win the championship. I still had two years left on my contract and I wanted to complete the job.

"I remember Jack made the statement at that time, 'It's ten thousand to one that you'll get the job back.' And I said, 'Well, I'd like to take that one shot.' We had built a home and had made so much progress with the team. I felt that once you start a job you should try to finish it."

As Redskins president, Williams had felt the impact of

trading with Allen earlier that year. Having drafted quarterback Gary Beban out of UCLA on the second round of the 1968 draft, the Rams would not offer nearly enough money to satisfy the Heisman Trophy winner. Informed of the impasse by Reeves, Allen said, with no apparent remorse, "It looks like we'll have to trade Beban." In an incredible exchange, Allen slickered the Redskins' number one draft choice from Williams, even though Beban's worth was fixed at the second round just weeks before. That added up to a short-term gain even Allen found hard to believe. What's more, Williams was stuck with the contract he himself had negotiated with Beban, a three-year no-cut arrangement worth $350,000. In return, the Redskins got next to nothing, Beban never adjusting to the pro game and Williams not to this day recovering his equanimity over the matter.

"He mentions the amount of the contract the Redskins had to pay — that bothers him more than losing the pick," Allen said. "Beban's still collecting on it."

"Gary Beban," Ed Williams said wistfully, getting to his feet and beginning to pace back and forth behind his desk as if he were about to deliver a courtroom defense. "Beban, Beban was a bad deal. It was Jack Kent Cooke's and my idea. Jack touted me on him and I got cracking with Beban's agent, Arthur Morse. I remember Bud Wilkinson told me before Beban got out of college that he would make a great defensive back, he was such a good athlete and had good speed. Poor Gary, he just couldn't cut it. I don't know why. George doesn't talk about it. He probably doesn't want to embarrass me.

"We do talk about a trade we didn't make," added Williams, again comfortable in his chair and contemplating a February snowstorm smacking his office windows. "Otto agreed to give the Rams Charley Taylor and Allen was going to give us a number one choice and three players who weren't even playing regularly for him, Tony Guillory, Willie Ellison, and Henry Dyer, three guys he wouldn't have missed.

"That's the one trade Otto wanted to make that I overruled, although, God knows, I should have stopped more of them, like that one when he traded Paul Krause to Minnesota for Marlin McKeever. Anyway, Graham was furious and Allen was on the other end of the phone egging him on, saying things like, 'I thought you were the general manager. What's Williams, that lawyer, doing interfering with you?' George told me that he could have won the world championship with Taylor, that it would have been what he called the greatest bank job of his career."

Having met Allen for the first time at a league meeting in Hawaii following the 1966 season, Allen's first in Los Angeles, Williams quickly became fascinated by the coach during a three-hour conversation, strictly on football.

"George is not the kind of guy you go out on the town with and laugh and expect to have a great deal of mirth," Williams said. "He talks football to the exclusion of everything else. There's really no other interest in his life. To most people, this can become very monotonous and it certainly circumscribes his area for friendships.

"Looking back, I think it was inevitable that he and Reeves would clash. Both of their interests were in football, that was the problem. I think Reeves resented Allen because he wasn't able to operate the ball club the way he had with previous coaches. Allen wouldn't stand for it. Then, too, Reeves fancied himself as the master of the draft. He disliked George intensely, but it made no sense to fire him off his won-lost record either the first time or the second time. I was very interested in him the first time because I was having a hell of a time getting stock for Lombardi and that was the only way I could get him out of Green Bay.

"The second time Green Bay went all out to get Allen. There were five teams in all after him. But I felt we had the inside track because of George's friendship with both Jack and me. Both of us felt, without question, that he was the man to get. I had become convinced the first time I met him that he was going to be 'the' coach of the NFL one day, and I said so to several people. I mean, look at his dedication. He works while other people in sports sleep."

To Williams, Allen's record in Los Angeles spoke for itself. The winningest coach in the conference, he had led the Rams to a third-place finish in 1966, first in 1967, second in 1968, first in 1969, and second in 1970. The 11-1-2 season in 1967 was the best in Rams history. That year he was named Coach of the Year by UPI and *The Sporting News* and shared the Associated Press honor. The record was 10-3-1 in 1968, in 1969 11-3.

Equally impressive was Allen's dedication to his work, which he had set down in a series of aphorisms that had come to be known as "Allen's Ten Commandments":

1. Football comes first.
2. The greatest feeling in life is to take an ordinary job and accomplish something with it.
3. If you can accept defeat and open your pay envelope without feeling guilty, then you're stealing.
4. Everyone, the head coach especially, must give 110 per cent.
5. Leisure time is that five or six hours when you sleep at night.
6. No detail is too small. No task is too small, or too big.
7. You must accomplish things in life, otherwise you are like the paper on the wall.
8. A person without problems is dead.
9. We win and lose as a team.
10. My prayer is that each man will be allowed to play to the best of his ability.

In Washington, Allen's mottoes, it was understood, would be severely tested. Of all the problems with this team, the main ones were the woeful defense and special teams, the Redskins punt-return average of less than two yards the year before Allen's arrival being an acute embarrassment.

There were no Merlin Olsens or Deacon Joneses on this

club. The entire defensive unit was enough to make a coach shudder, the worst part being the line, known for its docile rush. The linebacking seemed disorganized, the defensive backs small.

Prideful of his defense and special teams in Los Angeles, Allen promised a complete overhaul with new techniques and new personnel and often mentioned quarterback Sonny Jurgensen's disadvantage of having had to play for almost his entire career on teams notorious for their poor defenses.

"I stay familiar with every ball club in the league as much as I can," Allen said, "and I knew a lot about the Redskins. We had played them in nineteen sixty-nine in Washington and nineteen sixty-seven in Los Angeles and we had traded with them. I felt they had excellent offensive personnel and that if we could get a defense we'd have a chance to win. I thought that was a special challenge, making the changes on defense and making them that first year.

"So when Ed Williams called the second time around we set up another interview. We met at Jack Kent Cooke's ranch and, except for my attorney working out the details, it was pretty much settled there right away because of my friendship with Jack and Ed and because the Washington job was one you could improve on.

"One of the first things I did then was start quizzing everybody about the Redskins. That's what I always try to do, find out as much information as I can on the situation and about everybody in the program. I asked some questions at that first press conference. I'd ask fans on the street.

"One time I jumped into a cab and I said, 'Hey, how about the Redskins? What do they need? What do you think?' And the guy said, 'That Charley Taylor, he's a good one, they need another receiver like him.' I'll ask anybody because someone might hit on something that everyone else has overlooked.

"I remember even asking President Nixon, 'What do you think we have to do here to win in Washington?' All I can remember him saying was, 'I think you should have taken the job when it was offered to you the first time.' "

For his first day on the job, Allen scheduled a conference with Jurgensen. Like all new Redskin coaches, he seemed compelled to talk to Jurgensen first. Until Allen's arrival, the quarterback was regarded as "Mr. Redskin," the high liver who had arrived from Philadelphia in 1964 with a corpulence at his waistline evidencing the good life and a passing arm that could deliver victory despite even the worst betrayals by his defenses. The Redskins game plan could be summed up in one game under Graham in 1966 when they allowed the Giants forty-one points. But, behind Jurgensen, they scored seventy-two.

Graham had been more concerned with Jurgensen's stomach than his arm. Told to get rid of his belly before the 1966 season, Jurgensen did, weighing in at 192 after losing 31 pounds in five weeks, but it didn't help the Redskins win any games. "I don't throw with my stomach," he said with more than a little logic.

Lombardi went for Jurgensen's heart. "I want you to be yourself," Lombardi told him. "Don't emulate anyone else. Don't try to be someone you're not." He didn't want Jurgensen trying to be Bart Starr, and Jurgensen appreciated that. "Everything Coach Lombardi said made sense. I'm as happy as I can be."

Emerging from his talk with Allen, Jurgensen said, "I was very impressed. He seemed to be an extremely organized individual. He said defense is of prime importance. He said our major goals would be, one, to win and have a championship season and, two, to get our defense going." Then he added, laughing, "Coach promised me the defense will get the ball for us on the fifty-yard line or closer."

But the next few days brought forth a clear truth: the old order changeth. No longer would these be Jurgensen's Redskins, but Allen's Redskins.

A hint of things to come was contained in the announcement of Allen's new staff. He was importing five of his Los Angeles aides, Ted Marchibroda, Boyd Dowler, Marv Levy, LaVern Torgeson, and Joe Sullivan.

"To win a championship," Allen said, "you have to have everything going together, even the girl at the switchboard. The league is that tough and that balanced."

He didn't get the switchboard operator, but his personal secretary was enticed to cross the continent with her boss. Also joining the air shuttle east was a retired Long Beach policeman named Ed Boynton, known as "Double O," whose principal job was to be security.

When Allen assembled his staff with the Rams, he had set up operations in a hotel conference room, which he equipped with a blackboard and projector, near O'Hare Field in Chicago. Since most of the assistants he wanted were from the Midwest, he could fly them in and out and finish the job quickly.

"There were five head coaching jobs open at the time, which meant a new staff for each franchise," Allen recalled. "I might have lost an assistant if I had to wait an extra day. Good assistants make or break a head coach.

"I think if you're fairly well organized and put the time in you can do a lot of things at once. And that's what I was doing when I came to Washington: putting the staff together right down to the trainers and secretaries, planning our new building, and working on trades. I stayed up almost all night a lot of times and didn't sleep at all sometimes when I got to bed. Oh, cripes, a lot went into this."

On the night of January 27, the eve of the NFL player draft, the President of the United States gave a party for Prince Juan Carlos and Princess Sophia of Spain, and George Allen and his wife, Etty, were invited.

Normally, his friends say, Allen enjoys the social life of Howard Hughes, shunning his fellow man to concentrate on football. Yet there he was whispering to the President the likely events of the following day.

"I mentioned to him," Allen said, "that we were about to make a big trade. I still wasn't positive it would materialize but I told him we were on the verge of it. I had been talking on, talking on, talking on with the Rams, you see. We were on the phone at one spell for six hours straight. Hours and hours and hours of calls. You don't make a trade like that one in one phone call."

CHAPTER II

The Future Is Now

IT WAS JANUARY 28, 6 A.M., on the West Coast when the phone rang, awaking Marlin McKeever from a deep sleep. The voice on the other end said George Allen was calling.

"I knew he wasn't calling at six in the morning to check on my health," said McKeever, sensing he was about to become an ex-Redskin. "I knew something was up. Then George got on the line and told me he thought I'd be pleased. I figured he traded me to some West Coast team but when he told me the Rams I couldn't believe it."

The middle linebacker was going back to his original team. As the Rams coach, Allen had traded McKeever to Minnesota.

"When George calls," McKeever said, "I know I'm going somewhere."

This time he was part of the spectacular trade that introduced Washington to Allen's ways. One of the biggest deals in league history, it insured there would be, if not a winning at least a different-looking Redskin team in 1971.

Swapping seven draft choices in all, plus McKeever, Allen obtained six of his favorite Rams in return, including an entire unit of linebackers.

In Washington, the coach was back on page one of all three dailies just three weeks after his hiring. The reaction to the trade was one of staggering disbelief.

"Are you kidding?" people asked when they heard. "Traded seven draft choices? I'll believe it when I see it."

Switchboards at the papers were jammed.

"Did Allen really get six Rams?"

"Allen must be crazy. What's he trying to do?"

"Is it true one of those guys can't even walk?"

Indeed, it was. One of the six, linebacker Maxie Baughan, was about to undergo a foot operation, could barely stand up, and was in fact to spend the entire season on the injured-reserve list. The others were linebackers Jack Pardee and Myron Pottios, defensive tackle Diron Talbert, guard John Wilbur, and special teams' standout Jeff Jordan, plus a fifth-round draft choice which somehow snuck in there.

Allen gave up his first and third draft picks that day and numbers three through seven the following year. Later in the day, he traded that one choice he got from the Rams to Green Bay for Boyd Dowler, already an Allen assistant coach but whose player rights were still held by the Packers.

His sunken eyes telegraphing a lack of sleep, Allen nevertheless was overjoyed. "This is great, terrific for the Redskins," he said. "We've upgraded our defense at least twenty-five per cent. It's worth at least two victories. Our goal now is nine or ten wins."

He was reshaping the Redskins with his most faithful loyalists from the Rams, this being the second time he had traded for Pottios, Baughan, and Wilbur, whom he had previously imported to Los Angeles. And he had talked Pardee out of retirement five years before. So what if most of them were approaching middle age? Allen wanted experienced players.

Paralleling his initial moves with the Rams, Allen had accomplished precisely the same thing, an overhaul of the linebacking corps. As Ram coach, he changed all three linebackers before he had been on the job three months. From Philadelphia he brought in Baughan and from Pittsburgh he acquired Pottios. He went to the Texas A. & M. coaching staff to get Pardee, who had retired from the Rams. From Chicago, Allen imported the long-time defensive all-pro Bill George, who coached Baughan, Pottios, and Pardee in Allen's defensive system.

Though he never played for the Redskins, Baughan, in

turn, taught the young linebackers Allen's way of doing things, calling the Allen system the most complicated in football. There were ninety to one hundred audibles that could be called at the line of scrimmage, Pottios added. At thirty-five the epitome of a well-conditioned athlete, Pardee went on to become all-pro, and Pottios turned in one of his better seasons.

"The only time age will hurt a team," Pardee said the day he became a Redskin, "is when all the old players quit at the same time. This is what happened at Green Bay. George is not going to let that happen."

"What I've always tried to do," Allen elaborated after his first Redskin season, glancing periodically at an organizational table on his office wall, "is have a veteran backed up by a rookie or second-year man, something like that. For every experienced player, every old player, we usually have a young one behind him, being brought along slowly.

"You also have to get the right type of experienced players, the ones who can go on beyond the thirty age limit and still be efficient. We had people in camp who were old men at twenty-two, but if you get the Jack Pardees, the Rich Petitbons, you're all right.

"They take care of themselves, they know what it means to be prepared, and they can go on almost indefinitely. Actually, this is what Gordie Howe and Alex Delvecchio are doing right now in hockey and what Hank Aaron is doing in baseball. These are the kind of people we try to get, see. Even if they retire, it wouldn't hurt that much because we've been training people, some of them on the taxi squad, to step right into the job. They're not rookies and most of them have been in big games. But we don't believe in training players primarily in the games.

"I've seen it happen too many times where you're counting on somebody right out of college to help you and the guy never pans out. You get very few people who can come in their very first year and win for you, the percentages show that.

"What the Redskins needed were defensive players and this

is what we got from the Rams. We got football players who were winners, who would help us win at once, and I knew we couldn't get that in the draft. Even though we had our first choice, we were looking for a defensive lineman most of all and there weren't any available we wanted.

"I talked so long on the phone trying to get what I wanted that my ear got so sore I had to put the receiver on the other side and then put it back again to the other ear. I know I stayed up until four in the morning making the gad-danged trade, I know that because the guy on the other end of the line said, 'Boy, oh boy, what the heck time is it there? Boy, it's getting late here.'

"We kept getting off on tangents, talking about other players. You never get exactly what you want but in this case I got almost exactly what I wanted. I wanted Petitbon, too, but they wouldn't trade him, although I eventually got him.

"The trade was nailed down well before four in the morning but it's like buying a house or a suit, you know you're going to do it, it's just what shape you want or what color you want. It was just the matter of a few details, like I wanted one draft choice back from the Rams, a decent one, so we got a fifth which we in turn traded to Green Bay for Dowler."

The principal figure in the trade, Allen declared when he made it, was Diron Talbert, 6-5, 255 pounds, and only twenty-six years old, one of the most promising defensive linemen in pro football. Even Prothro admitted Talbert would have played regularly for the Rams and that he would be missed. As for Talbert himself, he was jubilant to be following Allen, answering the phone in his Seal Beach apartment that day, "Hello, Washington Redskins . . ."

"As we view it," Allen further stated, "Talbert was our number one pick in the draft. He'll move in and play for us next year, setting the pace for our defensive line. You draft a rookie and it might take three years for him to start. We need someone now."

In the White House idiom, one thing was perfectly clear about Allen's philosophy: "If you want something bad enough, buy it. Don't let it worry you that the other team will want more for a player than he's worth because they know you're interested. If they want another draft choice, give it to them. What do you care as long as you get the player you want. The future is now."

Happy to be a part of it, Talbert said, "This is the greatest thing that's ever happened to me in pro football."

In the following months, Talbert was to become the social celebrity of the Redskins, being seen in five-star restaurants and even escorting Ethel Kennedy on an evening out.

Improbable as it might seem that Talbert, a mustachioed, overgrown type, would escort Mrs. Kennedy, it was, said a teammate, "one of the high points of the season."

Picking her up at Averell Harriman's Georgetown home, Talbert and friend joined Ray Schoenke, John Wilbur, Myron Pottios, and their wives at the Kennedy Center to see singer Kris Kristofferson.

In all seriousness, one Redskin called Ethel Kennedy-Diron Talbert, "a natural match — in fact, I'm sorry it didn't blossom into something more serious.

"One thing," he added, "Allen is in favor of Diron getting married. Every time the coach sees a guy with little kids, he gets all excited. They make a guy more stable."

Seemingly more at home hunting Russian boar, Talbert did just that in Texas after the season. Less serious than the others in his party about tracking the prey, Talbert finally obliged one afternoon and went off with a pack of dogs to see what he could find.

Hearing all sorts of commotion down a ravine, the dogs having trapped a boar, Talbert moseyed down to have a look, when, to his amazement, the boar, all 450-500 pounds, took dead aim on him and roared directly his way.

Firing three shots from his pistol with the boar practically on him, Talbert watched with relief as it staggered up an embankment and expired.

On the plane that took the Rams home from a game in New York with the Giants, Allen's last as Rams coach, Talbert had told him, "If you're not going to be with the Rams next season I'd like to play with you wherever you are." The only unsigned Ram that season, he continued at loggerheads with the front office over money, making it easier to part with him. Happy at the prospect of getting what he considered his fair share from Allen, Talbert even threw a "Welcome to Washington" party the night he became a Redskin.

Noting the differing philosophies of the two teams, Allen told reporters, "I was in Los Angeles for five years and I knew they liked draft choices. I like players.

"Talbert is one of the best ten or twelve tackles in the league. He is more desirable than Deacon Jones or Merlin Olsen because his future is ahead of him. He sacked quarterbacks sixteen times by himself last season. Think of that, sixteen times.

"The three new linebackers will give us players who know the system. Despite his age, Pottios had his best season last year. Pardee is playing handball today to get in shape for next season.

"People in Washington haven't seen anyone on the special teams hit the way Jeff Jordan does. He's used as a blocker and tackler, not as a kick returner. He forces fumbles."

His loyalty to players he believes in knowing no bounds, Allen, in trading for Jordan, was bringing along a player any other coach would long ago have given up as a hopeless case, chronic knee problems having kept him in hospitals as much as he had played. Ironically, he plans someday to be a doctor.

"I'm thankful he's taken the time to stick with me," Jordan said, looking up from his bed in Georgetown University Hospital, where he had undergone his eighth knee operation after spending most of the 1971 season recovering from the seventh.

"He must see something in me. Maybe it's the way I hustle,

my attitude, the way I play football. I like physical contact. I get satisfaction from physically beating somebody, not in the sense of getting him down and stomping on him, but beating him head to head.

"If a coach likes the way you play, he'll usually stay with you. But I admit this is an extreme example. Sometimes I question myself why I keep playing. I guess it's because I've been so close to playing so many times, and yet I've never really made it in the sense I want to make it, as a starter.

"He'll always come up to me when I get down and give me a little pat on the back and a little talk to help keep me going. He has a knack of knowing when you've reached your limit, when you're fed up and just about ready to quit.

"It seems like every time I'm going to say, 'That's it, I quit,' he comes up and says, 'I was watching you out there today. Looks like you're picking it up.' He'll say just the thing to get you over the hump."

Satisfied with the acquisition of Jordan and the others, Allen skipped the rest of the college draft, leaving his aides to make the lower-round selections. "I'm going back to my hotel, drink a glass of milk, and get away from the telephone," he said. "We've already had our draft."

But the hubbub at Redskin headquarters persisted with a press conference featuring Billy Kilmer, the quarterback Allen obtained a few days earlier from New Orleans. Kilmer was Allen's first acquisition, a much-needed back-up to Sonny Jurgensen.

Not enthralled at the prospect of sitting on the bench nor flattered to learn that he had brought in trade only a little-known linebacker and a pair of throw-in draft choices, Kilmer did not greet his trade to Washington with smiles. But by the time he emerged from Allen's office, Kilmer seemed as caught up as everyone else in the atmosphere of expectation that filled the club's headquarters that day.

"I've admired Sonny for years," he said. "I know he's a fine athlete and a premier quarterback, but I've got to try to win that number one job." No one had even an inkling of the role Kilmer would eventually play in Allen's first season in Washington. Everyone was too busy analyzing the big trade, most concluding it was a steal for Allen. From 1600 Pennsylvania Avenue came the telegram, "Great trade. I am betting on the Redskins for the championship in 1971 or 1972."

While widespread celebrations broke out in Washington, "Welcome Los Angeles Rams" signs went up in store windows and the nickname "Ramskins" was forged. Allen's swashbuckling start indicated, to some, that he wanted to prove himself in a hurry. Actually, with seven years on his contract, there was no need to rush. To others, he seemed to be striking out haphazardly in a desperate attempt at quick riches. But, his aides pointed out, he moves swiftly only after calculating slowly.

Merely putting into practice his unorthodox way of getting good players, Allen remained very much the radical in the opinion of many, who did not perceive, in his theory of having young players mature not on his time but elsewhere, an essentially conservative philosophy.

For the Redskins, there had been enough building programs through the draft. Most often a disastrous exercise, the Redskins became known for an outrageously long list of first-round picks that for one reason or another contributed little or nothing.

Not to mention everyone, there were Yazoo Smith, Ray McDonald, Leroy Jackson, Richie Lucas, Don Allard, Ed Vereb, Jack Scarbath, names enough to demonstrate the hazards involved in drafting college players.

Similarly, defeat was a Ram tradition before Allen's arrival. They had all kinds of draft choices and a 4-10 record the year before he got there. And before that they were 5-7-2, 5-9, 1-12-1, 4-10, 4-7-1, and 2-10.

To Allen, it made common sense to trade in volume, getting known quantities. This was especially true, he felt, in the era of expansion, the common draft of all NFL and former AFL teams beginning in January 1967. It was possible that a team would be able to pick only the twenty-sixth best player available on its first turn, a chancy way at best to improve a team, Allen thought.

The year before Allen's arrival, the Rams had fifteen rookies on the roster. The year before, fourteen. Allen's thinking on rookies was as quickly apparent in Los Angeles as it was to be in Washington with sudden influxes of veterans he obtained in trades becoming the norm. Nor, as Pardee implied, was Allen so naive as to let all his players grow too old at once. A master of deficit spending, he merely would trade more draft choices, years in advance if necessary, for slightly younger veterans with good years ahead of them.

Probably his most significant acquisition with the Rams came in the summer of 1967 in the person of 300-pound Roger Brown, a find who enabled Allen to keep intact that season's famous "Fearsome Foursome" pass rush.

"This Ram defensive team has a chance to become the greatest of all time," he had said.

"No one ever won a championship without a great defense. That applied to the Yankees, even when they had their great hitting teams. It applies to basketball with the Celtics. It applies to the Toronto Maple Leafs, who have won the Stanley Cup three times in the last seven years with defense. It goes right down the line."

Going down his defensive line a few days later, however, Allen could observe a gaping hole. Tackle Rosey Grier fell while pursuing a quarterback in an exhibition game, severed an Achilles' tendon, and was to be lost forever. His team built on defense, Allen faced perhaps the major crisis of his Ram administration.

Moving dramatically one day later, after pondering the situation all night, he traded a first-round choice, a second, and a third to Detroit for Brown, who was thirty years old, five years younger than Grier, and who, as Allen forecast, had his best days ahead of him. With Brown in the line-up, the

Rams went on to their most successful season, 11-1-2, under Allen.

That year Brown was named second string on some all-pro teams and received several honorable mentions, the next year doing even better, making sixty-six unassisted tackles on a unit that set a fourteen-game NFL record for fewest yards allowed.

Crisis had brought out the best in Allen, who reacted to it with such intense concentration he was oblivious to almost everything, including his need for food. Fortunately, his secretary could be counted on in these times to supply him with peanut butter sandwiches and glasses of milk.

Except for the draft-day extravaganza, Allen's most fabulous trade with the Redskins, one that offers the most insight into how the Great Trader functions, was his twentieth and last of that initial season.

It was a deal that delivered former all-pro wide receiver Clifton McNeil from the Giants only two days after Charley Taylor was pronounced lost for the season and just four hours before the October 26 NFL trading deadline.

If McNeil lacked the ability to compensate completely for Taylor, one of the league's best wide receivers by virtue of his ability to block as well as catch and run, he served two significant purposes: an immediate uplift in team morale and a game-tying touchdown catch against Philadelphia two weeks later.

On the Monday after Taylor's left ankle was broken in the team's first loss, to Kansas City, Allen added to the general gloom by saying he saw little hope of a major trade before the deadline, noting, "Nobody wants to help us."

Apparently, the only solace Washington was to get was Richmond Flowers, claimed on waivers from the Dallas Cowboys, who had picked him number two in the 1969 draft.

Son of the former attorney general of Alabama, an NCAA hurdles champion at Tennessee, and a runner of a 9.3 hundred, Flowers had played both wide receiver and free safety, but had excelled at neither and had never been mentioned in the same class with the departed Taylor.

So on Tuesday, the last day for trades, reporters who showed up at Allen's suburban Xanadu were taken aback to learn that he had succeeded in getting McNeil, who led the league with seventy-one receptions in 1968 for San Francisco and had caught fifty as recently as 1970 for the rival New York Giants.

That was all they learned for a while, too, for as had become usual procedure, no one in the organization would say anything, secrecy being paramount, until Allen himself okayed every last word. Joe Blair, the team's publicity director, feared even to approach Allen and tell him that reporters had been waiting for upwards of two hours for some word of how the miracle had been pulled off. McNeil's home phone number was given out, but use of it revealed that the wide receiver had left for Washington hours ago, something the team presumably knew but neglected to divulge.

When the coach did appear, it became obvious that he had been under no small strain. He was unshaven and looked in want of sleep. He first tried to tape a television interview with CBS's Andy Musser, but responded to the first innocuous question with a long silence, finally asking Musser if he could please repeat it — he had a lot on his mind and couldn't concentrate.

When Allen began discussing the trade, his mood was one of exultation, making small jokes and barely containing his pleasure at the accomplishment. When asked what he had given the Giants in exchange, he said it was three draft choices, "medium range, between five and ten," adding wryly, "You know we didn't have any high ones left."

McNeil, he said, was exactly what the team needed, as well as being his type of ballplayer. "He's dedicated. He stays out after practice for extra work. He fits the mold, he's fundamentally a winner, he can help us in our policy that the future is now. That's what I call a good deal."

Allen said he had started making the phone calls that led to the deal literally as soon as the plane had landed after the flight back from Kansas City Sunday night.

"I talked to just about as many teams as time allowed, I just stayed on the phone," he said. "I contacted all twelve clubs in our conference. Green Bay had no receivers, the Dutchman [Atlanta's Norm Van Brocklin] had no receivers, the Saints had no receivers. Some teams are hesitant to trade with you when you're number one, even though we offered to help them with draft choices."

The preliminary details for the deal had been worked out late Monday night — McNeil was contacted while watching the NFL game on TV — and had been finalized close to noon Tuesday, barely before the 4 P.M. trade deadline. To do it Allen had stayed up until 1:30 Tuesday morning and gotten back up at 6:50 A.M., but did not seem bothered. "We had a deadline to meet and we met it," he said. "That's all that counts."

Heading out to do his daily laps around the practice field — "It's the only way I can relax: I haven't had much to relax about until now" — Allen showed his extraordinary good humor by inviting reporters to run with him. When they said they would rather talk to McNeil, Allen ordered it set up at once and further offered to break out his private stock of milk and graham crackers to help make the wait easier. "Whatever they ate last week," he said, superstitious to the end, "give 'em something else."

When McNeil showed up, he claimed to be as enamored with Allen as the coach was with him. "I've admired and respected him as long as I've known who he was," McNeil said. "He's kind of a magnetic personality, one of the most dedicated guys I've met, a player's coach. When he stood up for players when they had problems with their owners, my respect for him just swelled."

He claimed further he was "still mystified at the way Allen can come up with deals the way he has. I'm somewhat surprised. Employing logic, one of the last teams I'd be traded to is an arch rival like Washington."

The next day, others were mystified, too, for it suddenly developed that the Redskins were getting one of those draft choices back and sending to New York in its stead the aforementioned Mr. Flowers, suddenly very much expendable.

Why, people wondered, were the Giants now after Flowers, whom they had passed up on waivers for the regulation $100 before the Redskins had a crack at getting him? Allen's attempt at an explanation — "At that time they didn't know they were going to trade McNeil" — did not account for the Giants' apparent willingness to accept a mere $100 player in place of a draft choice, thought in most circles to be a pearl without price.

A more credible explanation emerged from New York later in the week. Allen, in his orgy of trades, had apparently lost track of which draft choices he could still call his own and had traded one he no longer had to the Giants. When the miffed New Yorkers found out about it, they claimed some other compensation, and Allen offered the travel-weary Flowers. Thus are great trades consummated.

Incidents similar to the missing draft choice also marked Allen's stay in Los Angeles and were, in the opinion of a Rams official clearly partial to Reeves, a primary cause of Allen's feud with the late Rams owner. "Dan felt he was losing face with the other owners because of the shady, little things Allen kept doing," the official said. "Like the time we were caught spying on Dallas. It was a matter of integrity. If he had shown any hint that he would improve in that area, Reeves would never have fired him."

Yet the controversy continued, spilling over into Allen's early days with the Redskins, with the fifty-eight-year-old Reeves, suffering from Hodgkin's disease, granting a deathbed, copyrighted interview to Mal Florence of the Los Angeles *Times* in which he accused Allen of lying, cheating, and disloyalty.

Reeves' outburst resulted largely in response to remarks by Allen in an article by Bill Libby that had appeared the week before in the *Times'* Sunday supplement, *West.*

"I operated in an atmosphere of hatred," Allen was quoted as saying. "Our whole team did. Reeves hated me. Hating me, he hated the team. He sought to split us so we'd come apart. Somehow, I held the pieces together.

"I do not believe any man in the history of sports has had to overcome as much as I have to accomplish as much as I have. I have been like a fine surgeon striving to bring a sick patient back to health, while the patient wished to die. That man wanted me to fail so I might quit or so it would be easy for him to fire me.

"Do you realize that wanting me to fail, to lose, he wanted the team to lose, the players to lose, the fans to lose? He was willing to see everyone else destroyed so long as I could be destroyed, too."

Reeves retorted by charging Allen with "a malicious lie" for saying the owner had not spoken with him in eleven months. He said Allen "placed the Rams in violation of the league constitution in 1970 by signing a player to a large bonus agreement outside the player's regular contract and never filing that contract with the club or league office."

Reeves said that the Rams never knew about the arrangement until the player brought the contract into the Rams office several months later and wanted his money.

Finally, Reeves said Allen contacted another club about its head coaching job for the 1970 season. "At the time he was talking about unity and morale on our team, he already had indicated his willingness to leave it for another job."

Reeves also added that Allen often tried to trade players without his consent and that one of the players, in fact, was Diron Talbert, whom Allen had recently brought to the Redskins.

Allen admitted the business about the illegal bonus agreement to be "partially true," the player turning out to be Jack Pardee, but Allen said it was a necessary action growing out of his first firing by Reeves in 1968.

"When he rehired me the player didn't want to come back. I couldn't locate Reeves at the time. So, I went to Pardee's home in Texas to sign him to a player-coaching contract. Jack already had received a college coaching offer. If I hadn't done what I did, we would have lost him.

"As for their not knowing about it, I told them after I did it. It wouldn't have happened if they hadn't fired me."

Allen denied he sought another job in 1970, but admitted talk of trading Talbert, apparently that being before the defensive tackle became a devoted Allen disciple. "Talbert's name came up because he wasn't attending to business at the time," Allen said.

Not discouraged easily despite the prolonged bickering with Reeves, Allen refused to be distracted from the task at hand, making the Redskins an instant winner, any more than he had been tempted by the location of his Rams office, in a golf shop right off the first tee. He never played golf once in five years.

In the midst of the Reeves controversy, Allen came up smiling, announcing a two-day free agent tryout camp for anyone at all who wanted to be a Redskin. Come one, come all, and they did, to George Allen's fresh-air amateur hour in a Washington public park, where the March winds whipped off the Anacostia River. There were 287 candidates, each more eager than the next to move up the future to the present. Among them were:

A would-be kicker, who told a reporter, "Don't use my name. My boss thinks I'm sick."

A 360-pound tackle, who drove a truck for Lombardi Transfer.

A flanker candidate who changed clothes appropriately in Flea Roberts' old locker. He told Allen he weighed 175. Actually, he weighed 150.

A fellow named Pat Nugent — not the former President's son-in-law — who said he spent more than $300 to get there from Hawaii.

A soccer-style kicker who brought along an agent.

A four-year veteran tuba player from the Redskins' band.

Twenty-four never got to the field for various reasons, including one who made history of sorts, being told personally by Allen that he was too old.

Even George Plimpton had been asked by a reporter how the candidates might make a good impression on the coaches. Plimpton urged running down a coach or wearing a Packers sweat shirt, or both.

Standing amid this swarm of Walter Mittys, Allen and his staff remained straight-faced, as if an all-pro would surely come driving up in his car at any moment. One never did, only six of the candidates even getting as far as the training camp at Carlisle, Pennsylvania. But on the brighter side for Allen, the tryouts proved a publicity bonanza, in sharp contrast with the bitter Reeves stories of recent days. Allen was bathed in favorable ink, getting more national publicity in his role of talent scout than the Redskins did the entire previous season.

Happy to be surrounded by football players, he then called a two-day early camp for rookies and a three-day early camp for veterans. It was April 15 when George Allen blew the whistle for the first time as Redskins coach at a prep school field in Alexandria. There was the mustachioed Diron Talbert, spitting tobacco juice, and Myron Pottios, hair covering his ears, his jaw bulging from a wad of Beechnut he had borrowed from Talbert. Lombardi might have reached a new decibel count at the very appearance of the so-called Ramskins, all, that is, except one.

Jack Pardee looked as straight as his coach. The only thing he seemed to have in common with the other former Rams, besides age, was his gaudy fatigue hat. It was polka dot, Talbert's was psychedelic. Pottios wore a painter's cap. All were distributed by Talbert, who popularized them on the Rams. "They're two dollars apiece," he said. "You just can't go giving away fifty hats."

Two of the other old Rams were there, Wilbur and Jordan,

plus a seventh who had gotten aboard the Allen shuttle from Los Angeles, Tommy Mason, about to turn thirty-two, the third oldest running back in the league. There were all kinds of new faces: tackles Mike Taylor and Errol Linden, linebackers Frank Richter and Mike Foote, defensive end Dave Cahill, and player-coach Dowler.

If the fans were gradually becoming convinced about Allen, so were the old-line Redskins. The coach concluded the drills by presenting each man with a pair of jogging shoes. The quarterbacks, running backs, and receivers were given footballs, as Allen bade farewell to each man personally, reminding them all to be in shape for the start of training camp in July.

All the while, Allen maintained his incredible pace, adding new players, subtracting other ones, trying to insure that the future, indeed, would be now. One of the players he coveted was the Rams' quarterback, Roman Gabriel, whose contract had expired after Allen's last season in Los Angeles.

Once a staunch Allen disciple, Gabriel lashed out at Allen in another story by Mal Florence, saying at one time he would have enjoyed going to Washington and that he fully expected to after Allen joined the Redskins, but not any longer.

"I have it from a very good source that he has told people that I have too many problems because of my divorce," Gabriel said. At the time, Allen merely winced and refused comment.

No more daunted by the Gabriel controversy than he was over Reeves' remarks, Allen continued to plot the moves he believed essential in making the Redskins a winner, calling the press conference that announced the team was moving its entire operation to an isolated site only two miles from Dulles Airport in Virginia, twenty-five miles from the city. At the time there was nothing there but woods, and reporters smiled knowingly and shook their heads while maps were distributed so they could cover the groundbreaking. Virginia governor Linwood Holton attended, welcoming the "Virginia Redskins," and less than four months later Allen's Shangri-la was completed.

Another Allen project that succeeded was having the league's inter-conference trading deadline extended. Realizing some of the old-line National League clubs that had traded with him in past seasons had grown wary of dealing again, Allen wanted to open up the American Conference as a ready source of player talent and so urged year-round trading.

When Al Davis of the Oakland Raiders heard that he said, only half in jest, "I couldn't sleep at night if I knew George Allen had that much latitude." Still Allen persuaded the owners to extend the deadline from April 15 to July 31, the additional time enabling him to consummate several more trades that figured prominently in the Redskins' turnabout.

Two players he added from the AFC, Ron McDole and Verlon Biggs, made up half his defensive line, the weakest part of the Redskins team the previous season.

To shore up the Redskins' woeful kick-return game, Allen dealt with San Diego for Speedy Duncan, the only active player who had returned punts and kickoffs for more than 5000 yards.

And on the last day of inter-conference trading, he obtained flanker Roy Jefferson from Baltimore in exchange for the Redskins' number one pick in 1973 and rookie receiver Cotton Speyrer.

Three minor trades raised Allen's total to thirteen in six months as Redskins coach, with the promise of more to come once training camp opened. With that date fast approaching, Allen could scarcely restrain his excitement at the prospect of locking into the sedate central Pennsylvania town of Carlisle with ninety-four football players. Carlisle was George Allen's kind of town, offering few distractions for the players. For most of their stay, the only movie theater in town showed *Willy Wonka and the Chocolate Factory* three times daily.

CHAPTER III

The Ice Cream Man

ON WHAT MEAT doth this George Allen feed, that he hath grown so great? No meat at all, really, more like ice cream, the vanilla kind. "I think he likes it because he doesn't have to chew it, it doesn't take any time," his wife once remarked. "Chewing would take his mind away from football."

This is the quintessential George Allen, a man who has quite literally channeled every moment of his life into winning football games. When in Los Angeles, he would periodically ask total strangers what they thought of his Rams, and when one gas station attendant innocently thought to reply, "Gosh, I don't know. I don't have time to keep up with football," the coach snapped back, "Nobody can be that busy."

Being a coach is not a mere job to him, but a life of total monastic dedication, to be approached the way the early Christian mystic Saint Simeon Stylites approached the sixty-foot pillar in the desert atop which he sat meditating undisturbed for thirty years.

"Nobody should work all the time," Allen will say modestly, then adding, "everyone should have some leisure, but I believe that the early-morning hours are best for this — the five or six hours when you're asleep. That way, you can combine two good things, sleep and leisure."

He has, for better and worse, made a philosophical commitment to victory that borders on the monomaniacal. He is the one sports figure who will never turn to politics, the man who says, "I enjoy team chapel services more than any church I have ever attended; I haven't missed one in years"; the coach who has said, "I get excited just walking onto the practice field. Every little thing about this game excites me."

Naturally, those facets of his life that cannot be directly related to winning football games have suffered. His irregular eating habits would terrorize Adelle Davis: he rarely has a complete meal, making do with endless peanut butter and jelly sandwiches, topped by ever-present glasses of milk and a generous supply of vitamins. Taking time to eat well is taking time that could be better used mapping zone defenses. Former Allen Assistant Coach Ray Prochaska once said, "If somebody would volunteer to feed George, he'd let them, and he might even get so he liked food." His nickname, "The Ice Cream Man," dates from commercials he did for a Los Angeles dairy, payment for which turned out to be 200 gallons of the stuff.

His conversation rarely touches anything outside of football — he has been called impossibly dull socially, a funnyman to rank with Bela Lugosi. The only time he has sat still for extended in-season interviews was in October of 1967, when Charles Maher of the Los Angeles *Times* did a classic series called "A Week With George Allen."

"To do this with you is agony," he told Maher. "I don't want to do anything but football. I don't want to talk about anything but football." And, after losing the game played at the end of that week, he told the *Times* man, "I wish you'd call off that series you're writing on me. I don't deserve it."

Still, Allen and his wife Etty cooperated enough to provide an unmatched look into that very small part of Allen that is not directly concerned with winning football games, a peek into the private life of a man who almost doesn't have one.

"I found George very thoughtful," Mrs. Allen told Maher. "And he had a very different way of thinking. He liked the real things in life. He's still that way. For instance, he likes nature. One of the things we both like to do is look at the ocean. George doesn't care for clubs and too much social life. He tries to stay away from artificial gatherings.

"George is very thoughtful, even though he is preoccupied with football. He used to bring flowers home to me, and he still does. Not all the time, but once in a while. He'll come in holding them behind his back. It's very touching."

Mrs. Allen said George used to putter around the house but hadn't had time for a while. "He doesn't even give himself a chance to relax," she said. "He's very intense. Very, very serious.

"There is one thing that relaxes him. Sometimes we'll take a walk along the beach and watch the waves. I know that George is actually relaxing then, that he actually feels and smells and hears. But that's about the only time he does relax.

"I do worry about the way he takes care of himself. I don't think he uses much common sense. He'll go all day without eating and stuff himself with vitamins.

"George hardly ever watches TV. He thinks it's a waste of time. He has to be doing something to improve himself all the time."

The coach himself revealed that, when he has time, his musical tastes run to Dixieland: "My two favorites are Al Hirt and Pete Fountain. I enjoy musicals, too. My favorite was *The Sound of Music.*

"As to books, I'm reading *Hawaii* right now. I enjoy reading books on human relations and leadership." And though no one would ever accuse him of having ordinary human vices, the coach admitted, "I tried smoking but I didn't get any enjoyment out of it. I'll drink in moderation. I like a little blackberry brandy before a meal. Brandy is good for your stomach."

The thought of Allen's having a hobby greatly amuses the people he works with: "Sure he's got one," they say. "It's football," and the coach himself has listed some of the six books he's written on the subject, books with spiffy titles like *Winning Football Drills*, *How to Train a Quarterback*, and *Pass Defense Drills*, as examples of his spare-time activities.

Actually, the coach does have one rarely publicized outside interest, a highly ironic one for a man whose team is under attack by Indian organizations for its derogatory nickname. Allen is a member and founder of the Red Cloud Athletic Federation, a group that has worked steadily over the years to raise funds, gather athletic equipment, and build a field house for a group of Sioux Indian children in Pine Ridge, South Dakota, efforts that have earned the coach an honorary chiefdom in the Sioux Nation.

The project started in 1965, when Allen, then the Chicago Bears defensive coach, got a letter from Gus Nemitz, one of his former players at Morningside College. Nemitz was an agent for the South Dakota welfare department and described, Allen said at the time, "the desperate need for athletic equipment, especially in football, at the mission school. He asked me whether the Bears had any old uniforms or pads, anything that might help out. And would I come to Pine Ridge with a Bear player to feature their first bona fide sports banquet?"

Taken by the chance to "keep kids in sports and out of trouble," Allen took Chicago linebacker Bill George up to South Dakota with him and was upset at what he saw.

"Gus wasn't exaggerating," he said. "I found that the school had forty-seven boys out for football last fall — and only three old balls to work with. Those forty-seven kids had fourteen helmets — and what helmets! I examined one — must have been the first of the plastics. You could punch your fist through it."

In the years since, Allen has worked consistently to raise funds for Pine Ridge, even trying unsuccessfully to schedule a Redskins-Colts exhibition slow-pitch softball game to channel funds to South Dakota.

As befits a man heavily involved in athletics, Allen maintains as much of an interest as he can in other sports. Though he used baseball analogies so often in talking about the Redskins that writers began looking upon him as kind of a frustrated Leo Durocher, next to football ice hockey is his favorite sport, and he often took his family down to the Los Angeles Forum in former days to watch the Kings play.

As far as participation, Allen's devotion to coaching has pared down the sports he can take part in himself to only one, an activity he would swear by if he was the type who swore: running.

"Track is great," he has said, "because it is an individual sport and you have to sacrifice so much to succeed." Every day after practice, Allen would take a number of solitary laps around the field, with reporters setting up a pool on how many it would be. As tireless a proselytizer as he was a runner, he told everyone who'd listen and even some who wouldn't what a fantastic relaxer running was, describing it as the only way he could unbend after a rough day of directing practice and attempting trades. "For you, watching a practice may be relaxing," he once told a doubting reporter. "To conduct a practice is just the opposite."

On a snowy day last February, the then nearly fifty-year-old head coach put on a heartening display of fitness. After running a mile in the thirty-two-degree temperature and falling snow, Allen in fifteen minutes clicked off fifteen exercises on a weight machine, one involving fifteen leg presses of 240 pounds each. Then he took on twenty-eight-year-old defensive end Verlon Biggs in basketball and beat him, five to three.

Suffering most from Allen's dedication to football has been his family, which he almost never sees, again an ironic situation because the coach is very much of a family man, saying often, "I'm a guy who has to have his family around him."

Allen is very conscious of the hardships his way of life has imposed on his wife, Etty, and their four children, George, twenty, Gregory, eighteen, Bruce, fifteen, and Jennifer, eleven. "The toughest part has been for my family," he told the *Times*' Maher. "It's like they don't have a father.

"My life has been football — football — morning, noon, and night. I've put it even ahead of my family, which is wrong.

But if you want to be totally successful, that's the way you have to do it. I'd do the same thing no matter what job I had.

"My wife is a great, great gal. Somehow she puts up with my being away from home. Some women wouldn't put up with that. You know, I won't eat one meal at home this week. I mean lunch or dinner."

At the close of the 1968 season, Allen again touched on this self-enforced separation. "I want to get to know my family," he said. "Having a father like me has been hard on them. I don't see them for the whole season. I don't keep track of the bills or the lawn or the cars or anything. Just football, football, football. It's been real hard on Mrs. Allen."

Allen met his future wife, the former Etty Lumbroso, during his first year as head coach at Morningside College in Sioux City, Iowa. With as interesting a background as her husband, Mrs. Allen is French, but was born and raised in Tunis, Tunisia, near the site of ancient Carthage, where her father was a wine importer. Besides English and French, she speaks Italian, Spanish, Arabic, and even knows a bit of Latin.

She was visiting friends at Morningside in 1950, and, Allen recalled, "She was introduced to me by the head of the speech department at a, what the heck kind of a thing was it, it was a play, a play at the community theater."

Allen flew to Tunis to propose, and there ran into a bit of a problem. "There are buses, there are Cadillacs, and there are camels in my city," Mrs. Allen recalled in 1966 as she was packing the family for a move from Chicago to Los Angeles. "I thought George should ride a camel for part of the way—and he did."

"Cripes, don't print that," Allen put in. "If the Los Angeles sportswriters ever find out I once rode a camel, they'll never let me forget it."

"He was different from anyone I had met before," Mrs. Allen said. "I didn't try to analyze then the reasons I was attracted to him. We were just in love. But I think I can see now why we were attracted to each other. For one thing, we had the same love of challenges."

The two were married on May 26, 1951, in Sioux City, Iowa, but Mrs. Allen did not see her first football game until later that year when her husband moved to California to coach the Whittier College team.

"The Whittier Poets — they even looked like poets on that team — played a SubPac [Navy] team, and got creamed, fifty-four to nothing," she recalled. "George came home and started working on his typewriter. I said, 'The game is over. What's this all about?' He said, 'I've got to correct all the mistakes.'

"I thought he was an oddball until I talked to the other coaches' wives. After a while I realized he had to be completely devoted to his work."

The realization was not easy in coming. A friend from the Whittier days remembers a birthday party for Mrs. Allen held one night at the local country club:

"George was sitting at the table, talking about football and diagramming plays, and all the men were listening to him and not celebrating. Mrs. Allen was getting madder than hell and finally she said she was going to run him out of the room if he didn't stop talking about football. 'Football, football, football,' she said. 'Even on my birthday.'"

Mrs. Allen admitted to Maher that "Sometimes I would get upset, because I had so much on my hands. Raising the children. But I think I've matured. I think I've come to accept it. I understand his responsibility to his job."

Not surprisingly, the Allens' three sons have all been successful in football. George, Jr., quarterbacked Palos Verdes High to a 7-2 season and was a scholarship player with UCLA's freshman team before transferring to the University of Virginia when his family moved east.

The other two, Greg and Bruce, formed a highly successful place-kicking combination for Langley High School in the Virginia suburbs. Using the family penchant for thoroughness, they even evolved their own set of foot signals to help with their timing.

Still, with his own experience as a guide, Allen is far from convinced he wants another coach in the family. "Mrs. Allen and I were talking about that recently," he said after his first Redskins season. "One of my boys, Bruce, is diagramming plays. We don't want him to be in coaching. You know, for every coach that succeeds, there are about a hundred who fail."

Allen's own coaching career evolved under far from favorable circumstances. He was born on April 29, 1922, in Grosse Pointe Woods, a suburb of Detroit. His father, Earl R. Allen, worked in a Chrysler auto plant in Detroit and was a native, as was his mother, Loretta, of Albany, New York. The family moved back to Rensselaer, New York, when Allen went to college — he remembers working as a lifeguard in the area for a couple of summers — and his mother and a married sister, Virginia, still live there.

"I was always interested in every sport and played football, basketball, baseball, and track," Allen recalled at his plush Redskin Park office. "I played some hockey because we lived in Saint Clair Shores, right near Lake Saint Clair, and we used to go out and play and skate for six, seven, eight, nine hours a day. I liked the outdoors, I liked to fish, and hike and camp and all those sports.

"I felt that if you could make a living by being in sports, what a great way it would be. And everything that I did real early was to try and learn more, to learn more about all sports. We were just an average family so I never had much of an opportunity to have the greatest clinics and teaching like we have nowadays. So we just picked up what we could, playing with the neighborhood kids. We didn't have any organized programs; I don't recall having any organized sports except for when we got to high school."

High school was Lake Shore High, where Allen says he never missed a day in four years and earned nine letters: three in football, three in basketball, and three in track.

"My best sports were really basketball and track," Allen said. "I wasn't very big, I only weighed about a hundred and forty-eight, a hundred and fifty pounds, something like that. I was all-conference center in basketball and [in 1938-1939] I was captain of the team."

In track Allen ran the 440 and long-jumped. "I set a school record in the long jump," he said, smiling. "It wasn't very far, twenty feet, two inches, because there wasn't anybody good then. I mean, if you jumped twenty feet in the long jump that was a pretty good jump.

"But all the time, I was thinking, 'Gee, this would be great, if you could get the right job this would be a great way to make a living.' I used to go to all the games, University of Detroit, Detroit Lions, University of Michigan. It was in the back of my mind, but I think that's in the back of every guy's mind. I can remember at that time that this was, this was something I wanted. Whether I could get it or not, I didn't know."

After World War II started, Allen joined the navy and, in 1943-1944, under a V-12 naval program, he attended Alma College in Alma, Michigan, for three semesters.

Founded by the Presbyterian Church in 1886 and having an enrollment even today of only 1300, tiny Alma nevertheless has a fascinating football history. Besides Allen, it produced Bob Devaney, coach of the national champion Nebraska team, and also had an unenvied part in the invention of the forward pass.

Jesse Harper, Alma's first football coach, moved to Notre Dame in 1913 and used the Fighting Irish's game with Alma to test the Gus Dorais to Knute Rockne passing attack that would stun Army in a historic 35-13 upset only a week later. Poor Alma was even more surprised, losing 62-0 to the Irish, a game followed in consecutive years by 56-0, 32-0, and 46-0 losses to Notre Dame before Alma wised up and dropped the series.

Another famous Alma graduate was Frank Knox, who played on Alma's first football team in 1894, and, as Secretary of the Navy under Franklin D. Roosevelt, was responsible for getting a V-12 program for his alma mater.

Unfortunately, Alma's male enrollment was only about 150, and the other V-12 schools the Scots played numbered 1000 men or more. So Alma was 1-5 in 1943, scoring only 14 points while giving up 130, losing two of three games to Central Michigan, and getting trounced, 54-0, by Western Michigan.

Allen's place on this team is downright difficult to detect. Careful research of the weekly editions of *The Almanian* published in 1943 failed to provide any mention of him as a football player, though he is mentioned often in "Cat Chatter," the college gossip column, and apparently had no small reputation as a coed's favorite.

"For the benefit of George Allen fans," one column notes, "he doesn't date up here because, 'I have to study so much, and, well, Saginaw is such a nice town!'" Another column notes with interest a sudden lengthening of his hair and calls him "a mighty sharp specimen," while a third, written after he left Alma, designates one Hank Brenner as "successor to George Allen, female heart throb number one."

Though unmentioned in the papers, Allen did in fact play at Alma, though largely in a reserve capacity, as a 156-pound right end, self-described as "just average" and remembered by teammates more for his personality than his playing ability. John Rosenkrans, now president of Eisenhower College in Seneca, New York, and the husband of a girl Allen once dated, recalled him as "an outgoing guy, very much of an extrovert," while the best player on Allen's team, halfback and Alma Hall of Fame member Rex Roseman, said, "he had quite a bit of the old fire he still has," and claimed to remember some speedy Allen catches in the Bunker Hill game, which Alma lost anyway, 32-0. Roseman's own career ended when he tried out for a New York professional team, was given a pair of shoes that were too tight, developed feet full of blisters but was too quiet to speak up and ask for the right size, and was consequently let go on the very last cut.

In the middle of 1944, Allen's sophomore year, part of his V-12 unit was transferred and the future coach ended up at Marquette, again playing right end. The team won only two games and Allen described his own contribution as "just fair." He also went out for track again, but noted, "I wasn't real good. I ran the four-forty but my best time was so slow some guys could probably do it walking today. I think I did fifty-two, four at Marquette."

In 1945 and 1946, Allen was athletic adjutant with the navy at Farragut, Idaho, where he did his first recorded coaching, leading teams that won three base championships in basketball, baseball, and softball.

In the fall of 1946, after getting out of the service, Allen entered the University of Michigan, and, though he was not to play the game anymore, took the first solid steps toward making football his eventual profession.

"I was going to go out for football," he said, "but they had so many ends. All the schools were loaded with talent then. I only weighed about one hundred and sixty. So I didn't go out."

Allen instead went out for wrestling, competing for Cliff Keen, a Wolverine legend who coached at Ann Arbor for a total of forty-four years. He did not, however, take his eyes or his mind off the highly successful varsity football team, which had put together a record of 70-16 between 1938 and 1947.

"I'd go to practice and watch things," he said. "I got to know Fritz Crisler. I thought he was the best college coach in the country then. I guess he kind of took a liking to me. In my senior year, he gave me a chance to coach the junior varsity and one-hundred-fifty-pound teams." The chance was successful, as Allen, working as line coach and general assistant to Cliff Keen, helped the 150-pounders tie for the 1947 championship with Ohio State in what was then the Big Nine Conference.

Allen graduated from Michigan in 1947 and "then decided to go to graduate school. I wasn't particular about what university I attended. I would have gone to Yankton College if they had the best football coach. That's all I was interested in. But I could see that Crisler was the best in the country, so I stayed at Michigan."

While there, Allen became a member of Sigma Delta Psi, a national honorary athletic and scholarship fraternity with rather arduous entrance requirements: "To get in you had to have a B average and you had to swim one hundred yards in one minute, twenty-five seconds, do a ten-second handstand, climb a twenty-foot rope in, I think, twelve seconds, do the one-hundred-twenty-yard high hurdles in sixteen seconds, throw a baseball two hundred fifty feet, punt a football forty-five yards, run a mile in five minutes, run the hundred in eleven flat, put a sixteen-pound shot thirty feet, do a seventeen-foot long jump, and high-jump five feet."

Allen also found time to earn his master of science degree, granted in physical education in February 1948. His thesis, written under the advisership of Bennie Oosterbaan, Crisler's successor as head football coach, was completed in June of that year and offers a rare glimpse into the making of the future terror of the National Football League.

The topic is "A Study of Outstanding Football Coaches' Attitudes and Practices in Scouting," a 118-page document, complete with a twenty-three-item bibliography, 176 pages of appendices, and endless carefully drawn reproductions of arcane diagrams and charts. With the amazing thoroughness that was to become his trademark, Allen deals in painful seriousness with scouting on the college, professional, and high school levels, delving into such weighty matters as how many scouts should be sent to a game, where they should sit, how many games they should attend, what and how much they should write down, and more. His conclusion, not surprisingly, was that scouting is an unabashed Good Thing.

Sprinkled throughout the work are hints of ideas that would characterize Allen's thoughts on football in later years. The deadly seriousness of his interest is indicated when he says, "If one begins to enjoy the game, he is not doing a good job of scouting." There was no such thing as a surplus of information on a future opponent, Allen felt, noting with scorn, "Many coaches believe that too much information from using many scouts can become too involved and not practical. It should be noted that information from a competent scout cannot become too involved if it is used properly. It is the *use of this information* that is important."

Allen was not without ideas of his own as to how the using should be done. "After all," he wrote, "coaching is a selling job — offensive movements are sold (play as well as formation adjustments) from scout reports. Coaches sell their defensive plans and adjustments from the scout's report. Psychological material is also derived from these reports, and results in a better selling job."

Mention was also made of one of Allen's best-known trademarks, a penchant for defensive football, especially as it relates to the professional game, something that Allen noted with remarkable clarity for that early a date.

"In professional leagues," he wrote, "teams are composed of selected personnel, usually the very best, and individual weaknesses are not frequent. It is also much more necessary to have good pass defenses in the pro league. A college team is likely to meet two or three top passers in a season, and stand-out receivers are limited. The professional league is different. Sunday after Sunday it is Baugh, Luckman, Christman, Waterfield, and so on, throwing to the finest receivers money can buy. Therefore, this makes pass defense one of the major problems in professional football and the principal objective of the professional scout.

"The intensive scouting, the movies, the close checking that results from playing teams twice a year also pose a problem the colleges escape. This also makes one type of pass defense inadequate in professional circles. There must be a switching defense with change-off, and it must be manned by smart operators. After both clubs study the movies and records of the first game, it is quite a guessing contest as to what the plan will be for the second encounter," a contest Allen was to prove especially adept at once he too became a professional.

As interesting as his comments was the method Allen employed in writing the thesis, and the probable reason for it. In his own words, scouting was "a very little-known field . . . no study comparable to this one . . . had been made." So, in a prime example of the brain-picking of more knowledgeable minds that was a constant leitmotif of Allen's early career, he wrote to fifty-six of the best-known, most knowing coaches in America, saying he would "appreciate receiving any forms or other information you might have so that I could gain the benefit of your experience in scouting football."

Ten cautious coaches, including Alabama's Paul (Bear) Bryant, Notre Dame's Frank Leahy, and Maryland's brilliant Clark Shaughnessy, soon to be Allen's mentor in Chicago, thought better of it and did not reply. But forty-six others did, including such legends as Army's Red Blaik, Georgia Tech's Bobby Dodd, Columbia's Lou Little, and the twin immortals, Dana X. Bible and Amos Alonzo Stagg. The quite aged Stagg noted pointedly, "May I say that I have not laid much emphasis on scouting of opposing teams . . . scouting has had very little to do with whatever success I have achieved," remarks Allen characterized as "perhaps the most interesting, as well as the most explicit reply."

Among the professional coaches who replied was future rival Paul Brown, then with the Cleveland Browns, who ended his letter with the "hope that your team turns out satisfactorily," and Chicago Bears head man George Halas, destined to be Allen's boss in ten years' time, who began with the typically brusque note, "Naturally you can realize how busy I have been and, as a matter of fact, still am." By the time his work was over, Allen could truthfully say, "This study has given the investigator an unusual opportunity to analyze the opinions of the most distinguished football coaches in the country. The writer also had the privilege of accumulating more material on scouting than any other one person."

That master's degree was the last step in Allen's educational career. Future night-school classes at the University of Southern California were to give him about half the credits he needed for a Ph.D. in education, but he never quite had the time to finish. Similar thoughts impelled him when he left Michigan: he was in a hurry to get down to coaching.

Not just any type of coaching, or on any old level either. "It's just a question of knowing what direction you want to go," Allen said once. "I've always known that direction. When I graduated college, I was offered a good job as a high school head coach. But I turned it down. People said I was nuts. But I wanted to start out coaching on the college level, even if it was as an assistant. I didn't want to put in the five or six years in high school waiting for a college job."

"One of the finest compliments I received," he said at another time, "was when Michigan offered me a job in the athletic department after I got out of school. It was a compliment because they had a lot of All-Americas they could have offered the job to.

"The job involved coaching track. I would have been an assistant. Since track was such a big sport at Michigan, I would have had to spend a lot of time on that and I would not have had time for football. And I had made up my mind I was going to be a football coach."

With typical thoroughness, Allen went through the Blue

Book of College Athletics, a comprehensive, nationwide directory, with an eye to schools that might have an eye out for him. "There were over a thousand schools listed, and a lot of them didn't have football, so I sent out form letters applying for head or assistant coaching jobs to something like six hundred and twenty-eight schools," the coach said. "Goshdarn if three schools didn't offer me jobs. One was in Cleveland — Case Tech. One was Trinity College in Connecticut. The other one was Morningside College — I'd never heard of Morningside — in Sioux City, Iowa."

Allen went out to Morningside, the alma mater of then Michigan president Alexander G. Ruthven, with the recommendation of former Michigan coach and then athletic director Fritz Crisler. "I was being interviewed for an assistant job," he said, "and I was there for two days and when I left they offered me the head job, which was a surprise." Surprised or not, Allen accepted the $3900 offered for coaching the Chiefs for the 1948 season, as well as assisting in baseball and teaching physical education, and officially began his ascent in his chosen profession.

Discussions of Allen's overall coaching career generally assume that the college portion of it, numbering three years at Morningside and six at Whittier College in Whittier, California, was as flamboyantly successful as the professional years that followed. This is not the case. Allen was relatively but far from spectacularly successful as a college coach, gaining results often improved upon by his immediate, though currently less prestigious, successors. He was not the most popular of coaches either, demanding from very small-time college players who were not used to such treatment the same type of intense dedication he was later to insist on from his professional charges.

"I once told George he'd never be a success in the college game," an acquaintance from those days related. "He wanted to concentrate on football, and football alone. In the world of teaching and academics, so much concentration was out of place. You have to dovetail, do different things, cooperate with other coaches, and this wasn't his desire. As far as his record, it's become a question of the older I get, the faster I ran as a boy."

Allen has said that he took the Morningside job because it presented the thing he loved most, a challenge. The Chiefs hadn't won a conference game in two years — a fact that is often misstated to indicate they hadn't won any games at all — and when Allen took over he at once understood why.

For Morningside, with a male enrollment of only 800, was by far the smallest school in the North Central Conference, a group that included conglomerates like the University of North Dakota, North Dakota State, the University of South Dakota, and South Dakota State. Far from being a big improvement, his first year at Sioux City saw the posting of a 2-7 record, the school's worst in thirteen years, including defeats in four out of six conference games.

The next year, 1949, Morningside played an eleven-game season, its biggest before or since, and compiled an impressive 7-3-1 record. A factor in that improvement was the presence in the backfield of one Connie Callahan, a Little All-America halfback who was the national collegiate total offense champion that year and holder of all Morningside's rushing and total offense records until the 1971 season ended.

Morningside's conference record, however, though nicely camouflaged by a very high number of outside games, had improved to only 3-2-1, and, according to a contemporary, "George began to see the handwriting on the wall. The conference was a great challenge; even if you won half your games you were doing pretty well. He had a better record than the previous two years, but he just wasn't going to win many in that competition."

Before the 1949 season, Allen had had head coaching offers from North Dakota State and Kansas State, but a salary increase to $5000 had kept him in Iowa for both that 7-3-1 season and the 6-2-1 1950 year, when he posted an identical 3-2-1 conference record. After that, there was no holding him, and he became California bound, leaving an overall 15-12-2 record, 8-8-2 in the conference, behind him. Four years after he left, a man named Clayton Droullard did what Allen could not, winning the North Central Conference title with a 5-1 record, and another fellow named Dewey Halford, the current Morningside coach, did it again two years after that.

Of all the anecdotes that have been gathered concerning Allen's years at Morningside, a surprising number concern transportation, the most-often-quoted dealing with one of his first penniless trips from Ann Arbor to Sioux City.

"I went down to a car agency," Allen recalled, "and asked them if they had a new car they wanted delivered to Sioux City. All they had was a second-hand milk truck they wanted delivered to Omaha. I had planned to borrow gas money if I could get a car — but when they said it was a milk truck, I audibilized. I said I'd need a ten dollar fee to deliver a milk truck."

In Omaha, so the story goes, Allen did not give up. He persuaded the milk company to let him drive on to Sioux City. And the vice president, after a short visit with the future leader of men, is even said to have sent a milkman along to drive the truck back.

Once established on the campus, and influenced perhaps by his small salary, Allen began a long career as a psychological motivator by vowing that he would not buy a car until he had experienced a winning season. He rode a bicycle everywhere and, as a symbol of the promise, the Morningside student body president borrowed it and drove it in the 1948 Homecoming Day parade.

After his 7-3-1 season the following year, he bought a new 1949 red Ford convertible, a car he was still driving in 1957 when he was hired as a Los Angeles Rams assistant. But the convertible top hadn't worked since a Sioux City sleet storm, followed by an unobliging freeze, had ruined it the second night after the purchase.

Even at that early stage, Allen's prowess as a ferreter-out of football talent had reached large proportions. During his last weeks at Michigan, he scouted for his future team, taking with him to Sioux City a reported nine high school graduates from Ohio and Michigan, more than a few of whom had doubtless previously planned to spend four years at Ann Arbor.

While in Sioux City, Allen made periodic visits further north to look for likely types. "I always used to go to state and city high school meets in Detroit," he said once. "We got a lot of our players that way. I got a fullback, a tackle, and a defensive back just by going to the finals of the city meet in Detroit one year."

There were rumors at the time that Allen, as one person put it, "had a problem in following procedures," that if he wanted a prospect bad enough he had perhaps a tendency to ignore recruiting rules and offer the player things that never materialized. Nothing ever came of this idle talk, and some Morningsiders feel that at its root is nothing more than mere sour grapes relating to Allen's later success, but it did apparently inspire the following obviously fictitious story that appeared in the 1949 issue of something called the *BamBoozler*:

"Yes," said tiny George Allen, "I got some Beauts."

He was speaking in this highly satisfied fashion about the football players he had recently signed up on his talent hunt to South America. He proudly displayed them (in cages of course) to all who had the courage to venture near.

"They look sort of wild," commented one observer. "Do they speak English?"

Said Allen, "English? They don't speak anything. They just scream at feeding times."

"How do you teach them plays?"

"They weigh four hundred pounds. I should teach them plays?"

"What else do they do?" persisted the observer.

"I don't know," said Allen in a puzzled tone. "Miss Webb amuses them between games."

Allen's contemporaries at Morningside, most of whom did not want to be quoted by name, still speak in tones of disbelief of the absolutely total dedication he brought to coaching even at that early stage. "I've known many coaches and athletes," said one associate, "and George was one out of twenty million."

"I suppose you'd have to call him a fanatic in his desire to excel in football, in just his willingness to do whatever was necessary to win," said another. "He lived, breathed, everything was football. He was really enthusiastic; you could just see him bubbling over. He brought an extra drive or intensity into the game at Morningside it didn't have before."

Occasionally, however, that vaunted enthusiasm backfired. "Sometimes, too much of anything is no good," said one cautious Allen watcher. "He really had lots of enthusiasm, but he was very theoretical. Some of the boys didn't get a full understanding of what he was trying to put across."

One of the few Morningside people who agreed to be quoted on Allen was Leon Shortenhaus, co-captain, along with Connie Callahan, of the 1948 Chiefs team, the very first Allen coached, and later a high school coach and scout for Morningside.

"I made all-conference end that year and it was mostly due to George Allen," Shortenhaus said. "I was real light and all and I had no business being that good. I would have been a mediocre ballplayer with any other coach."

Shortenhaus has heard the Morningside rumors "that he was just lucky, or that he used other people," but thinks the cause is that "some people here are more or less jealous of him more than anything else."

He does admit that Allen "wasn't easy to play for, I'll tell you that. A lot of times he was so intense the players felt he was going too far out. It took a little while for me to even relate to him. But after you caught on, he really helped you get the job done. There was just a part of him that got the best out of people."

The psychological techniques that made Allen unique as a professional coach were apparently with him even in his rookie year. "He kind of made you do things that you normally wouldn't be able to do," said Shortenhaus. "He made you feel like you were the most important man on the team. It made you feel good when you did something the way he wanted you to do it. He'd really praise you for those things right on the spot. He made you hungry for that kind of praise, so you went out and did your best.

"He was just so dedicated, just so thorough in everything that he did. He'd always make a real fine intricate study of the game, he didn't miss any facets, he planned his practices right down to the minute.

"He demanded respect through his knowledge, and he sure did know a lot. I think it rubs off. When players know they've got a coach who is thorough, they're going to be thorough themselves. You had to do it right if you played for him."

Even the personal touch, the show of individual concern, was part of the Allen technique as far back as 1948. "He gave me some personal things," recalled Shortenhaus. "Like when you felt troubled, when you had some problems, he'd show you where to find appropriate passages in the Bible. Things like that."

In order to leave Morningside and take the job at Whittier, Allen took a cut in salary to $4800, but made the switch anyway because "it was a promotion in area. They were playing about the same level of competition as Morningside, but Whittier was in an area that offered a lot more opportunity."

Along with the opportunity there were disadvantages: "I had a full teaching load besides coaching football. I'll tell you, I had so many jobs . . . I had classes in volleyball, tennis, wrestling, and I was the baseball coach. I taught a course in anatomy and a course in kinesiology and I had a corrective physical education class. And golf. And I taught a theory of football course and I used to recruit on Sunday."

And though Allen has said, "Every coaching job that I've had has been one where the team has been in last place or close to last place," the Whittier job was just the opposite. Allen's immediate predecessor, a campus institution named Wallace (Chief) Newman, football coach since 1929, had closed his career with 8-1 and 9-1 records and two successive Southern California Intercollegiate Athletic Conference titles for the Poets.

By contrast Allen, apparently victimized by losses via graduation, could do no better than 2-7 in his first season on the coast. The following year, however, 1952, was Allen's finest, as Whittier rose to 9-1, losing only to Air Force, 21-20, after outplaying the Falcons for most of the game.

The Poets won the SCIAC title too, but it was the one and only time that was to happen in Allen's six years at Whittier. By contrast, as soon as he left, the Poets became all but invincible, taking the title for eight consecutive years, the first three under Don Coryell, who later left to form yet another dynasty at San Diego State.

Though Allen's 32-22-5 record at Whittier is attributed by some to merely a "dry spell in talent," there was no doubt that, to quote an acquaintance from those days, "he was not the most popular of coaches.

"He was a rather demanding fellow. He wanted you to play for him twenty-four hours a day, or even forty-eight. And there were remarks about his practices. He believed in those, and he expected the players to work hard and do lots of drills. Most people had not been accustomed to that type of devotion. And he'd chew 'em out, in front of the whole squad, too, for not doing it. This isn't a good way to become popular."

On only his second day as Whittier coach, the absence of

complete harmony between the leader and his charges became noticeable.

"The first thing he did," recalled a friend, "was ask how many players owned cars. All but two raised their hands, and Allen just threw up his hands in disgust. He said at Morningside only two players had had cars, that you couldn't be in good shape if you rode everywhere. He wanted the players to give them up, to put their cars in the garage and walk. This didn't go over very big, this didn't do it at all.

"Some players just didn't warm up to the guy. He just isn't a funny guy—he's a broken record, talks football twelve months a year. But they all would have to admit he knew football—frontwards, backwards, and sideways."

One thing Allen learned at Whittier concerned the nonadvisability of taking chances on the field. "We were playing Cal Tech, the patsies of the conference; we don't even play them anymore," the Allen watcher recalled. "Whittier had a six-nothing lead in the very last minute, and Tech was backed up on its own one on fourth down. Their kid went back to punt—they have brainy boys over there—and noticed a ten-man rush, so he threw a pass that went for ninety-two yards. That taught George a lesson. You just don't gamble that way."

Always one to keep all his options open, Allen, who ran a boys' camp in the high Sierras during the summer months, wouldn't take the job unless he could have time off to visit a professional football training camp. In that way he got to know Sid Gillman, the Los Angeles Rams coach, and when Gillman had an opening on his staff in 1957, Allen leaped at it, leaving college coaching behind forever.

The job lasted but a year, with Allen opening a car wash in the San Fernando Valley after it was over. However, the taste for the professional game did not leave him, so he sold the car wash and drove to Chicago, supposedly even sleeping in his car one night, chasing his dream.

CHAPTER IV

Sounds Like You've Got Yourself a Hell of a Coach

IF THE TYPE AND EXTENT of control George Allen enjoyed over the Redskins was far from ordinary, so was the background of the man who wielded it. Throughout his professional coaching career Allen had hungered for such control and had become involved in one of the most bizarre episodes in NFL history on the way to making it a reality. Not even the churlishly imposing figure of George Halas, the most irascible man in the entire league, was too much for him to overcome.

In early 1966, when the two clashed, Allen was the author of four football texts and the most important assistant on Halas' staff, yet he was widely unknown, even in Chicago. But when things were over, though Halas was credited with a moral victory, it was Allen who came out on top.

This was no small triumph, for George Stanley Halas was at the time the seventy-one-year-old paterfamilias of the entire professional football oligarchy. Born the year the very first professional game was played, he was the only man still alive of those who had pioneered the formation of the NFL, the only man who could remember every single league game. He moved a team called the Staley Starchmakers to Chicago, changed the name to the Bears, and then as player, coach, and owner ruled them implacably for forty-six consecutive years. When you called him Papa Bear, you weren't supposed to smile.

Allen joined the Bears in the 1958 season after one year on

Sid Gillman's staff as offensive end coach for a team that would later see much more of him, the Los Angeles Rams.

Allen first came to Gillman's particular attention in 1955, when as coach of Whittier College, he spent some of his summer vacation at the Rams camp in Redlands. He was noticed at the time as the only nonprofessional coach who had such a strong desire to learn that he was allowed to move in with the Rams coaches, living with them for weeks on end, even watching game films in a garage. Every day, he followed Gillman from movie projector to squad meeting to late-night strategy session until the Ram coach gave in to sleep, sometimes at 3 A.M.

"At first," Gillman said, "I thought the kid was a little kooky, but then I discovered that what he did was part of an overall plan that made an awful lot of sense. He is a talented and very smart fellow."

Smart or not, a reshuffle of assistants at the end of 1957 left Allen free to go to the Bears, where the capacity for hard work he had absorbed from Gillman, sometimes known as the water buffalo of professional coaches, became evident.

He lived in suburban Deerfield, Illinois, and would catch a train called "The Hiawatha" to Chicago each morning, always burdened with a large carrying bag filled with upwards of twenty-five pounds of notes, charts, and other coaching paraphernalia for him to digest on the trip in.

It was a two-decker train, and Allen found he wanted to sit only in the top level, where an overhead rack was close enough to the seat to allow him to take things out of the valise without wasting the time it would take to get out of his seat. There were only eight of those seats available, but the story persists that Allen, in his mania for not having to waste any time, made sure he got one every day.

With the Bears, he was placed first in the personnel department, where his work was so much noticed that when Frank Korch, the club's chief talent scout, died during the 1958 season, Allen was made personnel director, supervising the signing and selection of college players and coming up with successive rookie-of-the-year draft picks in Mike Ditka in 1960 and Ron Bull in 1961. His draftees were to make up more than half of the Bears' 1963 world championship team.

Allen also became an assistant to the then defensive coach, Clark Shaughnessy, applying to him the same sponge techniques he had used in absorbing so much from Sid Gillman.

"I learned a lot from Clark," he said. "We'd go to the movies together, eat together, ride in planes together — and all the time we'd be talking football. I learned some things to do and some things not to do."

Shaughnessy was a good man to learn from, perhaps the greatest of all football minds, a major contributor to the development of the T formation and sophisticated defensive tactics. However, he chafed at the lack of independence he had under Halas' iron thumb and after a few run-ins with the man who loved to say "I am the Bears" abruptly left the team with three games remaining in the 1962 season.

Allen was the de facto coordinator of the defense for the rest of that season, and, though both Rams and Redskins press guides say he headed the Bears' defensive unit for all eight years he was at Chicago, it was only for the final three, starting with 1963, that he was the man in charge.

Halas, who put Allen in Shaughnessy's place in addition to keeping him at his personnel position, had apparently differed with Shaughnessy over matters of defensive strategy, with Allen benefiting from the conflict.

Halas felt that the Bears linebackers should be used to a greater degree on pass coverage, while Shaughnessy preferred extensive use of red-dogging. As the 1962 season wore on, Allen, previously in charge only of defensive backs, had been assigned more and more to coordinating the efforts of the linebackers as well. His success in this was noted by Halas when he appointed Allen defensive coach on February 12, 1963.

"Allen has done an outstanding job, particularly in improving our pass defense," the old Bear said, and quoted statistics which showed that opposing teams had completed only thirteen touchdown passes against the Bears in 1962 compared to twenty-eight the year before and that the team's pass defense permitted the lowest percentage of completions in the league, 46.8 per cent, while its backs topped everyone by returning interceptions for a total of 468 yards.

Allen's timing in getting the job proved ideal, for the 1963 Bears had perhaps the best defensive year of any club in NFL history, leading the league in ten of nineteen defensive categories, finishing second in eight others, and setting a team record for interceptions, thirty-six, which still stands.

As the man held responsible for this, Allen, albeit only an assistant, immediately became the hottest coach in the league, much sought out for his philosophies. His thoughts then bore remarkable similarities to what he would tell the Washington Redskins nearly a decade later, starting with the basic proposition, "You win or lose in this league on defense."

"We cut down and simplified a lot of things in the last couple of games last season," Allen explained in 1963. "We simply try to eliminate mistakes, concentrate on not giving up the easy score, the long run or the long pass.

"Then we work on the A-B-Cs. Every day in camp we stressed fundamentals, all of them, the techniques and everything basic. That's the laborious part of the game, but it's what pays dividends. You don't beat yourself."

The dividend in 1963 was the biggest in football, the NFL championship via a 14-10 victory over the favored and offensively superior New York Giants.

The Giants were leading, 10-7, at the half, but in the third quarter Bears defensive end Ed O'Bradovich grabbed a Y. A. Tittle screen pass, one of the five interceptions the normally accurate New York quarterback would suffer that day against Allen's superb defense, and ran the ball to the New York fourteen. The winning touchdown, a one-yard sneak by quarterback Billy Wade, followed and the Bears were number one.

In the dressing room and on national television afterward, everything was coming up Allen. An unidentified lineman grabbed the mike to tell those in TV land, "Allen is a helluva coach . . . we've got a helluva defense, and he deserves credit . . . he's a helluva coach we say."

Allen was then brought before the cameras, and the Bear team, oblivious to sensitive ears, sang the following unbleeped tune:

> Three cheers for Allen,
> Three cheers for George,
> Hooray for George,
> He's a horse's ass.

To top things off, in a completely extraordinary gesture, Allen was awarded the game ball. Among those the gift was not lost on was one Dan Reeves, owner of the Los Angeles Rams. "This was unheard of," Reeves said later, "giving the ball to an assistant coach," and admitted that when he went shopping for a new head coach for his own team that the game-ball tribute put Mr. Allen at the top of the list.

But before it became official that Allen, indeed, was Reeves' new coach, he became the subject of a tug of war between two famous franchises. In the most publicized court battle the game has known before or since, Allen and Halas locked into a legal scrimmage that threatened the sport's entire structure. The extent to which Allen's contract as Bears assistant coach was brought into the open and publicly scrutinized was unprecedented, and Allen became a household name.

It all started innocently enough. Two days before Christmas 1965, Reeves fired his head coach, Harland Svare, and set out to find the ninth coach in twenty-one years for a club that hadn't had a winning season since 1958 and was sardonically described by Los Angeles sportswriter Bob Oates as "a proud team that wins three or four games every single year."

Reached in Chicago the day Svare was let go, Allen was quoted as saying, "I haven't been contacted by anyone from Los Angeles," adding, "but I'm deeply flattered to hear that I'm being considered. Every assistant coach looks forward to being top man some day. I'm no exception." So much for modest understatement.

On January 9, 1966, Allen flew out to California to talk with Reeves, and the next day, wearing a black-and-white plaid sports coat with a button-down blue-gray shirt and knit tie, looking some said like a young Cary Grant, he was presented to the world as the new forty-three-year-old Rams coach.

Allen told reporters he had turned the job down as late as the morning before, but after leaving the Rams offices he "kept walking and walking around the block. I must have walked two or three miles."

Then, after an unsuccessful attempt to phone Halas, Allen met with Reeves in the afternoon and was persuaded to agree to terms, which included a $40,000-a-year salary, more than twice the $19,000 he was making in Chicago.

A proud Reeves boasted, "He is the number one coach in the nation," adding in what proved to be a very ominous note that Chicago owner-coach Halas, who still legally had Allen's services for two more years, "did not and still does not want me to sign George Allen. But I don't believe George Halas ever would stand in the way of an assistant coach moving up. Halas is an old football man and in the oldest traditions of the game a head coach never stands in the way of an assistant's advancement. How can we have a league if head coaches prohibit the advancement of their best men?" So much for great expectations.

For his part, Allen added he had told Halas that "an opportunity presented itself here which does not come along every day. I said that I would appreciate his cooperation if I accepted. He said he would think it over."

Halas did think it over, but as a man who valued personal

loyalty next to, if not above, the deity itself, what he decided was to stun pro football as nothing had before. He called Reeves' action "a flagrant case of tampering" and released a statement that sounded like the declaration of war it was:

"I am shocked that the Los Angeles Rams and their president, Dan Reeves, would attempt to pirate our coaching staff.

"It is rather widely accepted that the Bears could be an outstanding team in 1966, and we feel strongly that anything that would disturb our organization would dilute our chances. It would be unfair to the other coaches, the players and the fans.

"Within the framework of that thinking, the Rams were told Allen's legal and binding contract with the Bears had two years to go and we expected him to fulfill the terms of his agreement. In 7½ years with the Bears, George Allen has been an integral part of our coaching staff.

"He has developed into a position of significance in the manner comparable to that of a player who improves steadily and becomes a high caliber performer over a similar period of time.

"In all my years of pro football, the Bears never before encountered such a flagrant case of tampering with a coach under contract to us.

"The Rams' utter disregard and contempt for legal obligations present a serious challenge not only to the Bears but to the entire structure of the National Football League . . .

"It is unfortunate that Allen can be misled through specious representation by the Rams and flout the terms of a legal two-year contract. Distasteful though any altercation is, the Bears must take whatever steps are needed to protect our best interest."

Both Reeves and Allen reacted to all this with words of dignified shock, but both refused to attack the venerable old Bear, Allen going so far as to say, "George Halas is the greatest man I have ever known. I had to take this job because it was an opportunity I couldn't turn down. I'm really stunned. I can't believe Coach Halas would do anything to hurt me.

"When opportunity comes, you can't let it fly out the window. I've worked for this all my life. Of all the jobs that have opened, I've got the best in football.

"But this has been the toughest decision I've had to make. My sentiment was with the Bears. I worked for Coach Halas for eight years and he knows that I gave him one hundred ten per cent no matter what he asked."

Revealing more about what was to be an increasingly dense situation, Reeves, claiming, "We acted properly in this matter all the way and followed all the rules," disclosed that far from tampering with Allen, it was Allen himself who approached him for the job.

"Last Christmas, George called one of our staff men, Johnny Sanders [chief scout], and asked if the Rams might be interested in him as a head coach. Sanders called me the following Monday after Christmas and I instructed him to tell George Allen to ask George Halas for permission to talk to us. And, Mr. Halas gave him this permission.

"In football parlance that means forget the contract and go get the job.

"Later, Halas rescinded this permission and his objection was quite strong. Mr. Halas said he didn't want me to take Mr. Allen, or, if you prefer, Mr. Allen to take me."

This did nothing to calm Halas, who claimed he gave Allen permission to negotiate 1) just to tell Reeves thanks, but no thanks, and 2) to protect Reeves, once a good friend, from the very charges of tampering he was now leveling against him.

Neither was Halas pleased when Pete Rozelle, the newly minted NFL commissioner and former Ram general manager, put his two cents in as well, for Rozelle felt there was "no cause" to interfere in the Allen situation.

"It has been traditional with the NFL and throughout sports that assistant coaches are permitted to take advantage of opportunities for advancement," Rozelle said, echoing his old boss Reeves almost to the very word. "On the basis of this historical precedent and the facts now known, this office finds no cause at this time to interfere with the Rams' signing of George Allen. It is hoped that the matter can be amicably resolved by the two clubs."

Amicable resolution was the last thing on Halas' mind. On Tuesday, January 11, just a day after the Rams announced their prize possession, he sent an attorney to Cook County Circuit Court charging breach of contract and seeking a permanent injunction to restrain Allen from taking the Los Angeles job.

The Bears further alleged that Allen had in his possession information on Bears plays, scouting reports, game films, and two volumes wittily titled "Bears' Defense Manual No. 2" and "Defense Textbook No. 2," which could be used against the Chicago team should they reach the wrong, which was to say Ram, hands.

What powers there were in the league, always fearful that any entrance into court action would unleash the feared demon of antitrust action against their previously inviolate sport, had tried vigorously to dissuade Halas from this suit, but he would have none of it.

"I agree with Pete Rozelle that this is a matter between two clubs and not of league concern," Halas waspishly commented. "It is for that reason that we filed our suit. The suit stands."

Never a master of favorable publicity, Halas did not realize that two documents attached to his complaint would generate considerable sympathy for his once but nevermore assistant. One was Allen's letter of resignation, the other his Bears contract.

The letter, which began "Dear Coach Halas," masterfully conveyed an image of Allen as the American dreamer in the land of opportunity, the humble servant who could and should not be expected to turn his back on the chance of a lifetime.

"No man has ever owed more to another than I do to you for all you have done for me," Allen wrote. "No one has ever had a more agonizing experience in arriving at a decision than I have had in bringing myself to this final act of resignation.

"The opportunity which has been offered to me to become head coach of the Los Angeles Rams is one I feel I must accept. The job of realizing this ambition is marred only by the regret of leaving a team, and an association with you, which has given me the most rewarding years of my life.

"In accepting the challenge to take over the Rams, I do so with deep humility, knowing that my opportunity has come about only because of my personal growth which has occurred under your leadership during the past eight years.

"It is more difficult to even imagine myself in competition with the Bears. Yet, I shall attempt to compete with you and with the other NFL teams with the same spirit which you have most exemplified."

It was signed, "Most sincerely, George H. Allen."

Allen's contract was a document of a different sort, one that with its unusually astringent clauses painted a picture of Halas as an old flesh peddler that nicely complemented the one of Allen as a hardworking, poor but honest youth.

Though acknowledging his "exceptional and unique knowledge, skill and ability as a football coach," the contract prohibited Allen, under pain of instant injunction, from joining, without Halas' special consent, any other football team, college or professional, for the three years of the contract. And for another three years after its expiration, he was prohibited under similar threat from coaching in the geographical territory assigned to the Bears, that is, Chicago and its environs.

Allen also agreed that he would not do any work for anyone else without the consent of Halas in writing and that he would not author any articles without the Halas okay.

It was further specified that he would have to pay any fines that might be levied against him by Rozelle and was only to say nice things about the Bears if approached for comments by reporters.

When, with a speed remarkable in an era of coagulated justice, Halas' injunction came before Cook County Circuit Court Judge Cornelius J. Harrington at 10 A.M. the following day, Wednesday the twelfth, it was the terms of this contract with Allen that came under scrutiny in the Chicago courtroom. And the Bears assistant, the only man to testify that day, came well prepared for the battle, bringing as his lawyer Albert E. Jenner, a vice president of the American Bar Association and a legal aide to the Warren Commission that was investigating President Kennedy's assassination.

Though he said he was "flattered" that Halas considered him so essential, Allen said he "didn't realize I was that important," and attempted to down-play his unique status, saying, "Players make the coaches."

"Every year an average of fifty head coaches change jobs," he told the court. He said his projected transfer from the Bears to the Rams would not sabotage the Bears signal system and avowed there were no such things as football secrets, making it seem that any man off the street could be a professional coach.

Jenner, his attorney, also played this up, saying, "Let us turn to this red herring of football defense manuals. He [Allen] doesn't want them and the Bears can have them. What Allen has in his head, he has, and he's not going to be able to get it out."

As far as the contract proper, when asked by the judge if he had read the thing, a seemingly confused Allen said no, he had not, that "every time I signed a contract they would add another page."

He also testified that before turning to the Rams for solace he had: first, sought assurance from the Bears that he would be their next head coach, second, asked an option on 5 per cent of the Bears' stock, and third, asked the team to match any bona fide offer he might receive from other clubs. The answers he got from Halas were not to his liking, he said, the discussions "frustrating and misleading," prompting him to feel his dream of being Bear head coach was no more than a phantom.

"He [Halas] stammered and stuttered," Allen said, "and told me there were eight or nine men under consideration for the job and indicated I didn't have much chance."

Allen added that he had told the Bears if they would match the Ram offer dollar for dollar he would "get on the next plane" back to Chicago and stated further that Halas had not withdrawn his permission to negotiate with Reeves until after he had accepted the job.

Claiming that the clause which described Allen's talents as unique and the one calling for immediate injunction should Allen attempt to go elsewhere were illegal in that they prevented the coach from bettering himself, Jenner asked Judge Harrington to declare them void. The judge responded by continuing the case six days until the following Tuesday, when Halas himself was scheduled to testify.

Though Allen was extremely disappointed at the delay, feeling that all time until he could officially take over as Rams coach was time lost from the imperative job of finding capable assistants, the six days was to see a large public outpouring of sympathy for his situation.

Newspaper columnists almost to a man deplored the tactics of "Scrooge" Halas, with one fellow nominating the Bear owner for "the Heel of Fame."

Even some of the Chicago players came out to say, as if there were any doubts remaining, that Allen was one swell coach.

All-pro linebacker Dick Butkus, for example, then just a rookie lineman, responded with a horrified "Oh, no," when appraised of the possibility of Allen's leaving the fold.

"Gee," he went on, "I hope we don't lose him. He's a real good football man. I work with him all the time. Gee, I mean, I like to see a man better himself, but I'd just hate to lose him. He's such a conscientious football man, he prepares you so well. He eats and sleeps football . . . I mean, this is a coach."

Allen himself gave sympathetic interviews during the wait, saying that while he thought nothing but good thoughts about Halas — "He has been like a father to me. We've had the finest relationship" — the ongoing dispute was making him feel "like a man who has just given or is giving blood."

"Psychologically," he went on, "it throws you all off. I can't sell my home and I can't organize a coaching staff. But I'm not going to let it get me down. I'm all the more determined to do a good job with the Rams if the injunction isn't granted. I've received mail from all over the country and all of it was encouraging. I didn't realize so many people were interested in a coach."

The most poignant moments of the week came in connection with Allen's Tunisian-born wife Etty, whose birthday fell on the day before the hearings were to be resumed.

"It should be the happiest moment of our lives, but the bottom has dropped out," Allen said on that day. "For eighteen years I've worked for a job like the one with the Rams and now all this has taken all the thrill and honor out of it," he said.

"My wife, whose birthday is today, is under a doctor's care and must use sedatives. My oldest boy, George, comes home from school with a sick stomach. It is tragic, and in some ways it's a joke."

Mrs. Allen, in an interview after the whole mess was over, added, if possible, additional pathos to the situation when she said, "I will never forget the night they served the injunction papers. The only other night like it in my life was when the Nazis came and took my father away in the middle of the night.

"George was in Los Angeles when the man drove up outside the house around nine-thirty," she continued. "He banged on the front door and I was afraid to let him in because I didn't recognize him. When he got back inside his car and just sat out front, I called the police."

The much-maligned Mr. Halas seemed unconcerned through all of this, claiming, "We aren't trying to win a popularity contest." What he was trying to win was revealed when George Halas, Jr., the Papa Bear's son and the club's president, denied a midweek rumor that the Bears merely wanted some stalwart Ram player as compensation for their lost coach.

"Absolutely untrue," said Halas fils, explaining that the suit was for "settling once and for all whether a coach's contract is a contract for both sides.

"What do you think will happen to other contracts our league teams have with players, with television, with landlords of their parks, if this one is allowed to go unchallenged?

"We have been advocating this for a long time. It is an issue which must be resolved, sooner or later, and this is as good a time as any. Is George Allen's case a breach of contract or is it not, if he is permitted to sign with the Rams? That is the basic issue, and the only one."

Finally, the day of judgment was upon them. In a courtroom dotted with Bear functionaries, Halas and Allen sat on opposite sides of the aisle as the old man studied an envelope covered with notes he planned to use when called to testify. The call never came.

For after the opposing attorneys exchanged preliminary remarks, with Allen's man Jenner invoking the demon antitrust with words like "in restraint of trade," Judge Harrington spoke. Taking a goodly number of words to do it, he ruled that in fact a bona fide binding contract did exist between George Allen and the Chicago Bears and Allen was indeed guilty of breaching it.

"The court," he said, "after reviewing the pleadings and considering the evidence offered, has come to the conclusion that sufficient prima facie evidence has been offered to convince the court:

"That a valid and binding contract of employment was entered into by the parties for a term of three years, which has been sanctioned and confirmed by reciprocal performance of the parties for the period of approximately one year.

"That the evidence indicates that respondent Allen breached

the contract by negotiating for employment as head coach with persons representing the Los Angeles Rams without first receiving written permission which was specifically required under his contract with the Chicago Bears.

"And it does appear that the respondent Allen further breached the contract in question by committing himself orally or in writing to be employed as head coach by the said Los Angeles Rams during the remaining term of his contract with the Chicago Bears.

"The problem now before the court is whether the remedy by injunction which has been requested here . . . will be granted by the court."

The judge thought he was about to decide whether the court could stop Allen from moving, but before another word was spoken, the surprisingly nimble Halas showed a fine flair for drama by leaping to his feet and, ignoring objections from Jenner as well as pulls on the coattails by his own attorney, approached the bench and asked permission to address the court.

After being sworn in, Halas turned to the judge, a friend of some duration, and said, "I am most pleased that your honor upholds the validity of the contract. Your important ruling will uphold the integrity between National Football League clubs and will preserve the sanctity of contracts."

Ignoring frequent objections by Jenner and obviously relishing center stage, Halas went on magisterially:

"Validity was the issue here and your ruling will prevent the breakdown of organized sports and all sports. George Allen was a minor issue here. Now I want to drop this suit and give Allen his full release. He can go to Los Angeles, and he goes with my blessing."

The shock in the courtroom was complete. Even the opposing lawyers exchanged incredulous looks. Finally, Judge Harrington asked that Allen's release be presented in writing and left the courtroom.

"I didn't tell my attorney I was going to do it," a pleased-with-himself Halas said. "But that is what I had been thinking about once the suit started. I never intended to keep Allen here after validity of contract was established."

At this point, Allen crossed from the defendant's table and extended a hand.

"Thanks, Coach," he said.

Halas did no more than fix him with a seventy-one-year-old glare.

"George, a few of those statements you made on the stand I did not like," he said, referring to Allen's claim he had oral permission to negotiate for the Rams job. "They weren't true, George."

Then, showman to the end, he asked Allen to come to his office the next day, adding "and bring those books," a reference to the by now famed Bear defensive manuals.

Asked by a reporter as he was about to leave if he would ever consider Allen as a head coach for the Bears, Halas began, "Well, I'll tell you, my boy," adding after the correct dramatic pause: "He won't be!"

Allen was much too relieved to be bothered by such histrionics, claiming that he hadn't even heard Halas make his grand declamation. "He wasn't talking very loud and I didn't hear him say it," he said. "It took me completely by surprise. I thought we would be in court all today and the next day."

And about those books? "I returned them several days ago," he said, later jokingly telling a photographer taking pictures in his basement not to include a stack of notebooks in the shot because "Halas will think they belong to him . . . I've already turned in my last eraser."

Papa Bear, however, was still in a state very far from humor. The day following his surprise courtroom reversal, Halas, with George, Jr., sometimes known as Muggs, at his side, called in the media to give his version of the case. "The fans and the press have a right to know," he said. "But until the case got out of court, there wasn't anything I could say."

Now properly unmuzzled, Halas had plenty to say. He claimed the entire situation "started with a subterfuge and ended up in chicanery," and, in a kind of last hurrah about the deterioration of principles and integrity in the face of a take-over by big business, reserved a special boo for NFL leader Rozelle.

"When Commissioner Pete Rozelle made that ill-advised statement, where he advocated substituting 'phony tradition' for a legal document," Halas gruffly stated, "we were all the more determined to go through with the lawsuit."

An inveterate note-taker who invariably answers phones with pad in hand, Halas produced a detailed record of what he said were his transactions with Allen and Reeves over the last two weeks, claiming that his former protégé made four propositions to stay with the Bears after he had come to terms with the Rams.

At various times, Halas said, Allen offered to remain with the Chicago team if:

He could become head coach when Halas retired.

He could be released for three or four years to coach the Rams and then return to the Bears as head coach.

He could purchase a 5 per cent option of Bears stock.

The Bears would match the Rams $40,000 per annum salary offer.

"One part of the chicanery," Halas said, "was that Allen did not tell Reeves that he was not available. The chicanery was that Reeves and Allen together connived to break a contract."

What Halas told the world forms a fascinating picture of power brokers at work, beginning with the statement, "Now chronologically, here is how it happened.

"On Tuesday night, December 28, George Allen called me from the Roosevelt Hotel in New Orleans [where he had gone to sign a draft choice] and Allen said at that time the Rams called him stating they were interested in him as far as the head coaching job was concerned. So Allen said he wanted permission to talk to Reeves.

"In an effort to prevent the stigma of tampering on Reeves, I told Allen it was okay to talk to Reeves, but also to inform Reeves that he was not available . . . And I told Allen the reason why he was not available. Most everybody expected the Bears to have a good football team in 1966 and I did not want our organization disturbed as it would dilute our chances.

"The next day, December 29, I talked to Dan Reeves and chided him because the Rams had called Allen without my permission. Reeves said he did not call Allen but that Allen called the Rams on December 25, Christmas Day, so I told Reeves the same thing I had told Allen. I did tell him that I didn't want the stigma of tampering on him so I told George Allen it would be okay for him to talk to Reeves but he was to tell the Rams he was not available.

"Reeves said the Rams were very much interested in Allen, and if the Rams did decide to hire him, would the Bears please release him. I said, 'Dan, I'd have to say "Please" right back at you and repeat that Allen is under contract to the Bears.' Reeves knew definitely at that time, December 29, that Allen was not available . . .

"When I talked to Allen the evening of December 30, about 11 P.M., Allen said that Reeves would like to know about him coming with the Rams and that he had to call him back.

"I said, 'George, I don't know why Reeves is asking you that again. I told Reeves yesterday that you were not available. So call him back and tell him that you are not available.' And Allen said, 'Well, will I get more salary?' And I said, 'Well, when you come back we'll talk about it.' . . .

"Allen came in the office on January 5 and he again wanted to know if I would let him out of the contract. I reiterated what I had told him on December 28. Then he said he would remain with the Bears if I promised him the head coaching position with the Bears when I retired.

"I told him I could not promise that. At this time I offered him a bonus for 1966 because of the talent scout work he had been doing. I did not know at this time, until he so testified later, that on January 4, a day earlier, he had agreed orally to take over the Rams head coaching job.

"If there was any uncertainty in my mind up to this time about retaining Allen, it all disappeared when he testified that he came to agreement with Reeves on January 4.

"On Thursday morning, January 6, Allen came in again and I talked to him in my office, and I held a similar conversation with him. He said he was going to take the Bears contract with him to an attorney . . . I still did not know at this time that he had agreed to coach the Rams.

"He came to the Bears office on Saturday afternoon and . . . made proposition number two. He said, 'If you let me go and coach the Rams for the next three or four years then I will return to the Bears as the head coach. I will agree to that now.' I had to laugh that off.

"Then he submitted another deal — that he would remain here if we would give him the option to buy 5 per cent of the stock. I told him that could not be done.

"So Allen laid a letter of resignation on my desk, indicating what it was, and I said we would not accept his resignation as he had two years to go on his contract. So he said he would go home and talk it over with his wife. He left the letter of resignation.

"Then he called me at 7:50 A.M. Sunday morning, January 9. He wanted to know if I would reconsider his request for the option to buy 5 per cent of the stock, and that he had a plane reservation for Los Angeles, but would cancel it if I would agree.

"I told him that we would not do it. So at 10:30 P.M. Sunday night, Allen called me at home from Los Angeles . . . and he made a fourth proposition to me. He said if we matched the salary that the Rams offered him he would catch the next plane to Chicago and not keep the appointment he had with Reeves in half an hour. I said, 'That is impossible.' Allen then said, 'What do you suggest?' I said, 'Come back to Chicago and fulfill your contract.'

"He made four propositions to me after he had already agreed with Reeves on January 4 to coach the Rams.

"When he handed in his letter of resignation on Saturday, I attempted to call Reeves because all this while I had not heard from him since I talked to him on December 29. That was the only time I had talked to him. I assumed he had understood what I had told him about Allen not being available.

"The part that amazed me was that Reeves was negotiating with Allen all this time. I couldn't reach him on January 8, Saturday, and left word at his office and at his home for him to return the call.

"On Sunday, January 9, at 2 P.M., Reeves telephoned me. I told him that I was astonished that he had been negotiating with Allen, and that I had not heard from him. Didn't he know that Allen had a legal three-year contract with two years remaining? I expected him [Reeves] to respect that contract.

"I asked him three times, pointedly: 'Have you talked to the commissioner?' He replied every time: 'I am placing a call to the commissioner.'

"On January 10 the commissioner called me, said he had talked with Reeves, and that he would not cite Reeves for conduct detrimental to football.

"That is when I became real concerned about the entire matter, not only Allen and Reeves, but the entire approach to our sport . . .

"Reeves said he thought he was going to sign Allen anyway. Well, of course that left us no alternative except to go to court . . .

"So you can say the real villain in the case was Reeves, with Allen and attorney Albert E. Jenner unwilling victims in a plan that could have caused a breakdown of the National Football League."

The reactions of those damned herein was more curt than the damnation, with commissioner Rozelle speaking first and saying, "I will comment to Mr. Halas directly and privately."

Then there was a public statement by Allen that began,

"Many statements in Mr. Halas' release, none of which are under oath, are completely incorrect.

"I testified under oath in court as to what happened. On the other hand, Mr. Halas did not choose to support his suit by testifying in court where he would have been subject to cross-examination by my attorneys.

"Mr. Halas filed an ill-advised lawsuit, which he withdrew. The suit has been dismissed and my attorneys advise me that nothing other than the fact the case was dismissed has any legal effect or precedent."

Still, though both coaches expressed a commendable desire to get back to the old x's and o's, the affair and the rancor it aroused refused to settle, surfacing again when premier defensive end Doug Atkins announced he was retiring because of the unseemly treatment given Allen as well as his own problems getting along with Mr. Halas.

"This situation that my friend, George Allen, has been involved in," Atkins said, "helped me make up my mind to wind it up with the Bears. It was the last straw.

"Halas has become too unreasonable," he continued. "He's impossible to deal with. I always got along great with Allen and he did a fine job of handling the Bears defenders. I'm in good shape and I could play a few years more, but because of present conditions I intend to quit."

Despite it all, Atkins changed his mind and remained for another year, but Halas' opinion of Allen was never to mellow. Asked for an appraisal of his former coach later that year, he hesitated for a moment before responding, "I would say he's a good organizer. He also prepares a good defense. That's about it."

And would he have trouble getting along without his number one assistant?

"Aw, that's a lot of baloney. He was a loyal assistant while he worked for me and that's all. I've been in football for forty-six years and I've somehow managed to get along."

For most of football, the first look at how well both coaches were to fare came in the second game of the 1966 season, when Allen's Rams hosted Halas' Bears on a late September night and, after being behind by three points at the half, outscored the Chicagoans 17-0 afterward for a 31-17 victory. Allen was so excited he couldn't sleep that night despite drinking four glasses of milk to calm his nerves.

The new Rams coach took a special delight in detailing how he outfoxed the old Bear in his own specialty, defense, by substituting the simple for the complex.

"The Bears were looking for shifts, red dogs, and odd man spacings," he said. "We didn't give it to them. They spent time on things during the week that we didn't use."

As befitted such an emotionally pivotal game, the Rams-Bears contest was filled with unusual happenings, so much so that Allen commented, "I've never seen a game that had so many things." Among the events he was talking about were:

A ninety-four-yard kickoff return by Chicago's Dick Gordon that didn't produce a touchdown, a forward pass that was fumbled by one receiver to another for a twenty-six-yard gain, three runs totaling 211 yards in a space of two minutes, seven fumbles (four lost) by the winning team, sixteen penalties, two consecutive Ram goal-line stands in which the secondary broke up six consecutive passes, and finally, Chicago's Mike Ditka, an Allen draft choice, wiping out a fan who ambled onto the field in the game's waning moments.

Stranger still was the intractable Halas' behavior before the game, as related by a perplexed Allen:

"Some man from CBS wanted me to pose with Halas and I said, 'Heck, yes,' but he refused. If that's the way he wants it, then it is his prerogative. I usually go up to shake hands with a coach after a game even if I win. But, if he feels that way . . . it's not even worth thinking about."

Nor did Halas give Allen as much as a glance after the game. With the Ram band playing "Happy Days Are Here Again," the old warrior walked from the field alone, staring into the stands.

Several of Allen's former defensive stalwarts on the Bears greeted their ex-coach in the foyer leading to the two dressing rooms. Offering congratulations on the victory, wearing happy expressions not normally associated with members of a losing team, were Dick Butkus, Dave Whitsell, Bennie McRae, Richie Petitbon, and Rosey Taylor.

The final word on the confrontation that wouldn't die was to come, ironically, from Vince Lombardi, then at Green Bay but fated to be the man whom Allen would replace with the Redskins.

At a league meeting after Allen had gone west, Halas was on his feet and subjecting Reeves and everyone else to a graphic lecture on Allen's moral shortcomings, going on and on about his opportunism, lying, scheming, cheating, lack of character, and more.

In the middle of it all, Lombardi leaned toward Reeves and, in a loud stage whisper, informed the Rams owner and the world, "Sounds like you've got yourself a helluva coach."

CHAPTER V

The People's Choice

HAVING SUFFERED THROUGH seven straight losing seasons, even Rams owner Dan Reeves was impressed with the job done by his first-year coach, George Allen. Trading for veterans, curbing Hollywood distractions by moving the team's practice site to Long Beach, working countless twenty-hour days, Allen won immediately in 1966, as he promised.

Getting off quickly, the Rams took four of their first five games and finished the season with an 8-6 record, with Allen receiving a loud ovation from his players in the locker room after the final game, a defeat.

Not only was there no hint of the animosity that was to mark their relationship, Reeves' early public utterances concerning his new coach were even characterized by their effusive praise.

"It was amazing after the heartbreak of a loss that they could come up with a hand like that," Reeves marveled after that final game of 1966. "Later, when I went around to say a few words to individual players, about sixty per cent of them volunteered how great George and the rest of the coaching staff had been this year.

"George has always been able to get the most out of his football players. One reason is that he takes time to work individually with players. He listens to their problems. When you have the regular workload of preparing for a game, it's hard to give that individual attention. But George does it. He becomes close to his players."

As in Washington, it was also a matter of having the right players to get next to. Trading furiously before that first season, Allen acquired seasoned veterans and spotted them in key defensive positions behind the already Fearsome Foursome front line of Deacon Jones, Merlin Olsen, Lamar Lundy, and Rosey Grier.

For linebackers, Allen talked Jack Pardee out of retirement, got Maxie Baughan and Myron Pottios in trades, and picked up Bill George after his release from Chicago. To bolster his secondary, he swapped for all-pro cornerback Irv Cross from Philadelphia.

"There's no substitute for experience on defense," Allen proclaimed, and his acquisitions brought along that commodity and more. If they were not the best in the league at their respective positions, they were reasonably close to it and worthy of the younger players' respect.

Declining from the outset to consider his first year one of traditional "rebuilding," even though the 1965 Rams finished 4-10 and last in the then seven-team NFL Western Conference, Allen declared, "I'm thinking of nineteen sixty-six, not nineteen sixty-nine or nineteen seventy. We want to win now. Let the other years take care of themselves."

To succeed, he said, the Rams would have to be "good, lucky, have great morale, and be willing to pay the price." There was only one thing he could be sure of in the early months, "paying the price."

"We'll pay it," he vowed. "We'll pay it."

They paid it so well that Allen's Rams moved up close to the top in all defensive categories after being last or close to it in the 1965 statistics. In sharp contrast with previous seasons, the Rams ranked first in defense against rushing and pass completions and allowed only 212 points, second to champion Green Bay.

If the Rams were not yet to be likened to Lombardi's Packers, they at least had proven quickly a resiliency under Allen they lacked in previous administrations. After their first defeat, 24-13 at Green Bay in the third game of the season, they came back to whip San Francisco, 34-3. And they refused to stay down in the midst of a four-game losing streak in midseason, recovering with a four-game winning streak.

As if the Rams' postseason ovation wasn't testimony enough to Allen's accomplishments, the players on the West squad Allen was named to coach in the Pro Bowl echoed the favorable sentiments.

"He's a great coach," said Gale Sayers. "I didn't have much contact with him while he was with the Bears. But I know one thing. When he left us, the Rams went to third and we went to fifth."

Even the normally staid Johnny Unitas claimed to be impressed. "I think the play book we have for this one game is bigger than the one we had at Baltimore for the entire season," he said.

In the final stages of 1966, the Rams defense gave promise of matching Allen's 1963 Bear defense, which allowed only 144 points, at the time a modern NFL record. In three of the final four games, the Rams gave up the meager total of sixteen points, leaving Allen anxiously counting the days to the next training camp.

Increasing Allen's anticipation was the thought of Roman Gabriel, just turning twenty-seven and about to blossom as a high-quality quarterback in his sixth pro season. Ending a two-quarterback dilemma that plagued his predecessor Harland Svare, Allen named Gabriel number one in 1966 ahead of Bill Munson, and the durable Gabriel responded with club records in passes and completions.

"Gabriel," said Allen, the memory bringing a rare smile to his face even five years later, "was like this, you see," raising his hand in a gradual ever-increasing ascent like an airplane taking off for parts unknown.

The Rams were not to disappoint him. After moving the

team's training camp to Cal State at Fullerton, Allen got them off to the fastest start of any of his teams, six straight exhibition victories and three more winning efforts as the regular season began.

Seemingly lost in thoughts, striving to overlook not even the faintest of minutiae as the mounting successes only sharpened his desire for more, the modestly built Allen displayed a tendency to wander absent-mindedly into the path of charging football players. Against the Vikings in the Coliseum, he was flattened near the sideline by running back Dave Osborn, resulting in a scurry of aides to where the coach lay, near a water bucket.

An East Coast writer, visiting the Rams' Long Beach practice field later that season, witnessed similar near calamities. On the same day, Allen was jarred by Gabriel, fading for a pass, and later by Jack Snow, running a pass route.

In addition to collecting bruises, Allen had, by that time, built the Rams up to close contention with traditional Western Conference powers Green Bay and Baltimore. In fact, after twelve weeks of the season, plus the exhibitions, the Rams had a 16-1-1 record. But 1967 marked the advent of a new divisional structure in the NFL, the Rams being bracketed with Baltimore in the four-team Coastal Division. And the Colts had done even better, going undefeated in the regular season, 10-0-2 compared to the Rams' 9-1-2.

A game behind Baltimore with two games remaining, both in the Coliseum against none other than the Packers and Colts, the Rams seemed on the verge of elimination from the race, unprecedented as their record for a Ram team might be.

Reacting as he usually does to challenges, with something like the 110 per cent effort he asks of his teams, Allen put the Rams through unusually thorough workouts leading up to the Packer game. A typical one lasted two and a half hours and featured tumbling exercises, violent hitting among the linemen, diving catches, sixty-yard passes by Gabriel, and wind sprints.

"This is why we're in such good shape," he told the eastern

writer without looking up from his stopwatch. "We do more running than anybody else. Roger Brown never ran so much in seven years at Detroit." And Allen had the facts to support his conditioning theories: the Rams had outscored their opponents 106-38 in the fourth period.

Noticeably pale and gaunt and, at 172, fifteen pounds under his normal weight because of his poor eating habits, Allen said, "I had a cup of coffee and a piece of toast this morning. I didn't eat lunch. Didn't have time. And I'm not hungry now."

He added that he was looking forward to a good dinner with his wife at home on Friday night. That was Wednesday. Until then, home being forty-five minutes away in Palos Verdes, he would endure in a nearby motel after spending all of the night and most of the early morning hours watching films and organizing strategy. "She's been very understanding," he said of Mrs. Allen.

Never taking his eyes from the field as practice wound down on the outfield grass of the Blair Field baseball park, Allen said, "We're trying to get rid of the Hollywood image. I want conscientious, dedicated players. If they're not, I'll get rid of them.

"When we're traveling, I don't want to stay in the downtown areas. I'd rather get out in the suburbs, away from it all. This year we didn't lose any road games. It's the first time the Rams have ever done that."

Adding that it took him only one week to decide to revamp the Rams, he said, "You have to live with yourself now. I'm not interested in nineteen seventy-one. I wasn't interested in a long-range building program. Trading for veterans is not so much of a gamble if you get people like Maxie Baughan and Irv Cross and Bernie Casey."

Casey figured largely in the Rams' improved attack in 1967. Recognizing the need for offense, especially a wide receiver, Allen seized the opportunity to land Casey in a deal for an expendable running back, Tom Moore.

A long-time San Francisco veteran, Casey had been traded

to Atlanta, where he refused to report. Allen promptly relieved the Falcons of their problem and solved one of his own. The presence of the 6-foot-4 Casey, a poet, artist, and actor of some talent, eliminated the frequent double coverage Jack Snow had been given on the other flank the previous season and opened up the Ram attack, which climbed to second in the league in scoring in 1967.

Unfortunately for the Rams, Casey spent only two years with the club, retiring in his prime after the 1968 season to devote his life to the arts, to Allen's profound consternation.

"Bernie was different," linebacker Jack Pardee was to recall years later, himself unable to quite comprehend what Casey had gone and done. "He always said he didn't like football. But I find that hard to believe, as good as he played.

"After the season, he'd say he didn't like to play. Others would say it but they didn't act it. Bernie was the only player who said it and acted it the same way."

Having lost Casey, one notable player Allen failed to lure from retirement, the Rams never again under Allen had a wide-receiver threat with such a capacity to loosen up a defense.

But they would have, had it not been for one trade Allen would have rather had back.

Seeking to strengthen his running game before the 1969 season, Allen obtained veteran Izzy Lang from Philadelphia, including in his shipment to the Eagles an until-then little-known receiver, one Harold Jackson.

While Jackson blossomed into one of the league's best receivers at Philadelphia, Lang proved no bargain in Los Angeles, as did the receiver Allen chose to keep over Jackson, Wendell Tucker, who, after some short-lived heroics in 1969, flattened out.

"Coach Allen didn't feel he could keep both," Pardee recalled. "They were both the same type of receiver. They were little and had speed. You can't have a whole team like that. Coach Allen chose one and had to let the other go. Tucker had a little more experience. He had one good season, then started having problems after that."

But in 1967, Casey was one of the key offensive threats for the Rams, and it was he who caught the winning touchdown pass in the last thirty-four seconds to beat the Packers in one of the most memorable of all Ram football games. Seemingly beaten in the final minute, the Rams blocked a Green Bay punt, the ball rolling to the Packer five-yard line, and scored on the pass twenty seconds later to win, 27-24.

Hundreds of fans heading for the Coliseum exits turned around in wonderment and scrambled back to their seats. There were some literally running back into the stadium, through the empty seats in the sealed-off end zone portion of the huge arena. Others never did see the finish. Having given up hope, they were in the parking lots, some beyond.

One man said, "I heard a roar and ran for the car. I turned on the radio and the announcer was saying, 'We won, we won.' He was sobbing. It was unreal."

The victim of the blocked punt was the left-footed Donny Anderson. Allen, not surprisingly, had had his men practicing blocking left-footed punts that week.

Still one game behind Baltimore, but miraculously still in the race, the Rams, by virtue of an earlier tie with the Colts, could win the Coastal Division outright with a victory the following week. Although their records would be an identical 11-1-2 in that event, the Rams would win it on the basis of more points scored in the two Ram-Colt games.

If the Green Bay game wasn't Allen's finest hour in Los Angeles, then the Colt game promised to be. Immediately after the Packers were beaten, a sign was posted in the Rams dressing room: "Get the Colts." Unbeaten though they were, the Colts clearly would be in the uncomfortable position of losing all chance for a share of play-off money against a team at an emotional peak so acute Knute Rockne himself would have been impressed.

Back in Long Beach and filling his nervous stomach with an eggnog milk shake at the lunch counter in the golf shop, which also houses the Rams offices, Allen talked about his "total defense" that he hoped would stop the passing of Johnny Unitas.

"The Rams could always stop the run," he said, "but they used to be last in interceptions and giving up yardage on passes." What Allen did to compensate was to install 300 variations of formations and 150 audible signals. The average Ram play book weighed fifteen pounds.

His milk shake finished, Allen rushed from the building and, taking cranelike strides across the edge of the golf course on the way to the adjoining practice field, said, "Come along, but I've got to keep moving.

"When you've been in the coaching business long enough you usually can look back and find a reference to help you prepare," he continued, growing as expansive as a few seconds permit. He likened his plans for stopping Unitas to those he used as Bears defensive coach in stopping Y. A. Tittle in the 1963 title game.

"They're very similar circumstances," he said. "Unitas and Tittle are much alike, except Unitas is a little quicker at getting the ball away and he runs a little better."

Decorated with posters that said, "The difference between mediocrity and greatness is extra effort" and "Always remember, anything is yours if you are willing to pay the price" and "100 per cent is not enough," the Rams clubhouse looked more like that of a college or high school team.

Why Allen was not laughed all the way back to Morningside College was explained by Lamar Lundy, defensive end and dean of the Ram players. "What he has done," Lundy said, "is give the older players a feeling that they are important. He stopped all the building programs and made us feel we were more than just people filling in until other younger ones came along."

Also appealing to most players was his soft-sell approach. "I let Carroll Dale get behind me and score that thirty-yard touchdown pass last week," cornerback Clancy Williams said. "In nineteen sixty-five if I had done that I would have been chewed out. So I came back to the sideline and Allen said quietly, 'Clancy, you can't give him the inside.' That's where Dale likes to run, and I moved over after that."

And so, on December 17, 1967, George Allen's Rams put together the game of their lives. The Fearsome Foursome overran Unitas. Gabriel, knighted by Allen the year before as the undisputed number one quarterback, completed eighteen of twenty-two passes for 257 yards and three touchdowns, in the process setting the club record for touchdown passes in a season that surpassed such Ram legends as Bob Waterfield and Norm Van Brocklin. The final score: 34-10. The Rams had won the Coastal Division title.

"I knew it was going to be this way," Roger Brown said afterward. "I knew it wasn't going to be close. It was going to be the one with the momentum that was going to win."

Brown also stated that Baltimore hadn't really known what pressure was, reasoning that it was easier for the Colts with an almost season-long, one-game advantage than for the Rams, who experienced the weekly desperation of trying to keep pace.

Having handed Baltimore its only defeat of the season and taken the title, the Rams reacted almost as if they'd expected to win, in marked contrast to the jubilation that had followed the blocked punt and victory over Green Bay. "I feel great," a subdued Gabriel said, "but I jumped up and down all I could last week. It doesn't show, but I feel happy for the whole club."

In fact, the Rams had expended more emotion in those two weeks than most teams do in a season, and, in some cases, quite a few seasons. If Vince Lombardi's task before the Western Conference play-off game in six days was to rally his heavily injured Packers after two defeats and hold them together for one last championship effort, Allen's was even greater.

Having to face Green Bay, Baltimore, and Green Bay on successive weekends was enough of a chore, but now Allen would be taking his team, critically drained of emotion, into what promised to be a frigid afternoon in Milwaukee.

"I've tried to convince our team that cold weather is Ram weather," he said, after being named the Associated Press co-coach of the year, along with Baltimore's Don Shula. "In other years, I think the Rams were beaten before they took the field on cold days out of town." He also warned that many of the Packers had played little in their meaningless last game.

Up in Green Bay, Lombardi was turning the oddsmakers' choice of the Rams by three to his own psychological advantage in what Jerry Kramer described over the phone that very day as one of Lombardi's greatest pep talks.

"He came in this morning," Kramer said, "and there was that gleam in his eye. He said, 'We're wounded. We're hurting. They're picking L.A. But they better be ready to play a football game when they come into Milwaukee. We're going to take it to them.'

"I felt a little better after that," Kramer added. "I was seriously worried before this morning."

Though the Wisconsin temperature climbed into the high fifties on the Thursday morning before Saturday's game, the chill hit just as quickly that afternoon as gray clouds moved in. By the time the Rams worked out in Milwaukee Friday it was hardly picnic weather, twenty degrees.

With the game as a backdrop, some striking similarities in the Allen and Lombardi coaching methods seemed apparent. Opposite as they might be in temperament, they had employed precisely the same technique to revive their respective franchises.

Both shored up last-place, ten-game losers by trading for veterans, Lombardi having brought in Fuzzy Thurston, Willie Davis, and Henry Jordan among others after taking over the Packers in 1959. Both Allen and Lombardi had settled on one quarterback. And both produced winning seasons in one year and division titles the next.

By late Saturday afternoon, the parallel could be extended. Just as Lombardi's second team had failed to go the route in 1960, falling short in the title game, so too Allen's second Ram squad came up short.

With a temperature of twenty-two degrees and a chill factor somewhere near zero, Allen, clad in a lightweight blue Rams windbreaker to remind his men it was really Rams weather after all, watched his team bow, 28-7. Among the Packers, however, there was high praise for Allen's team, particularly from tackle Bob Skoronski, who said, "It didn't take an ordinary game to beat them. In fact, we may have played better than we were even capable."

The season over and almost everyone gone from the stadium, Allen walked underneath the windswept stands to find Lombardi and congratulate him. As he came upon the Packers bus, its doors shut and it pulled away.

Unnoticed, Allen stood there a moment, a cold, solitary figure, shoulders hunched, a portrait of despair in the enclosing darkness. It had been a lost weekend from the moment of their arrival, which had coincided with a temperature plunge of forty-six degrees.

If this was the game Allen would carry with him until next season, there was also the consolation that his theories on building a football team could not be all that misguided. For all the elderly veterans he had obtained, the Packers were older and balder and, up to then, still better.

But before the 1968 season, there remained one more game for the Rams, the most meaningless of all pro football games, the now-abandoned Runner-up Bowl in January, the Stupor Bowl. Two teams whose seasons have been ruined are told to report to Miami and put on a good show.

Characteristically, Allen took it seriously. He established history one day, becoming the first and last coach to ever hold two prebowl workouts between the rising and setting of the sun. "This is nineteen sixty-eight and we want to start off on the right foot," he reasoned. And the Rams did, crushing Cleveland,

30-6, to complete their season with a remarkable 18-2-2 record.

In the off season, claiming to have had the best-conditioned team the previous two years, an opinion no one was about to challenge, Allen stepped up his training program anyway, dispatching the team's trainer all around the country to check out the players, not once but twice.

The string of goals Allen set for 1968 was not much greater than 1967, the coach commenting modestly, "You can't improve much on near perfection." As examples, the 1967 goal for interceptions had been twenty-eight. The Rams intercepted thirty-two. He made a 1968 goal of thirty. He kept his standard for opponents' rushing average at three yards after leading the league with 3.1 the previous year.

More than a strict defense, what had enabled the Rams to move up in 1967 was their markedly improved offense. Having scored 289 points in his first season, the Rams were to lead the league in 1967 with 398, Allen adding that his team improved from about 50 per cent to 75 per cent on successful third-down and short-yardage situations. While the Rams quarterbacks had been dumped fifty-four times in 1966, the total was reduced to thirty-one in 1967.

Just about the best Allen could hope for in 1968 was to maintain the Rams' level of play, and he came close. The Rams finished 10-3-1, good enough to win almost any division except the Coastal. Stubbornly refusing to lose week after week, Baltimore went 13-1 on the way to their Super Bowl disaster against the Jets, relegating the Rams to a second-place finish.

Along the way, however, Allen again demonstrated his knack for bringing his teams to emotional summits. Trailing the Colts by half a game with three weeks remaining in the season, the Rams faced a severe challenge against the Vikings in Minnesota. Not only had the Rams never won there, compiling an 0-5-1 record in the North Country, Allen had experienced there his most embarrassing defeat as Rams coach, a 35-7 loss in 1966.

In addition, the Rams had been hit with such a virulent outbreak of flu that their Bloomington motel looked more like a hospital ward on the eve of the game. Undaunted, Allen, calling the Rams "a complete team" because of their improved offensive capabilities over two seasons, predicted his men would win the last three games and repeat their title with another last-game victory over Baltimore.

Responding to still one more challenge as a snowstorm struck the morning of the game, the Rams got out of their sickbeds to humiliate Minnesota, 31-3, prompting an instant celebration that began at the final gun and grew louder as the players rumbled down the tunnel to their dressing room.

"No little ol' fever is going to keep me in bed," said Deacon Jones, who got his temperature down from an alleged 105 to an alleged 102 by game time, then made ten unassisted tackles. "I couldn't take a deep breath. My head felt big. My chest was congested. But my philosophy is, 'If I can walk, I'm going to play.'"

"All man . . . a great man," chortled Allen, downing his milk. "We broke two jinxes. We won for the first time in Minnesota. And we won in the cold and snow." Then quarterback Gabriel said, "We beat two jinxes. We won in Minnesota. We won in the cold." Any more questions?

Nevertheless, Allen's prediction went awry the following week when the Rams fell out of the race by losing not only a down in the fourth quarter on an official's error but a spirit-crushing 17-16 game to Chicago, then bowing in a meaningless final game to Baltimore, 28-24.

The season ended all too soon, and a heartsick Allen expounded on his grief to the Los Angeles *Times'* Charles Maher.

"I just have no desire for material things," he said. "Food, entertainment, anything. I just don't want it." Nor, he revealed, could he even sleep.

"It's been that way ever since the goshdarn Bear game," he said. "This is one of the things Vince Lombardi told me got to him the most when he was coaching. He just couldn't sleep. He said it took him until Tuesday to get unwound, but by that time a coach has to start getting wound up again.

"A coach has to be realistic, but when you've lost your last two games by a total of five points, it can't help but leave you emotionally drained.

"So much has been accomplished. Yet, when you lose, it all seems to go down the drain. I suppose it's a shame to take these things so seriously. Maybe you think I'm crazy for taking them so seriously. But I think everybody has got to take his job seriously.

"So many people are content to be the paper on the wall. It's not the money that interests me. Money means nothing. The only thing that counts if you're a coach is to be able to feel you've accomplished a lot with the team. And I thought we were going all the way this year.

"I won't be going down to watch the Super Bowl. I feel we're as good as any team that will be playing in that game. I wouldn't want to go down there and see somebody else play in it."

Allen having compiled a 21-4-3 league record over two years, there was not a hint of what was to come in a matter of days in the form of a startling greeting from owner Reeves. Indeed, it was written in Los Angeles, "For Allen, the Ram picture today is about as bright as any in football . . . A Ram coach probably is the most independent coach in America, college or pro. In 23 years, Reeves never has interfered in the football department. His coaches always have had 100 per cent authority . . ."

Exactly one week later Allen was fired.

The coach was stunned, as was almost an entire city. At 8 A.M. on the morning after Christmas, Reeves called Allen and gave him the news.

"You have no idea how shocked and hurt he was when he was fired," his wife, Etty, said at the time. "When Mr. Reeves woke us up that morning, George just stared at the phone. All he could remember afterward that Mr. Reeves said was, 'You're fired.'

"It was brutal. It was so unexpected, too. But the brutality, that's what hurt. So different than Paris. Before going to the guillotine, they always gave a man a cigarette and the chance to say a few prayers."

Rare though it was to fire such a successful coach, Reeves nevertheless dismissed the action with a simple announcement to the world that he had done it because of a "personality conflict."

It had flared into the open a month before when Reeves publicly censured Allen for his remarks criticizing the rain-soaked Kezar Stadium playing field after the Rams were held to a 20-20 tie by the 49ers. Bitter words were then exchanged the following week when Reeves went to the locker room to congratulate Allen on a dramatic last-minute victory over the Giants. Allen declined Reeves' handshake, then later angrily took exception to the owner's public criticism.

There was one other occasion when Reeves had been noticeably upset at Allen. In 1967, the Rams had been caught spying at a Cowboys practice in Dallas. Allen tried to make a joke of the incident, but Reeves found nothing to laugh at, regarding the occurrence as a loss of integrity for the entire Rams organization.

As shocking as the news of the firing was to the public, however, there were long-festering disagreements between Reeves and Allen, kept secret by the Rams organization, that foretold some sort of inevitable break between the two.

First, that the Rams were spying on the Cowboys in 1967 did not come as all that much of a shock to Reeves, for it was common knowledge within the organization, according to the testimony of a club official, that, in fact, the Rams were out gathering information on other clubs as early as 1966, Allen's first year.

"We had guys on the road that first year," the official said.

"There was one guy who's gone on to be a prominent NFL figure who we'd see in cities where we were playing."

Another area of conflict beginning as early as 1966, which Allen would not mention for obvious reasons, involved his coaching province, the question of who would play the games. Reeves disagreed with Allen's almost exclusive use of Roman Gabriel at quarterback, resulting in a restless number two, Bill Munson.

"When I traded Bill Munson," Allen said, "that was really against the management's policy. They didn't want me to trade Bill Munson." Actually, the Rams had little choice, Munson having played out his option in 1967, something Reeves had hoped to forestall by persuading Allen to play the quarterback more.

Even from the very outset of Allen's term, the Ram hierarchy realized they had a coach of a different breed in their midst. Calling all football outposts in search of talent in his first month on the job, Allen ran up a $3000 phone bill. The Rams office quickly discovered that it was nothing for Allen, off in Chicago assembling his coaching staff, to call in three or four times daily if there was something on his mind.

Reeves' protestations about integrity notwithstanding, the friction and unhappiness, as is often the case in professional sports, had money as its root. Operating as he does, quite literally, on the win-at-all-cost theory, Allen did not hesitate to spend lavishly on salaries and all sorts of equipment, in short, anything he thought was needed to win. Be it bonuses or blocking sleds, Allen could be counted on to use Reeves' money to get them for his players.

"He brought up things we never dreamed we needed," a Rams official said. "We had so many contraptions at training camp we called it 'Disneyland North.' Over the years we tested every kind of blocking dummy imaginable.

"Once we had a tackling dummy known as 'Joe the Bartender.' It was like a big balloon, weighted at the bottom, and about seven feet tall, his arms outstretched and something like a helmet on his head.

"He'd be the simulated receiver. A coach would throw the ball at him and the linebackers would hit him, and he'd bounce right back up. He only lasted a couple of sessions."

That Reeves played a significant role in the development of the college player draft, a source of talent largely ignored by Allen, and that their ideas of social life were poles apart neither helped the relationship nor ultimately caused its wreckage.

Of far greater significance were Allen's ready and ample cash outlays, including bonuses for games well played, funds to untangle financial woes of newly acquired players, even bonuses to players for napping in their hotel rooms the afternoons before games.

Lacking the authority to do many of the things he did, Allen simply did them anyway.

"First of all, a coach has to know what he wants to do and when he wants to do it and if you don't have that authority then you're always going to be frustrated," said Allen, after a season of enjoying that very control with the Redskins.

"Now in L.A. I did a lot of things I didn't have authority to do, but the only reason I did them is that many times I couldn't locate Dan Reeves and by the time I'd get an answer it might be too late, you see. If we're going to make this trade or aren't we, well, we can't find Dan. He's out somewhere under the weather and you might not see him for a month.

"So I did some things there that upset him but they were all things that turned out to be correct. We didn't make many mistakes in L.A. and I took the authority into my hands and I would do it again because if you don't do it and you lose you're going to get blamed anyway."

At Christmas 1968, however, none of this intramural feuding mattered to Rams fans, who had been treated to three highly successful seasons, or to the great majority of the players, who were enjoying the fruits of victory under Allen.

Thus, Reeves badly underestimated the highly charged reaction of the Los Angeles populace and players that he was to detonate with his announcement of Allen's firing. Immediately, Ram veterans threatened retirement, calling Reeves' action "unbelievable."

Gabriel's reaction was as forceful as any. "I don't know if it's worthwhile to come back here," he said. "If Allen goes somewhere else and there is a chance I could join him I would." According to Gabriel, of the fifty-three Rams, including taxi squaders, no more than three were opposed to Allen and no more than five were neutral.

The next day a citizens' committee to return Allen to the Rams was formed, and switchboards at the Rams office and the local papers were jammed with calls protesting Allen's dismissal.

Two days after the firing, an emotional Allen, his eyes reddened from lack of sleep or tears or both, appeared with a dozen of the Ram players at a press conference in the Sheraton West Hotel.

Speaking first to the assembled media, Allen outlined briefly his version of the feud with Reeves:

"When I first arrived here I got the shock of my life when I saw the Rams training facilities at San Fernando Recreation Center. They were the worst facilities I had ever seen in my life. The locker room was a disgrace. I wouldn't even have the Russians train there.

"I couldn't eat for three days after seeing it. I told Reeves that these facilities were for a last-place club. This was our first personality clash. Mr. Reeves is a man who doesn't like to be pushed, and I don't blame him.

"But I wouldn't take no for an answer. You have to fight for what you think is right in this world and I was fighting for my players. We then got the facilities we wanted at Long Beach.

"The second personality clash occurred when I saw our summer training camp at Chapman College. The players held meetings in the cafeteria while people were washing the dishes. I finally got a new site at Cal State, Fullerton, one of the best in the league. These are the personality clashes; I don't want to go into the others.

"If I put on any pressure or pushed, it was only to improve the football team and existing conditions, nothing else. I hate to see it go down the drain. I feel we could have built a football dynasty here."

Backing up Allen, figuratively and literally, were quarterback Gabriel, Ram legends Deacon Jones and Merlin Olsen, end Jack Snow, tackle Charlie Cowan, defensive end Lamar Lundy, defensive backs Eddie Meador, Claude Crabb, and Ron Smith, and linebackers Jack Pardee, Doug Woodlief, and Tony Guillory.

Capsulizing their feelings was Deacon Jones, the Rams' so-called "Secretary of Defense," who declared, "The last time you'll see number seventy-five play is in the Pro Bowl game if Allen doesn't come back." Linebacker Maxie Baughan and fullback Dick Bass sent messages that they, too, would retire if Allen were not rehired.

Making the firing all the more incongruous was a $20,000 Christmas bonus Reeves had given Allen, not enough to prevent the owner from being hung in effigy on the front door of the Rams offices. The citizens' committee claimed it had received messages of support for Allen from 2500 persons. A players' committee, led by Meador, demanded and got a meeting with Reeves.

Under the mounting and unprecedented pressure, Reeves relented. It was New Year's Day when Reeves called and invited Allen to his house.

"We sat there and talked," Allen recalled, "and I could see that, really, I was going to take him off the hot seat. Not only the players, it was the fans and everything. He was on the spot.

"Later he told Bud Furillo of the L.A. *Herald-Examiner*, 'Boy, I got out of this lucky,' you see, because I came back, I didn't ask for anything, I kept the same contract, no extension of the contract, everything the same. Bob Reynolds [Rams vice president] said, 'George, I tell you, I've never seen anything like that, for a guy to come back and keep his word like that . . .' Because I was in the driver's seat, see, I could say, 'Hey, listen, I want a forty-thousand-dollar raise, I want four more years,' he was on the spot.

"I understand he tried to get Vince," which, in fact, Reeves did, calling Green Bay the day he fired Allen, "but, hell, Vince wasn't going to come into a situation like that.

"So he couldn't get anyone who would satisfy everyone. So he didn't take me back because he loved me. He took me back because I wanted to come back and he had to."

Five days later, January 6, 1969, Allen was rehired to complete his original contract, ending one of the most bizarre chapters in the history of any sports team.

Attending a press conference at the Century Plaza Hotel, Reeves and Allen shook hands and Allen read a prepared statement expressing his gratitude to the players and happiness to be returning "as Dan's coach." For his part, Reeves said Allen would remain as coach the next two years barring any "flagrant violations" of either league rules or "understandings" between the two men. He added that he and Allen would try to meet at least once a week in an effort to avoid differences.

While Merlin Olsen and others contended the whole affair would solidify the team, which, indeed, went on to win a second Coastal Division title in 1969, center George Burman, who was a Ram then and later a Redskin under Allen, offered quite another view. As loyal as they come to Allen, Burman nevertheless cited an adverse effect on the players as a result of the Reeves-Allen feud.

"That sort of action is fine," said Burman, referring to the support he and the other players gave Allen at the time of his 1968 firing. "But it was also the beginning of the end. There was never any doubt about how the situation was going to be resolved. Everybody knew that eventually George had to go and that it would likely be at the end of his five-year contract.

"So it was like playing for a guy who was virtually gone. It became harder and harder for a player to cope with the situation. A player feels an allegiance to the coach and the owner. I really felt loyalty to both. I play for one, the other pays me. What do you do, take sides? You didn't know exactly what to do. It bothered me. It bothered everybody.

"When the players stood up for Allen, it wasn't a slap at Reeves. It was just them saying, 'Look, we're winning. This is the first chance we have to go somewhere and you want to bring in a new coach and a whole new system.'

"I believe L.A. wants to develop its talent from within. They'd rather not win a championship with talent obtained from other teams. The supreme thing is to go all the way with forty original draft choices. I felt that was the way Reeves wanted to do it and his friends are still in the organization. George felt it was a waste of his time to concentrate on techniques, teach them from the ground up.

"So there was a lot of pressure between coach and management. This put George on edge and the whole coaching staff on edge. L.A. had its definite ideas, and it wasn't George's way of doing it. The owners have a right to do it any way they want. So it was only a matter of time before George had to leave.

"Here in Washington, management says, 'Here, you're the coach, we believe you have a way to win, so go and do it.' This has relieved George. He's a lot more relaxed, if you could ever describe George as relaxed.

"The result is that from George on down through the whole coaching staff there is a more relaxed approach. I felt there was more openness in the Redskin camp. The coaches were less ready to give you a hard time for what you might say or do. This was one thing that helped us to get the togetherness we eventually had.

"My coach, Mike McCormack, was a new experience for me.

He was completely open and friendly and willing to help. He'd only get uptight if he felt we were really doing something wrong. They treated us more like men than infantile football players.

"Since there was less tension with the Redskins, the attitude among the players was better. Players in L.A. got on others in other positions. I didn't see any of that here. The situation there became more uncomfortable, more of an impossible situation for the players.

"In nineteen seventy, there were many reasons why the players didn't stand up again. It had been very difficult for the players to put up with the coach-management friction. By that point, everybody knew it was inevitable.

"By then, the feeling developed among some, 'What can I do?' Maybe some were glad to see him go because of the uncomfortable situation. Others just couldn't tolerate the situation anymore. You reached a point where you didn't want anything to do with it.

"You wanted to support Allen as much as you could but after a while you're afraid to take a stand. I don't think there's such a thing as a blackball around the league as such, but certainly, maybe at a meeting, one owner can say to another, 'Look, this guy's goddamn trouble.' And when a player's getting older, getting marginal, he's got to be careful. The owners can put the word out on players. The NFL's a cartel, and that's the function of every cartel there ever was.

"At the time of the first firing, we were coming off the play-offs in nineteen sixty-seven and we had just missed them in nineteen sixty-eight, and we should have been in them, and we had the feeling we really had something going. It was new and exciting.

"In nineteen seventy, I suppose some of the guys felt we had four good shots in a row. Twice we lost in the first play-off game. Twice we just missed the play-offs. There was a different feeling. It wasn't Camelot as it had been in the beginning. After the nineteen seventy season, I know I was pretty flat."

Little wonder, for once Allen was welcomed back by Reeves the Rams were to be engaged in two more years of pressure races. Making two more deft trades to improve his attack for the 1969 season, Allen brought in kick returner Alvin Haymond and mammoth tackle Bob Brown, both from Philadelphia. Acquired from Chicago, Rich Petitbon moved into the defensive secondary.

To nobody's surprise, Allen called the Rams' opening game of 1969 "crucial," and no one could take exception because it was against the arch-rival Colts in Baltimore. Though former Colt Haymond saw the opportunity for "vengeance in a sense" and vowed to break off not one but two long returns, the victory the Rams were to achieve was confected in traditional Allen style of defense and opportunism.

Converting a pass interception and a fumbled punt into ten points, the Rams rallied to win, 27-20, in a game that established the tempo of the season for both clubs: the Rams going on to win their first eleven games and the division title, the Colts suffering through one of their worst seasons in recent years, 7-7.

Restoring order in his stomach with the customary cup of milk, Allen, calling the victory "number one, at least right now," uttered virtually every one of his patented wall mottoes in the span of a few seconds amid the wild locker-room celebration.

"This is the story of the Rams . . . forty players working for each other . . . blood and guts . . . scratching and fighting . . . Nobody gave us a chance . . . This is a lesson that you should never give up."

"Bubba who?" Burman shouted.

"Shut up," said first-string center Ken Iman, eyeing reporters nearby.

But it didn't matter. The coach was saying the same thing. Asked about the play of new tackle Bob Brown, who opposed the best-known Colt lineman, Bubba Smith, Allen came up with an identical "Bubba who?"

Sitting quietly in front of his locker, safetyman Meador, who had led the players' committee to have Allen reinstated, said earnestly, "You can't imagine how happy we are. I used to play on some Ram teams that didn't win many and this is so satisfying. We worked so hard preparing for Baltimore I can't even tell you who we play next week."

Over in the Colts locker room, linebacker Mike Curtis said, with some anger in his voice, "We've been sliding through the exhibition games and we tried to slide through one more. I can't speak for everybody; there's been a lethargy."

While the Colts were never to recover, the Rams used their opening-game victory as a springboard to a successful season, which ended in a Western Conference play-off game at Minnesota, a visit Allen would like to forget.

Having lost the last three games of the season to finish with an 11-3 record, Allen, hoping to shake the team from its slump, elected to travel to Minnesota a week in advance to get "acclimated." Training in cold, wind, and snow, the Rams had a perfectly miserable Christmas holiday.

Sensing the mood of the team, the story goes, Allen struck upon the idea of having a group of youngsters from an orphanage join the Rams for dinner one night that week, not only to show the kids a little holiday cheer but to impress upon the players who were feeling a bit sorry for themselves that their sacrifices weren't all that great.

The whole thing didn't turn out quite the way Allen had hoped, with one of the youngsters jumping out of the bus as it pulled up to the Rams camp and fleeing across an icy field never to be seen again. Nor did the children seem all that pitiable, one, when it came his turn to step up on a chair and introduce himself, singing out loud and clear, "I'm Eddie Peterson—'Fast Eddie' to you studs."

The contest itself also turned out to be a fiasco for the Rams, who lost a 17-7 half-time lead and the game, 23-20. That proved to be as close as the Rams would come to a conference title under Allen.

In 1970, the Rams became part of the National Football Conference's Western Division as the league was realigned once again, this time to include the old American League teams, and their chief concern became the 49ers.

Engaging them in a pressurized race like those with the Colts the previous three years, the Rams pulled into the division lead by beating the 49ers, 30-13, in the eleventh game of the season, only to get knocked back to second place two weeks later with a 28-23 defeat by Detroit in a nationally televised Monday-night game. Thus, a last-game 30-13 victory over the Giants in New York was not to be enough, with the 49ers clinching the title with a victory of their own later on in the day.

At that point, with only a matter of days remaining on his five-year contract, there was nothing left for Allen to do but await Reeves' inevitable decision. It came on December 30, 1970, one day before Allen's contract was up. On his deathbed, Reeves announced it would not be renewed.

In terms of wins and losses, Allen's Ram record was one of the most enviable in any sport: 49-17-4 in regular-season games, 23-6 in exhibitions, a club-record eleven straight victories in 1969, and a four-year road record of 23-3-2.

There were also the memories, for Allen and those around him. "I have mixed feelings about the man," said fullback Lester Josephson one day in 1972. "He has his faults but he is a fine football coach. We got along fine and I have to be grateful to him because he gave me a chance to play.

"There's something basically different about him. It may be just his dedication and will to win. The main ingredient of his success is hard work. I know early every day he'd be in the office and he'd still be there late at night. He never went home, just to the motel near the office.

"If you ever had a problem, personal or otherwise, he'd come to you and talk about it. This personal approach sort of led you to a feeling that you should do something extra for him, go one step beyond.

"Everyone has shortcomings. There are certain rules and regulations that have to be followed and perhaps he didn't follow all of them. I think that was because he might have wanted to win too much. You can argue winning a lot of ways."

Having been unusually involved in the Allen era from the very start, the Rams' current assistant to the president, Jack Teele, who served as intermediary between Reeves and Allen in the 1969 and 1970 seasons, will not soon forget the experience.

When the club's search for a coach narrowed to three men in 1966, Reeves asked three Ram officials to act as "advocates" for each. Teele selected Allen.

"I was impressed with the fact that the Bears had won a championship in nineteen sixty-three and Allen had won a game ball," he said. "I talked to Jon Arnett and Johnny Morris, each of whom had played for him on the Bears, and he was eventually hired.

"Elroy Hirsch was the direct liaison man with Allen until Elroy left for the Wisconsin athletic directorship in nineteen sixty-nine. Then John Sanders, the director of player personnel, Bill Barnes, an adviser then and now the president of the Rams, and I worked with Allen. Toward the end when Dan was very ill, if George couldn't reach him he would generally come to me.

"If he were alive, Dan would have the perfect coach in Tommy Prothro. He would have worked well with him because they thought the same way on things. There was a certain segment of the public that thought the Rams would cave in without George Allen. The results are not definite yet, but both the Rams and George are doing well.

"George's strengths are tenacity and a singleness of purpose. He used to wear other people down on trades. If some guys might be up three nights in a row until midnight making speeches and attending banquets, George would go four nights if it would help him. He would do what he had to do to achieve the things he wanted to achieve.

"There are some great memories — the blocked punt against the Packers that helped keep us in the running in nineteen sixty-seven, that week before the Minnesota play-off game in nineteen sixty-nine when there was so much snow on the practice field at Macalester College we had to get orange paint to line the field. You don't go through things like that without remembering."

Nor did Allen. If there was a legitimate pride in a lustrous record, there was also the frustration of never having made the Super Bowl. If there was satisfaction in the support he received from some of the players to the very end, there was the disappointment of others publicly criticizing him. One of these was Gabriel.

"We had a great relationship," Allen reminisced after his first Redskin season. "It was like father and son. I think the reason we had a great relationship is that Gabe needed someone to help him and he was about ready to quit football, he was about ready to jump his contract when I came to L.A. He hadn't played and they'd even considered switching him to flanker, after they had him there for a week or so.

"When I traded Bill Munson, Gabe knew that I was in his corner. Coming back on the plane after we beat the Giants and were waiting for the San Francisco score, we talked about what we might have done and what we didn't do and also that probably I wouldn't be back with the Rams because I hadn't heard from Reeves.

"And wherever I went I wanted to bring Gabe and wherever I went he wanted to come. Then somebody told him I didn't want him because he had too many problems and when it appeared like I wasn't trying to get him, which was not true, because I did try to get him, and repeatedly tried and couldn't make a trade for him, he signed his new contract, showing his loyalty to the management.

"When somebody said, 'Hey, I thought you were going with George Allen,' well, it hit him like a ton of bricks," said the coach, his voice trailing off, not wishing to recount Gabriel's verbal blasts.

There were others, too, Allen tried to take along to Washington. "I asked for Deacon early," he said, "and I was interested in guys like Tom Mack. I tried to get Lester Josephson, he would have helped us, and I tried to get Larry Smith, and then earlier I tried to get Jack Snow, before we had Roy Jefferson. I tried to get Coy Bacon . . ."

There was no doubt, talking to him that day after the 1971 season, that George Allen had left his heart in Los Angeles, that perhaps, of all the personal challenges he says bring added joy when surmounted, this was, for him, the hardest.

"We loved L.A.," he said. "We'd built a home there. We had our friends. The kids had gone to school. My boy had quarterbacked Palos Verdes High to a seven-two season. He had a scholarship to UCLA.

"To pull up stakes and have a beautiful home like we have and have to leave it to live in a condominium is quite a psychological blow. Just to show you how hungry we are to find a home, yesterday we were driving around looking for homes in a snowstorm; people think we're nuts. We aren't going to be able to find a home here like we want. We're going to have to build a home.

"Dan Reeves told me that was the last coaching change he ever wanted to make when I accepted the job and we won big and set an all-time record attendance-wise, not just the Rams but a league record, and then to have to leave because the owner was an alcoholic and also became ill and was an absentee general manager, that was what was frustrating.

"If it had been a normal situation that wouldn't have happened, we wouldn't be here talking. I'd still be in L.A. and we would have won a Super Bowl by now, because last year's team was good enough to win the Super Bowl."

CHAPTER VI

Exhibitionism

FOR THE FIRST TIME EVER, the main gate to the Redskins practice field in Carlisle, Pennsylvania, was locked. Noticing a reporter trying to get in, Ed Boynton hurried over and asked for identification. Known to the players as Double O, Boynton was a fifty-nine-year-old retired Long Beach policeman the security-conscious Allen brought with him from Los Angeles to watch for spies of a football variety. Since Allen took the business of security seriously, so did the vigilant Double O.

"See those houses over behind that fence," he said, pointing across the Dickinson College field. "Anyone could be there watching this practice." With the Rams, Double O once chased a suspect from the chem lab on the second floor of Wilson High School, just across the street from the team's practice field.

"Another time I found this fellow behind a fence," he said, "and asked him his name. That sort of stopped him. Then he said Tingelhoff. It was right before a Viking game. I just smiled and showed him the way out."

Another of Double O's jobs was patroling the team bench during the games, ousting intruders. Like his coach, Double O reviews game films to see how he did and once discovered a figure he didn't recognize at a Ram-49er game.

"Who's that codger?" he wondered. "How did I miss him?" Then it dawned on him. It was himself.

Showing game films one night on the eleven o'clock news, Washington's ebullient sportscaster, Warner Wolf, exclaimed,

"Hey, look at that guy looking right over Allen's shoulder. Looks like George Halas." It was, of course, Double O.

Spy machinations being what they were in Carlisle, Double O had to content himself by chasing an occasional stray dog.

One day a reporter peered through the fence and asked Double O if he had a password. "Abracadabra," he said, opening the gate.

Once inside, a visitor was confronted with all sorts of other equally strange sights that marked a George Allen camp as the only one of its kind.

There was Allen himself, jogging around the running track every day after practice, followed by his assistants and even a wire service reporter and the team photographer. More amusing still were the ponderous quarter-mile footraces of 250-pound Mike McCormack and 240-pound LaVern Torgeson, with the two kicking in on the final straightaway to the roars of whatever crowd was on hand.

There were all the gaudy hats introduced by the former Rams, Speedy Duncan owning the brightest collection and even staid old Sonny Jurgensen getting into things a bit with a conventional Redskin cap.

Then there were new-fangled weight machines brought in by Allen where mammoth bodies strained daily. It became a small joke that Allen traded for so many Rams to teach the others how to work the machines.

Maxie Baughan, undergoing rehabilitation after his foot operation, rode Double O's bicycle around the practice field every day. Wearing a striped railroad engineer's cap, he would ring the bell on the handlebar when starting his last lap.

Assistant coaches roamed the field with walkie-talkies. The coach's aide-de-camp, Joe Sullivan, sounded the horn of authority.

In the middle of this scene was George Herbert Allen, blowing the whistle around his neck at precise intervals, sending skirmish lines of players on forty-yard wind sprints, squinting into the sun after them, rubbing his hands together gleefully, loving every golden minute of this monastic drudgery.

This was the field Lombardi strode only two years before, his voice rising above even the clang of coupling box cars on the railroad spur across the street. "Hey, Mister, get a move on, nobody walks around here." Or to reporters, inching too close to the action, "Don't anyone step over that line."

You couldn't hear Allen on the field no matter how hard you tried. You could see him watching, his eyes darting one way, then the other, but he let his assistants do most of the talking.

When he had something to say, he would take the man aside, put an arm on his shoulder, trying, it seemed, to make the fellow feel he was downright essential to the operation. Later that day, Allen explained his philosophy this way, "You can get as much accomplished talking sensibly, so there's no point in tearing people down. I didn't like anyone yelling at me when I was a player.

"I don't believe in it. It's not my style to be yelling and screaming. I say, if you make a mistake, forget it. I don't believe in tearing down. I believe in building up. You have to be yourself."

If Allen preferred to issue corrections quietly, calmly motioning his weary athletes to repeat a drill, he could also make changes without uttering a word.

When he took the Rams to camp for the first time, he was aghast at the leisurely way the "Fearsome Foursome" worked its way into shape, Deacon Jones, Merlin Olsen, Lamar Lundy, and Rosey Grier casually tossing a big medicine ball among themselves and considering that a good day's work. Allen hid the medicine ball. Much to his surprise, the four were out the next day throwing it around. It isn't easy to hide a medicine ball. Allen tried again. Again someone found it. Finally, after three or four days, the players got the message.

But if Allen's decibel count in camp was low, the goals he wrote into the play books for the Redskins' defensive unit were clearly stated:

"We must intercept 24 passes this year. Last year the Redskins intercepted only 15 and were 12th in the league. We've got to return those intercepted passes 360 yards. Last year the return yardage was only 204.

"We'll have to dump the quarterback 50 times, not the mere 29 of last year. A minimum of four touchdowns by our defense is what I project. And we should be geared to allow only 200 points by the opposition, not the 314 they scored last season."

In the textbooks issued to candidates for the special teams, Allen's second passion, were a page of seasonal goals, among them: a kickoff return average of at least twenty-four yards, eight turnovers in the kicking game, four blocked punts, four blocked place kicks, six downed punts inside the opponents' ten-yard line.

Paralleling his relationship with players, Allen projected himself as friend and colleague of reporters, although in the latter case he acted out a strange dichotomy. In post-practice press conferences he was totally cordial, if not informative. On the other hand, he dictatorially barred the press from the locker room, a practice he continued after the team moved into its Virginia campsite.

Feigning cooperation to the utmost, he often turned questions into his own questions, never really divulging many of the secrets of his heart. When it came to being pinned down to specifics, he proved as elusive in his football parlance as Charley Taylor running pass routes.

To the writers, Allen would constantly extol the virtues of his weight machines and the unusually pleasant July weather and urge them to jog with him.

"When you make the Super Bowl," one replied.

"I'll remember that," Allen said, trotting away.

The most unusual interplay between coach and writer involved George Solomon of the Washington *Daily News.* Their almost daily exchanges began one day early in camp when Allen, who often speaks in baseball analogies, likened one of his players to "the hustling center fielder" of the Washington Senators.

"Elliott Maddox!" said a justly amazed Solomon. "He's a nice fellow, but he can't hit," an observation that the averages confirmed. Maddox was batting .180 that morning.

"I'll bet you five dollars he hits two hundred," Allen said, observing that Maddox somehow often got to third base and that things can happen for a team with a runner at third and that's why he liked him.

Thus, at every morning press conference, whether Solomon was there or not, Allen inquired of Maddox's progress. In the event that no reporter bothered to check the box score, which was almost always, the Redskins' relentless publicist, Joe Blair, supplied the answer.

"Two hits last night, Coach," he'd say, his face aglow. Maddox finished the season at .213 and Solomon paid off. More important to Allen, he avoided countless questions that summer with his soliloquies on Elliott Maddox.

Cordial enough though he was, Allen had a knack for exasperating reporters on deadline by keeping them waiting so long. Always the last off the field, he supervised a series of post-practice stretching exercises he incorporated from his background as a wrestler and called "warm-downs," a perfectly natural procedure, he felt, for anyone who had "warmed up."

Having enjoyed the sight of all those bodies hard at work, he then would do his own exercises of sit-ups, leg lifts, leg splits, and two or three laps around the track. This routine, he explained, "Relaxes me. My job is tension and crises. Two, it gets my blood circulating so I become clear-headed. Three, by exercising myself I can do a fairer job of arranging a training pace for the players." The former Mr. Universe, Bruce Randall, called Allen "the best-conditioned coach in the National Football League." Appointed Redskins' "strength coach" by Allen, Randall helped plan off-season training programs for the players and demonstrated proper use of Allen's favorite weight machines.

Once with the writers, his exercises completed, Allen preferred to do much of the talking, a convenient alternative to answering questions. One of his favorite subjects was his preference for veterans over rookies.

"One," he said one morning, "rookies today are demanding more and appreciating things less. The veterans will like our new facilities at Dulles. The rookies probably will take them for granted.

"Two, veterans don't make mistakes or, rather, not nearly as many.

"Three, veterans take care of themselves. They come to camp ready to play. They might come in a little heavy, but they know how to take off, say, seven pounds and do their job."

To Allen's embarrassment, one veteran who should have known better, Verlon Biggs, reported more than seven pounds overweight — much more. How much more remained one of the mysteries of camp. The overstuffed Biggs blamed his condition on late-night TV snacks. It was obvious Biggs had watched a lot of TV.

Put on a grapefruit and protein diet by Allen with instructions to shed to 270 pounds in ten days, Biggs made it with an assist from the coach's awesome work schedule. Allen even had the team practicing on Sundays, a break with Redskin tradition, but he rationalized it this way, "Football players have plenty of time to rest in the off season. Not many folks have a six-month vacation."

Setting the pace himself, Allen was up at daybreak to begin round-the-clock meetings with his assistants. The last thing he did before falling asleep at night was study accumulated information on all his players posted on a bulletin board, which he had ordered placed in his bedroom.

Even meals seemed an intrusion on his schedule. Once he boasted, after a particularly pleasing afternoon pass drill, "Tonight I can enjoy my dinner."

What's more, Allen kept the Redskins in literal motion with a series of bus trips to other teams' camps to hold scrimmages. At high noon on July 22, the Redskins' two-bus caravan began rolling down hilly, one-lane country roads toward Westminster, Maryland, and a joint workout with the Baltimore Colts.

Such as it was, this was Allen's first road trip with the Redskins and even though it was merely a seven-on-seven passing drill with no tackling allowed and only thirty Redskins involved, George Allen was thinking about winning.

"It's my favorite drill," said Allen, who had persuaded the Colts to partake. "We'll be able to play two football games in an hour. One game takes place at each end of the field."

About 500 curious spectators, many having driven up from Washington, relaxed on the grassy hills surrounding the Western Maryland College field. Johnny Unitas, recovering from a torn Achilles' tendon, laughed with well-wishers and happily signed autographs for swarms of youngsters.

The only person who seemed to take the proceedings seriously was Allen. "I think we outpointed 'em," he said afterward. What really made his day was the weight machine he discovered in the Western Maryland gym. Every question a reporter asked was punctuated with a clang.

So pleased was Allen that he decided to do it again the next day. This time he persuaded the Philadelphia Eagles to join in. The site would be the Eagles camp in Reading, Pennsylvania, there would be tackling, and the whole squad would be going. Joe Blair, the publicity man, phoned the itinerary to each of the reporters, who were just returning from the first trip and greeted the news with less than exultation.

Meticulous though he usually is about even the smallest detail, Allen nevertheless ended up with a bus driver with a bad sense of direction. Getting lost and taking almost two and a half hours to cover the eighty miles from Carlisle to Reading, the Redskins literally sprang from their buses and tore into the Eagles, Allen pronouncing them "defeated."

He then promised yet another pre-preseason scrimmage, adding that he hadn't set the date yet. "A minor technicality," reserve quarterback Sam Wyche quipped.

Allen's quest for competition almost knew no bounds. He began talking about the Pittsburgh Steelers, who were encamped at Latrobe, Pennsylvania, and the Cleveland Browns, in Hiram, Ohio. "We'll play anyone," he said, regarding the scrimmages as the best way to prepare for the exhibition season. Under Allen, the Redskins were getting ready to get ready.

About that time, the coach himself became a training camp casualty, accidently run down in practice by Speedy Duncan. Hit from the blind side, Allen was upended and dropped spinning to earth like a top run amuck. "When you get hit like that it takes your breath away," he said once he could talk. "Somebody asked me how I was and all I could do was wave. I thought a rib was broken."

In fact, one was. Allen was taken to Carlisle Hospital after practice and x-rays revealed the fracture. Another x-ray taken a couple of weeks later when the pain persisted turned up two others that were broken.

But Allen perceived in his misfortune a good omen. In his first Rams camp, he broke his hand on a metal chair while emphasizing a point. Since the Rams won eight games that season, Allen reasoned that a broken rib should be worth ten.

Fractured ribs and all, Allen ushered the Redskins back to the buses a few days later and it was off to Reading again and another scrimmage with the Eagles. If the Redskins did not "defeat" the Eagles as badly this time, Allen at least witnessed that Redskin rarity known as a goal-line stand. The new front four of Ron McDole, Manny Sistrunk, Diron Talbert, and Verlon Biggs was asserting itself.

In Carlisle that night, only hours before the inter-conference trading deadline, Allen pulled yet another surprise. His fifteenth deal brought wide receiver Roy Jefferson from the Colts in exchange for the Redskins' number one draft choice for 1973 and rookie receiver Cotton Speyrer.

Checking out of the Baltimore camp, Jefferson was attired in a burgundy jump suit, prompting Don McCafferty, the Colts coach, to remark, "I see you're in the Redskins colors already."

Allen did not seem half as cheery as he surveyed his new man's jump suit, a beige purse, and a pair of extraordinary muttonchops. He eyed Jefferson warily, then led him by the arm to one side of the field where they talked for about five minutes. Was Allen, who prefers blue button-down shirts, laying down a code of attire for the mod Jefferson?

Hardly. Allen was not so foolish as to alienate his newest prize, as personally unsettling as the sight of a man carrying a purse might be to him. Allen even went to the opposite extreme with Jefferson, stressing individuality.

"He said anyone can play for him," the receiver said. "He wanted me to know each individual is a part of the team, but can still retain his individuality." The next day Jefferson showed up for lunch wearing another jump suit and a peace button that read, "Turn on to Jesus."

Still, the feeling persisted among close observers of Allen's Redskins that if a player practiced a boat-rocking brand of individuality and happened to be considered marginal as well, he had better be ready to move on. Such was the case of tackle Steve Wright.

Gifted with a singular outlook on life, Wright was known for a droll detachment. If he saw something funny, even in the august game of football, he laughed. He had exasperated the best of them, including Bear Bryant and Vince Lombardi, and it was clear from the outset that Allen did not have time for Wright's aggravation, even though he was, at the very worst, the third best offensive tackle in camp.

It was at his own personal, parting press conference that Wright, asked what he would remember most about Washington, uttered the cutting line, "Central Liquor."

Allen seemed to shun Wright from the opening day of camp when the 6-foot-6, 250-pounder emerged from the locker room exercising his little finger and remarking, "I don't want to overdo it this early."

One day Allen was holding court with the press and interrupted himself to point out two players working on the weight machines. "They're working on their own," the coach said proudly. "That's John Wilbur and uh . . ."

His voice trailed off. He never mentioned Wright's name even though the ever-present publicity man, Joe Blair, right at the coach's shoulder, said, "Steve Wright, Coach." It was as if Wright wasn't there.

And soon he wasn't. "I wish they hadn't waited until after wind sprints to tell me," he said. Part of still another Allen trade, Wright went on to have his best season in Chicago, which sent special teams man Mike Hull to the Redskins. This was only fitting, for the eight-year veteran Wright's disdain for special-team play, an Allen fetish, was a strong factor in his release.

August brought rain, six straight days of it, to Carlisle. The weather was hot and humid, tortuous for the players. Verlon Biggs, struggling with his weight, could be seen with his finger on the water-cooler lever for a full two minutes. "I've finally found a place with lousier weather than Buffalo," Ron McDole said.

Allen refused to be slowed by the weather, or anything. By day, he directed his charges. At night, he sat up dreaming of trades. It was 1:30 in the morning in fact, three days before the first exhibition game, when he struck again, this time acquiring strong safety Rich Petitbon, yet another former Ram.

Like most of the others, Petitbon was on the far side of thirty, with twelve years experience dating back to Allen's days in Chicago. Rams' coach Tommy Prothro was appalled at Petitbon's physical condition and lack of speed. There was no way Petitbon could be of any help to his team, Prothro felt.

Allen thought otherwise, declaring Petitbon "the greatest strong safety in modern pro football history," adding that he would move immediately into the Redskins defensive backfield. The holdover safety, Rickie Harris, demurred. "I'm not going to hand him or anyone else the job." But he knew he was gone.

Not surprisingly, Petitbon's philosophy coincided precisely with Allen's. The new safety arrived in camp declaring that Prothro, the long-time UCLA coach, wasn't cut out for the pros and that the Rams were in for a long season.

Petitbon was to take special delight with his performance in the first league game, in St. Louis, when he intercepted three passes in the Redskins' 24-17 victory. Amazingly, it was the best game Petitbon ever played. Sitting on a stool in front of his locker, he took particular pleasure in reminding reporters that Prothro had recently traded him.

"I guess he's an expert on the pro game," said Petitbon, an almost sinister look in his eyes.

The eighth player Allen had imported directly from Los Angeles, Petitbon was the fourteenth ex-Ram in the Redskins camp and sixtieth player altogether.

"I count sixty-four," one reporter persisted one day.

"You must have failed math," Allen said, slightly edgy with the first exhibition game approaching.

That was a bad day for reporters all around. A *New York Times* writer fell down while jogging on the running track, and others had little success in their interviews with Allen, who seemed lost in his own thoughts, presumably about the forthcoming trip to San Diego and that first game. Gulping down a cottage cheese lunch, he declared, "I want to win them all."

He had never lost an opening game of any kind, exhibition or regular season. But, then, he had never coached the Redskins. The score that night: San Diego 19, Washington 10.

Sonny Jurgensen didn't play because of a bruised right thumb, nor did Larry Brown, whose knee aggravations, which were to linger all season, had begun with a blow to the left knee in the first Eagles scrimmage. In addition, fullback Charley Harraway came out of the game with a slightly torn knee ligament, Diron Talbert suffered a severely twisted ankle, some of the veterans wore out, and Billy Kilmer completed only eight of twenty-seven passes.

Allen responded with a grueling two-and-a-half-hour practice under a boiling sun, remarking afterward, "I didn't think it was a long practice. It's never long when you're not winning."

But what disturbed him most about the defeat was a bad snap from center that turned the game around in the Chargers' favor. It sailed over the punter's head and out of the end zone for a safety and after the ensuing Redskin punt the Chargers added a touchdown. Allen called it "a nine-point play."

Worse, the snapper was a rookie.

The Redskins had a dramatic history of being unable to master the center snap. During a 1970 game, with the Redskins in punt formation deep in their territory, spectators in the end zone seats at Robert F. Kennedy Stadium had stood up hoping to catch the snap after a long and particularly embarrassing afternoon for a since-departed center.

Having seen for himself the Redskins' capacity for the absurd, Allen promptly got a new center, a veteran and yet another ex-Ram, for what had become the customary payment, two draft choices.

Allen's newest recruit was George Burman. Ironically, it was the second time in a month Allen had dealt for him. The first time Burman said he was going to retire and write his thesis for a labor economics doctorate. "We don't give up," the coach observed upon finally luring Burman into camp.

Having been drafted by the Chicago Bears when Allen was an assistant, Burman was joining the third team on which the two had been together. Only one thing troubled Allen, the mustache Burman had recently grown. The coach hinted it should be shaved off. Would Burman comply? Preferably not. Individuality prevailed in the case of a center who could be counted on to snap the ball properly.

That problem solved, Allen began focusing on the Denver Broncos, who proved to be the Redskins' first victim under Allen. With Jurgensen playing with his injured thumb and Brown and Harraway out of the line-up, the Redskins looked anything but impressive, giving up 222 yards while gaining only 94 themselves and just managing a 17-13 victory.

Worse, the trip to Denver resulted in Allen's first crisis as Redskins coach. Four players missed the second bed check, in fact stayed out all night on the eve of the game, among them Jurgensen himself, long the symbol of Washington football and a night-life expert. The others were Kilmer, Brown, and Harraway.

Ironically, Allen had talked about "total dedication" to reporters that very evening.

"There's just such a short period when you have to commit yourself to winning," he said. "Careers don't last forever, and the season is short. There's plenty of time in the off season for the other things. I don't think it's enough just to be satisfied that you're in the National Football League. To me, being in the National Football League means something only if you win."

Each of the offenders was fined $500 by Allen, but of more lasting importance the coach at this juncture established in no uncertain terms that these were his Redskins, Jurgensen being accorded no special privileges whatsoever.

Allen had publicly lauded Jurgensen after their first meeting, declaring he was going to be "the John Brodie of 1971," that all he needed was a defense to give him good field position, and here was Jurgensen a month after the opening of training camp setting out in open defiance of the coach.

"There wasn't any doubt in my mind that Sonny was challenging the situation a little bit," Allen said in his office after the season. "He had been hurt, he didn't play the week before, so he was restless and he kind of sets the pace.

"See, this team depends so much on a guy like Sonny and as Sonny went the team went. If Sonny didn't like the color of this chair, the team didn't like the color of this chair. And if Sonny wanted to do this, Sonny did it.

"So I made an announcement to the ball club that here we were after losing last week's game to San Diego and this was only our second game as a new group and that I was very disappointed that we had four people break curfew and each would be fined $500 and there was no way they'd get that money back.

"And then I said, 'I'll tell you one thing, before this is over we're going to have one hell of a football team,' and then I split them up."

Allen tapped on the desk nervously as he reconsidered Jurgensen's challenge to his authority, then said softly but forcefully, as though suddenly conscious of his own power, "We'll do things the way I think they should be done and if someone doesn't want to do them that way they won't be here. It doesn't matter who it is."

Having made that point to the players, Allen then watched them play two remarkably similar games in front of their fans in Washington. They took a 20-0 lead and coasted past St. Louis, 20-13. The next week Baltimore took a 20-0 lead against them and coasted, 20-14, all of which left the Redskins with a 2-2 exhibition record and the fans with enough evidence that the future was still where it had always been.

It was at this uncertain point, with the Redskins stubbornly refusing to jell, that Sonny Jurgensen, the fifteen-season veteran Allen was counting on to direct the offense, suffered a broken bone in his left shoulder on a freak play in the fifth exhibition, a humid, rainy Saturday-night game against the Dolphins in Miami.

On the next-to-last play of the third quarter, with the Redskins playing their worst game yet and trailing 20-3, Jurgensen saw one of his passes intercepted by Dick Anderson. Seized by frustration, the quarterback later admitted, he set out in determined pursuit of Anderson, only to break his shoulder making the tackle.

"Roy Jefferson was open," he said dejectedly in the Orange Bowl locker room, his arm already in a sling. "I was mad at myself for making a bad throw. I wanted to get the man who made the interception."

Jurgensen reacted angrily to one reporter's suggestion he

would have been wise to avoid making the tackle. "When somebody intercepts a pass, it's instinctive to try to tackle him," he snapped. "I can't ever recall trying to get out of the way, and I don't intend to start now."

The next day Jurgensen was flown to Oklahoma City for an operation, the prognosis being that the quarterback would miss at the very least five league games and perhaps the entire season, and Allen called the development, figuratively as well as literally, "a severe blow."

News of the extent of the injury prompted recollections of seer Jeane Dixon's July prediction that Jurgensen was not destined for a happy season.

"Sonny Jurgensen," she had written, "will retire from active football in the not-too-distant future and take a job where he will be giving advice and/or instruction. He will not be a full-time player this coming season, but will still be important in an advisory role. A great change is coming in his life, but he is not one to complain because of it. September of this year will bring him great opportunities."

The injury also prompted a telegram delivered to Jurgensen's Mount Vernon home from the White House, which read, "My thoughts, as those of countless friends and fans, were with you when we learned of your recent operation. We will all be praying for you and hoping for your quick return to the best of health and to the game through which you have captured all the hearts of sports enthusiasts."

For seven years, the name Jurgensen was the only one that counted in Washington football. Now attention shifted dramatically to Allen, whose ability to turn adversity to advantage was not yet that well known in the east, and Billy Kilmer, thrust into the number one job by Jurgensen's misfortune.

Never confused with Jurgensen as a pure passer, Kilmer brought to Washington the reputation of fierce competitor and ruffian type who could and liked to run with the ball. He did regularly out of the single wing at UCLA, and later the San

Francisco 49ers installed the shotgun formation for the express purpose of capitalizing on his running ability.

The fact that Kilmer could literally carry the ball, which he did ninety-six times one season for the 49ers and ninety-three the next, did nothing to assuage the fears of total team collapse by Redskin fans, long enamored of Jurgensen's more conventional ability to throw a football and throw it as well as anyone in the game.

Under perhaps the severest test of his ability to capitalize on misfortune, Allen seemed stunned in the locker room in his initial contemplation of Jurgensen's injury, but he snapped back quickly.

Early the next morning, Allen called Kilmer to his room in the motel at Dulles Airport, where both had stayed after arriving back from Miami at 3 A.M. Sunday.

"I imagine he thought he was going to be traded, or something," Allen said, "because I don't think he knew at the time the seriousness of Jurgensen's injury. I was the only one who knew that.

"I told him how bad it was and I said, 'This is the reason we brought you in. This may be the biggest opportunity of your life. I want you to work hard and be dedicated, and it certainly can be a most rewarding year for you.'

"I also told him it was a break for him that we had one more game left before we got into league play because it would give him a little more time to work on our system."

His grave expression immediately after the game notwithstanding, Allen insisted that not for an instant did he feel the season had ended before it began.

"We weren't playing very well at the time," he recalled. "We weren't even playing very well on defense. I approached it this way, that jeez, what an unusual opportunity we had now, that it could be rewarding for everybody, that the only way we could win was to work together and help each other.

"That's what I told the team when we met at eleven-thirty on

Monday morning. I said our team was built with selected, experienced personnel and that for every man we had we usually had a good man to replace him.

"But the big thing I emphasized was, 'We just have to stick closer together now than ever before. There's no way you can win if you don't.' "

Stressing the necessity of team unity in conversations with reporters, in part for the benefit of the players, Allen observed, "Around town people have been saying the Redskins season is dead without Sonny Jurgensen. I hear the bookmakers have made the Bengals favorites by a touchdown on Saturday night.

"The owner of another club called me and said he had problems with injuries until I told him about Jurgy undergoing surgery. Then he said he didn't have any problems at all by comparison.

"But the fellows are banding together. They are going to have to do more. They realize the only way they can achieve success and win is for everyone to work together and do more than his share."

Preparing for the Cincinnati game, there was a bona fide atmosphere, one could sense for the first time, of enthusiasm and expectation. Allen's talk to the players had at least somewhat convinced them they could rally around Kilmer, and Kilmer echoed Allen's message that all was not lost.

"I have no doubt we'll play a good game against Cincinnati," the quarterback said. "I've been getting a lot of work in with the first unit. I think it'll pay off. I don't pretend to be able to fill Sonny's shoes, but with my experience I can get the job done. I'll do things in my own way."

Backing up the tough talk that Saturday night at RFK Stadium, Kilmer threw two touchdown passes, including a forty-two-yarder to Jerry Smith in the final quarter that gave the Redskins a 17-17 tie with the previously unbeaten Bengals. A hint of what was to be a frequent Kilmer tactic during the season, the crucial pass was delivered in a situation normally reserved for a fullback plunge, third down and inches. Faking to the back and straightening up close to the scrimmage line, Kilmer found Smith ten yards beyond the defenders and ready to turn the medium-range pass into a long scoring play. "He threw the ball beautifully," said Roy Jefferson. "We can win with him."

Though Allen had suffered his first losing preseason record, 2-3-1, the Redskins at least looked prepared to open the season. It was a vastly different team from the one Allen inherited, even a historic one. As closely as the league office could verify, the 1971 Redskins were the first not to have a single rookie on the roster.

In all, Allen had made nineteen trades and added seventeen new faces to the forty-man roster. In his annual State of the Redskins message, before a luncheon crowd of 2100 team worshipers, Edward Bennett Williams outdid himself in his customary preseason effusiveness and dropped one-liners faster than Johnny Carson.

"At age four, Coach Allen received a six-year-old dog for a birthday present. He promptly traded the dog for two twelve-year-old cats . . .

"Tim Temerario, our director of player personnel, is working on the nineteen seventy-six draft . . ."

Even the faintest of heart seemed to realize that if the Redskins were going to continue being losers, at least there would be a different group to be held responsible. And that losers they would be the Redskin faithful had on the word of no less an authority than Alex Karras, whose last angry roar at pro football engulfed Washington as well as Detroit and the Lions.

Five days before the league opener, Allen found irresistible the temptation to pluck from the waiver list the most famous Lion of all, who had been summarily cut from the roster after thirteen years with the same club. But instead of joining Allen's corps of defensive tackles, Karras ridiculed the Redskins' chances with Kilmer instead of Jurgensen as their quarterback.

"It would be ridiculous for me to go," he said. "If I thought they could do anything it would be different. I've played long enough without a quarterback. I've played without one all of my career. It would be a nightmare to go there and lose again. I've been losing all my career."

CHAPTER VII

The Over the Hill Gang

"TELL ALEX KARRAS I said hello," said George Allen, his face gorged with victory as he stepped out of the Redskins locker room in Busch Memorial Stadium. The Redskins had officially begun the Allen era by beating the St. Louis Cardinals.

For the sixth straight year, an Allen team had won its regular-season opener, and the way it did this time could not have been more pleasing to a coach who had staked his reputation as master rebuilder on a slow-to-jell defense reshaped at no small expense and viewed with growing skepticism.

With an anxious and customarily large September television audience sitting in judgment in Washington, the Redskins' previously sporadic defense came together on precisely the right day after a summer of uncertainty.

Taking the ball away from the Cardinals seven times in a 24-17 victory, the reconstructed Redskins supplied the evidence that Allen's emphasis on defense had its merits and that Allen had brought in the players to make his system work.

Particularly symbolic of the rebuilt defense was thirty-three-year-old safety Rich Petitbon, the former Ram, who intercepted three passes, and thirty-five-year-old Jack Pardee, the defensive signal caller, who not only distinguished himself that day but would quickly become the symbol of the entire Washington defense.

Forming the heart of this newly respected unit was a collection of aging veterans, most of them discarded by other teams, bound by a common desire to show people they could still play the game. These were the charter members of Washington's "Over the Hill Gang." Offensive players were also allowed in, the only prerequisites for membership being sufficient age and/or rejection by some other club, and Allen's team was stocked with candidates who qualified on both counts. In all, eleven of the forty active players were thirty or older, and almost all had plenty to prove.

Liking it just that way, Allen reacted with an I-told-you-so attitude immediately after the opening game with the Cardinals, comparing Petitbon's three-interception accomplishment as a strong safety to a baseball player hitting four home runs in a single game. Taking immense pleasure in the put-down of a reporter who had suggested Petitbon looked "unspectacular" in the exhibitions, Allen chortled, "Was he spectacular enough for you?"

"For you guys who think Richie Petitbon is too old," Allen continued in the dressing room, "he did a pretty good job. You can write and cover pro football games for the next fifteen years and you won't see a strong safety make three interceptions.

"And Jack Pardee called all our defensive signals. Pardee's thirty-five and Petitbon's thirty-three. Now if we could just get a few more guys with a little more experience . . ."

Praising his "Old Geezers," another nickname that would become a Redskin trademark, Allen exulted, "I think our team came together today," an observation he reaffirmed after the season was over.

"Gosh, I think the turning point was that goshdarn opener," he said. "Oh, I tell you, that was an important game to win because St. Louis was tough, particularly on the road, and because we hadn't done anything up to then. We were just struggling.

"It's unusual to say the turning point of the season was the opening game but I think in our case it was. I think it set us on fire. We had Billy Kilmer as our quarterback and we didn't know what we could do. I knew we could play better than we had shown but whether we would or not was something else."

Even for Allen, it had been difficult to get a fix on this team, so improbable was the mixture of players. In addition to the seventeen newcomers on the active roster, he had assembled a passel of new recruits listed as either taxi-squad members or injured reserves.

Among these reserves was one Dave Cahill, a defensive tackle who had played briefly under Allen in Los Angeles and been picked up as a free agent. Then twenty-nine, Cahill liked to tell audiences, "Coach Allen told me as soon as I turn thirty I might have enough experience."

Those new men deemed ready by Allen were, on defense, ends Ron McDole, Verlon Biggs, and Jimmy Jones, tackle Diron Talbert, linebackers Jack Pardee, Myron Pottios, and Bob Grant, and safety Rich Petitbon; on offense, receivers Roy Jefferson and Boyd Dowler, guard John Wilbur, center George Burman, quarterbacks Billy Kilmer and Sam Wyche, and halfback Tommy Mason, plus Speedy Duncan and Mike Hull on special teams.

In addition to the eight former Rams who opened the season, there were still other Los Angeles imports more or less in Cahill's category: Maxie Baughan, who continued to pedal his bike daily and study films for Allen; Jeff Jordan, actually pale from being indoors so much rehabilitating his knee in Allen's sweatshop; and, finally, a linebacker named Mike Foote, who once belonged to Allen's taxi squad in Los Angeles and now had something uncertain the matter with his knee.

Diverse as it was, the group was further characterized by age and, in many cases, controversy. Besides Pardee, thirty-five, and Petitbon, thirty-three, Dowler was thirty-three, and Pottios, McDole, Kilmer, and Mason were thirty-two. As for the controversy, Biggs had played out his option with the New York

Jets, Petitbon had feuded with Rams coach Tommy Prothro and called the Rams camp a "joke," McDole had fallen from the good graces of the since-departed Buffalo coach John Rauch, and Jefferson had waged a war of words over his contract with Colts owner Carroll Rosenbloom.

As confected by Allen, the Redskins were clearly one of the strangest assemblages of athletes imaginable. It was enough to worry even their originator, who admitted after the season his concern about unifying the motley crowd.

"When you have as many different personalities from around the league as we had," he said, "it's very difficult to get them to think as one. I think that was the biggest thing we had going for us, we had forty men working together. Now I know that sounds kind of corny, but I'll tell you you can't win without it, there's no way.

"So this is going to continue to be our biggest problem without a doubt. You see, every year it's more difficult to win — nobody wants to trade with us because we made too much progress in a short time — and every year it's more difficult to keep the same football team working together.

"I fear that right now. Not a day goes by as I approach a season, never a moment passes, that I don't keep thinking about the coming season and what we have to do to win."

In like fashion, his goal as fixed as his coach's, Jack Pardee before long became known in Washington as he had in Los Angeles for his singular devotion to duty. Setting the pace for the entire team, Pardee played the best football of his life in the first five weeks of the season, intercepting five passes and accumulating three game balls in that time, and proceeding to be named to several postseason all-league teams. The farthest over of the Over the Hill Gang in terms of years, Pardee was to Allen what Bart Starr had been to Lombardi at Green Bay, the coach's physical extension on the field.

Cited by Allen after the opening-game victory in St. Louis for "calling a perfect game" as defensive leader, a tribute that was to be repeated almost weekly, Pardee put into perspective, while accepting congratulations in the dressing room in Busch Stadium, the importance of the victory.

"We needed this game to prove to ourselves we can do the job," he said. "We needed it very badly." Just how badly he kept to himself until after the season, when he continued to report almost daily to Redskin Park to work on Allen's body-building contraptions in an effort to put on weight before his thirty-sixth birthday and another season, his fifteenth.

Taking a brief rest from the machines one day in March, he said, "I have to admit I was starting to doubt," the confession sounding almost like literal heresy coming as it was from Allen's primary disciple. "To have a good defense, the players have to be good enough to stop the run. We hardly stopped anybody in the exhibitions. If you can't stop a simple run on first-and-ten you've got to start wondering.

"I remember coming back east for the early camp and I told a reporter the reason I came was that I wanted to be on a winner and that we had a better team here than the Rams. They thought it was funny on the Coast. But I was serious about it.

"To me, the first year Coach Allen took over in Los Angeles, I wasn't as convinced as I was here that we were going to win the Super Bowl. But then when we got to training camp it seemed like the team was fighting itself from being good. We had injuries. There was always something to keep us from coming together. It would have been enough to make anybody except Coach Allen panic."

The one team the Redskins had managed to stop, and stop convincingly, was St. Louis. Holding the Cardinal runners to minus seven yards in a one-sided exhibition, the Redskins picked up all the confidence they needed for their league opener in St. Louis.

"From the earlier game," Pardee said, "we knew we could beat them. Their plan had to be to get Jackie Smith, one of the better tight ends in the league, on Richie Petitbon. We not only took away their best weapon, but their whole plan backfired on them psychologically when Richie intercepted three times and stopped three different drives."

In the opener, as in all the games to follow, Pardee played with a shoulder separation that limited his tackling ability. Hurt in the exhibition with the Cardinals by ramming into MacArthur Lane, Pardee nevertheless played as usual, keeping intact his personal record of missing only two games because of injury or illness in twenty-three years of football.

Not even a severe attack of flu, which caused him to lose fifteen pounds before the Kansas City game, could keep him out of the line-up. Further weakened by playing with a soaked, heavy uniform on a wet field, and matched against 6-10 tight end Morris Stroud, Pardee still managed a winning effort even if the team didn't that day. "I just picked a bad week to get sick," he said.

Having finished the season underweight at 210, Pardee recalled that the flu had dropped him under 200 one season with the Rams and the worrisome prospect of playing in such an emaciated state was keeping him busy on the weights all winter at Redskin headquarters.

The kind of player coaches dream about and rarely find, Pardee, like Allen, literally moved into the Virginia countryside, renting a five-acre farm in Oakton, Virginia, near the Dulles campsite.

As dedicated as his leader, Pardee's entire existence centered around the Redskins. He watched no television except for the Monday-night football games, attended no movies or theater, but rather devoted almost every waking moment to football. In the mornings, he studied scouting reports. In the evenings, after his five children had gone to bed or were doing schoolwork, he watched game films.

"To me that's the fun of it," he said one day during the season. "I study at home. I guess it's just the way of life I'm used to. I can't imagine playing any other way.

"I like getting up Sunday with the butterflies in my stomach. I can't eat. I haven't eaten the day of the game for the last nine or ten years. This is the reason I'm still in football. It still excites me that much.

"It becomes more so as the years go on, being involved, doing well. When you win, it becomes a bigger challenge every week. As you get closer to your goal there's more pressure and what the game is all about is being able to take the pressure and still win."

Having played on Ram teams of another generation, with Norm Van Brocklin and Elroy Hirsch, Pardee preached the assets of age from personal experience. From day one in camp, he repeated his theory that old players would never hurt a team, that a team collapsed only when all the old players retired.

"After Lombardi left, Phil Bengtson couldn't keep the old Packers from quitting," he'd say. "They had to replace five, six, seven players at once. That's what got them in trouble."

Playing better than ever at thirty-four and thirty-five as if to prove his point, Pardee cited his familiarity with other teams and players around the league as the partial cause. "It's not hard for me to go over fifty to one hundred pages of reports or even more and remember almost every detail," he said.

"I know the best points of most of the players because I've seen them before. A good background makes it easier to remember. There's another advantage to being around a while. They say you win ball games by eliminating bad plays. By being a veteran you shouldn't have so many of those."

"Calendar age," he insisted, was meaningless, claiming that players in their twenties often had "old" bodies. As for the older players, they would be replaced gradually by younger ones who had gained experience on the taxi squad or as reserves.

"We have some young linebackers now who could play twelve to fifteen years if they want to," Pardee said. "But

Coach Allen isn't going to put them out there until they're ready. There's no sense in having them make their mistakes in the game."

According to Pardee, Allen's predecessor as Rams coach, Harland Svare, "thought I was too old at twenty-seven," and following the 1964 season, not a good one for Pardee, he retired. There were reasons for the off year, however.

Pardee had been treated for cancer earlier that year and undergone an eleven-and-a-half hour operation for a malignant mole on his right arm. "When I went to training camp," he said, "I actually had an open wound.

"I wasn't as strong as I had been the year before when I made all-pro. I wasn't playing as well. And there were changes going on. The Rams were on the youth move again and I couldn't agree with everything they were trying to do. As a player, you either get on board or get off. I wasn't enjoying football, so I got off."

Returning to his native Texas in 1965 — he had grown up, the youngest of seven children, in the west Texas town of Christoval, where his high school class numbered eight and there were only enough kids for a six-man football team — Pardee took a job as an assistant coach at his alma mater, Texas A. & M., where he had played under future Alabama coach, Paul (Bear) Bryant.

When Allen took over the Rams in 1966, Pardee knew he would be returning to Los Angeles. As a rookie in 1957 he had first met Allen, then the Rams offensive end coach.

"At that time," Pardee recalled, "they were using Lamar Lundy on offense and George was working with him. I wasn't playing much so he'd work Lamar out against me mostly."

Following a good season in 1963, Pardee went to the Pro Bowl, where the two met again, Allen serving as defensive assistant under George Halas on the West squad.

Having been impressed with Allen both times, Pardee was an easy mark when Allen began to entice him out of retirement.

"He'd call me every day," Pardee said. "He flew me in to Los Angeles to see him. George is persistent."

But more than that, Pardee felt, the quality that has made Allen a success is his thoroughness. "A player would have to feel bad if he didn't take advantage of all the things prepared for him before a game," he said. "The book keeps growing on each team and player. That's why Coach Allen keeps us in meetings, to learn all we can about an opponent. He'd rather have us 'overlearn' than 'underlearn.' Maybe you could even say it was 'overkill.'

"In a sense, he motivates with all this work because along with all the study and review there's always something extra, something that's new and not boring, that will help us know more about the team we're playing. From all these things — the training films, the play books, the pages of scouting reports — there is something in there to give us the edge. I'm willing and I think most players are willing to work to get that edge."

Working as diligently as he does on their behalf, Allen can embarrass a player into cooperation, Pardee seemed to be saying, a notion that Myron Pottios also suggested in training camp when talking about his struggle to diet. "If I ate like a pig," Pottios said, "the coach would be disappointed."

To Rich Petitbon, who began his pro career in Chicago when Allen was there and had since spent ten of his thirteen seasons with him, the coach gains the players' allegiance largely through the generous contracts he gives them.

"To win you have to keep the players happy," Petitbon said. "To keep 'em happy you've got to pay 'em money. That's something George Halas really didn't believe in, but Allen learned from Halas' experience."

Citing what he considers the second major ingredient in Allen's success, Petitbon called Allen a "disciplinarian," though he doesn't look or sound like one.

"This is one of Halas' good points he picked up," Petitbon

said. "He's not a stern disciplinarian like Halas, but it's something he gets done in his own way, and something you must have."

The way he does it is with the strictest set of fines in the league: $1000 for losing a play book, $500 for breaking curfew, $100 per pound overweight, and he counts down to $25 to the quarter pound.

In addition, said Petitbon, Allen makes a player feel not only wanted but important, and recalled an "amazing transformation" in defensive end Doug Atkins when Allen took over the Chicago defense in the Bears' 1963 championship season.

"Most of the guys on defense didn't know what was going on before George took over because they couldn't understand Clark Shaughnessy's complex defenses," Petitbon said. "Shaughnessy was a genius. He knew more football than anybody in the whole world. He was far, far more advanced than anyone. But he couldn't relate to the players. He couldn't get down to their level.

"Doug Atkins had been more or less overlooked. George made him feel wanted. He'd go over everything with him. Any time he'd put something new in he'd check it out with Doug. I'm not sure Doug knew a zone defense from a man-to-man. All he was interested in was where to line up and get the quarterback.

"Well, that year it was amazing. First thing you knew Doug would be taking his tablet into the meetings and taking notes. Before that he used to sit in the back and blow bubbles. On the field, he was a one-man pass rush. We won the championship on defense and he was the best thing we had going. He must have knocked out about eight or nine quarterbacks, I mean put 'em on stretchers.

"I think that was George's biggest accomplishment that year, getting Doug together. You know, being a psychologist is George's strongest point as far as coaching goes.

"He takes time to find out what makes everybody tick. If

everybody's different, athletes are more so. Athletes are the biggest group of prima donnas in the world. And when you have forty of them you've got problems. George recognizes this and takes the extra time to keep everybody happy."

Eager to join Allen's collection of "Geezers" in Washington, Petitbon arrived predicting doom for the Rams under Prothro and reiterated that opinion on request throughout the season. During the following winter and spring, his feelings had not mellowed a bit.

"He brought in all those college coaches; it was a joke," he said, his voice edged heavily with sarcasm. "Frankly, most of the players knew more than they did. The only way I can describe the training camp is that Prothro was trying to teach himself the pro game. Training camp was a waste.

"The defensive backs did one thing, the safeties did another, the linebackers did another. They seldom came together as a group on the field and they seldom came together in meetings.

"They were even teaching defensive backs blocking techniques. Lot of good that's going to do.

"I believe Prothro is one of the most egotistical people I've met. He's going to have a tough time. I don't think he's dedicated enough to do what he has to do to win. I'm not saying that you have to be concerned with football all the time. But he has a lot of outside interests. You can't rearrange your schedule to play in bridge tournaments."

Like the resolute Petitbon — who added another interception in the Redskins' second game against New York to the three he picked off in the St. Louis opener — there were others on the Washington roster with something to prove. Disgruntled on other teams or labeled as "problems," these outcasts were welcomed by Allen and assimilated into his Over the Hill Gang.

Meriting honorary membership in the "gang" was reserve defensive end Jimmy Jones, only twenty-four. Thinking him of no further use after a knee operation, the Jets parted with him cheaply, happy to accept a draft choice Allen had no intention of keeping anyway.

Considering himself underpaid, Jones also had the feeling he was not really part of the Jet team. Charging that the coach, Weeb Ewbank, had his favorites, and he obviously wasn't one of them, Jones said, "You could tell Ewbank was interested in a particular person. You could see the favoritism every day. You felt like you were second-rate.

"You'd read all the publicity about Joe Namath and only Joe Namath. I'm not saying I need publicity, just that it affects you somewhat reading about one person. It's best I'm away from there.

"When I came to the Redskins I had something to prove to myself and I guess to prove to the world — that I could still play. I had a little bitter taste in my mouth from not getting a chance."

In contrast, when he arrived in Washington as a typical Allen reclamation project, he felt that "George really seemed enthused over being able to obtain me. I could see it in his eyes talking to him. He made me feel I was the starting end. He made me feel part of the team.

"We talked about Deacon Jones and he told me he hoped I could put on some weight but that Deacon had the same trouble, that he was so light George wouldn't tell people how much he really weighed."

Liking Jones' speed and maneuverability, Allen was willing to take the small gamble on the troublesome left knee that the Jets wouldn't. Having injured the knee and undergone surgery after the 1969 season, Jones suffered a reinjury in 1970, forcing him to miss eleven games. After that, he said, "They wanted to get what they could for me. After the season I got a call from Ewbank checking on how I was and I got the distinct feeling that the next call I got from him would be a notice of being traded. The next month he called back and told me I'd been traded."

Before his last season with the Jets, Jones also was stung by a brown spider and hospitalized and poked in the eye by somebody's thumb in a basketball game, causing him to miss almost the entire training camp with torn blood vessels.

All things considered, Jones said, "I think they figured I was accident prone, I really do," the nicest thing he could manage to say about the Jets management.

Happy to pay for yet another knee operation after Jones' first season in Washington, Allen considered the trade a huge success because it enabled him to team Jones with another swift defensive lineman, Bill Brundige, and wheel them into the lineup for their quick rush in obvious passing situations.

His specialized talent becoming apparent in the third exhibition game, against St. Louis, Jones got two third-down cracks at quarterback Pete Beathard and threw him for losses both times, with Allen excitedly calling Jones' heroics "home runs."

By the opening game, again against St. Louis, it was apparent that Allen's pains had succeeded in impressing upon Jones that he was as valuable to the team as any of the other thirty-nine players. Sent in on a third-down passing situation deep in Redskin territory, Jones attracted two blockers and still was the only one to almost reach quarterback Jim Hart, who threw a touchdown pass anyway. Full of his mission to dump the quarterback, Jones snapped his fingers, as though he had been personally responsible for the score.

As did most of his teammates, Jones considered that opening game the crucial one of the season, "the most exciting game for me. There was uncertainty beforehand, but the locker room after that game was something to experience.

"It was like we had won the Super Bowl. We were releasing all that doubt. Everybody gained confidence that day. It gave us more confidence in Coach Allen. He had said we would be winners, but everybody was wondering. It was a confidence vote for him."

And if he could not quite catch up with Jim Hart, Jones more than atoned for it the following week by getting his quarterback in New York, the victim being the usually super-mobile Fran Tarkenton, harassed all afternoon in a 30-3 Redskin rout.

With the Giants already overrun, Tarkenton lost his composure to an unprecedented degree on the team's last play from scrimmage in the third quarter when it seemed he was about to be dragged all the way out an exit tunnel by Jones.

Retreating from his twenty-five-yard line, Tarkenton was back-pedaling toward his end zone when Jones caught him by the jersey and began escorting him toward the goal line, depositing him finally like the week's laundry, in a heap.

Before the official could mark the ball for a fourteen-yard loss, Tarkenton threw it at Jones, hitting him in the back of the helmet, perhaps his most accurate pass of the day.

"The guy had been talking all day and said some things I didn't appreciate and I threw the ball at him," said the scrambled Tarkenton, his day of frustration culminating on one play.

What had Jones said?

"Words I don't think you can repeat in a newspaper," Tarkenton told reporters. "He was on top. I guess he could afford to talk."

Denying he ever used profanity on a football field, Jones said, "I was so hyped up all week, getting in and getting Fran Tarkenton. I just walked past him, patted him on the back and said, 'Way to go.' The next thing I felt was the ball hitting me in the back of the head."

Whirling, Jones swung at Tarkenton, but it was Tarkenton who drew the penalty and later a seat on the bench, withdrawn from the one-sided encounter for most of the fourth quarter. Making no attempt to hide his envy with still another bleak season facing him in New York, Tarkenton offered unstinting praise after the game for George Allen.

"Look what he's got," marveled Tarkenton, at the same time telling exactly what the Giants didn't have, "three guys on the defensive line who were all-pros, two all-pro linebackers, an all-pro receiver in Roy Jefferson, a Boyd Dowler as an experienced receiver, and a Bill Kilmer at quarterback as a back-up.

"They're two and nothing now. Could you ever imagine Washington winning before without a Jurgensen in the line-up? Allen's put together a fine veteran ball club."

Feeling precisely the same way, the Redskins whooped it up in their dressing room, with Jones observing, "This means that last week was really bona fide. Everyone was standing up together on the sidelines. We really came together."

A large part of that togetherness involved the huge defensive end, Verlon Biggs, like Jones a former Jet happy to be in Washington. "I'll tell you the difference between this Redskins team and the Jets," he said. "Everybody feels a part of this team. Everybody is a star. You've got to have forty guys out there, not eleven or two or three."

Having played first-string in all of his six years with the Jets and having become known for some crucial defensive plays along the way — he tackled Oakland's Daryle Lamonica on fourth and ten late in the 1968 AFL title game and caused a fumble by Baltimore's Tom Matte in the 1969 Super Bowl — Biggs felt alienated by the Jets, and by Ewbank in particular, for repeatedly ignoring his salary requests.

Seeking a $35,000 contract, hardly an outrageous figure for one who graded out as the Jets top defensive lineman of 1970, Biggs played out his option and got his money from George Allen, who was glad to pay — just as he was glad to pay handsomely defensive tackle Diron Talbert, who had refused to sign his 1970 Rams contract, and defensive end Ron McDole, to say nothing of linebackers Pardee and Pottios and safety Petitbon, all pulling down in the neighborhood of $50,000 a season.

Once stocked with defensive players in the near-minimum $18,000 to $20,000 pay bracket, the Redskins were moving up an estimated $300,000 in salaries over one season. "We traded for dissatisfied veterans and built almost our whole front defense that way," said team president Edward Bennett Williams. "That cost money."

So, too, did Roy Jefferson, who became available when Baltimore refused to renegotiate his $50,000-a-year contract, the most ever paid a Colt wide receiver. Then there was Maxie Baughan, Allen's faithful disciple, who was said to have made $50,000 with the Redskins in 1971 while not getting in for a single play because of his foot injury. After the season, he signed on with Georgia Tech as an assistant coach.

In the case of Biggs, Allen catered to his smaller cravings as well as his desire to be wealthy. For example, Allen flipped him a game ball after the victory over the Giants to signify Biggs' successful return to New York, although any number of others could have qualified for the postgame honor.

Attending to another detail the Jets ignored almost completely, Allen arranged to have Biggs address a luncheon the following day in New York, a speaking engagement worth $250. Having made only two appearances as a Jet for a total of less money, Biggs could say, and did, "I'm making more in one day in New York than I did in six years."

Nor was it long before Biggs appeared as a car salesman on TV, his place in the hearts of Washingtonians assured. Looking back, he said, "I don't owe New York nothing. I think I was the most underrated player in the league. I didn't expect to be front page, but I did all those things, played on all-star teams, did everything I possibly could, and it didn't mean anything. I made plays that would have gotten other guys headlines. I didn't get a mention."

If Biggs and Jones had sufficient incentive for the New York game, Allen took no chances with the others, constantly reminding them of the Redskins' historically miserable road record and particular ineptitude in Yankee Stadium.

Citing a "New York jinx," Allen repeated to the players all week that the Redskins had won only one of their last eleven in

New York, had failed to win their first two regular-season games since 1955, and had lost eighteen of twenty-eight road games the previous four years.

Motivational aids close at hand, Allen had only to mention some of the ludicrous scores by which the team had lost in New York — 49-34, 44-14, 30-0, 53-0, to name just a few — and stress the 1970 fiasco, in which Washington managed to squander a nineteen-point lead in the fourth quarter and lose, 35-33. Upon taking over the Redskins, Allen emphatically volunteered, "We won't lose any more nineteen-point leads."

Stressing that his players be "physical" — they responded with a fight on the first play from scrimmage and 173 yards in penalties — Allen also told his defensive unit to keep up a stream of vocal reminders for Tarkenton that his was a lost cause. Under one pileup, a Redskin reportedly went so far as chiding Tarkenton for deserting his teammates in summer camp while trying to get a better contract.

Having a far more satisfying game was Tarkenton's counterpart, Kilmer, at thirty-two a member in good standing of the overage crew with credentials as a double castoff, discarded by both San Francisco and New Orleans.

Enjoying his first big game as a Redskin, Kilmer completed twenty-three of thirty-two passes, including eleven of fifteen in the first half, for 309 of the club's 427-yard total offense. Fooling the Giants with his favorite play, a surprise pass from a short-yardage situation, Kilmer connected with Charley Taylor on third and one for a seventy-one-yard scoring play that erased New York's early 3-0 lead.

Still another castoff who helped demoralize the Giants was thirty-two-year-old defensive end Ron McDole. Once 316 pounds while playing in Buffalo — "I was the golden egg" — the newly svelte McDole, 265 pounds but still round enough to pass for a 300-pounder, pressured Tarkenton all afternoon.

Looking more like forty-two than thirty-two, McDole was obtained from the youth-conscious Bills for three draft choices, the trade coming as no surprise to him. Though a team captain, McDole admitted having "a lot of communication problems" with Coach John Rauch and observed, "The players kept getting younger and younger. I don't begrudge a young fellow a job if he earns it. That's the way this game works. But I don't think anyone should be handed a job just because he's young."

An admirer of Lou Saban, since returned to Buffalo as head coach, McDole recalled the Bills' descent from AFL prominence after Saban's departure. "Our offense started to slide and holes began appearing in the defense and there was no one left to fill them up," he said, a bit nostalgically.

"It seemed all the guys around me the last few years were young kids. They're fine but throw them in together they're going to make mistakes. On every play one of these kids would make a mistake and we'd wind up with a mess on our hands.

"I can understand Allen's logic for playing experienced people. When we were winning at Buffalo everyone knew what they were supposed to do. Take a guy like Pat Fischer. In any situation he's going to adapt and not panic. A rookie or second-year man won't react that way."

Classmates at Nebraska and later rookies on the St. Louis Cardinals, McDole and the thirty-one-year-old cornerback Fischer were reunited on the Redskins, McDole hypothesizing, "I told him we probably came here to die together." Little Fischer even served as big McDole's godfather when the lineman converted to Catholicism.

Uncertain about his future in football as he headed toward the Redskins training camp — "It was like going off to an all-star game in a sense" — McDole said he was reassured at Allen's first team meeting when the coach said, "I believe in experienced players because they make fewer mistakes."

"I took that to mean that the job of left defensive end was mine until I lost it," McDole said. "I felt better knowing it wasn't a case of having to fight off ten guys for the position.

"You know, I think you could play till you're one hundred

for him if you could get the job done. But then I've talked to some guys who used to play for him and they've told me he'll get rid of you in a minute once you're not doing the job."

Steady and dependable on the field with a personality to match, McDole adopted a bemused attitude toward Allen from their very first contact, an Allen phone call twenty minutes after Rauch had notified McDole of the trade.

"He was welcoming me to the team," said McDole, laughing. "He was very optimistic, very enthusiastic. He said, 'Glad to have you aboard. We've finally got you on a winner. You've got to be tired of losing in Buffalo.'

"My first thought was, 'Winner? The Redskins didn't do much better than we did. What do you mean winner?' But then I thought about all the good players he brought in.

"It turned out that the age factor is what really brought us together. It brought us together the way we had it in Buffalo during the good years. If you don't have that unity you're not going to win any big games.

"They said the older guys were over the hill and that type of thing helped us all the more. The Over the Hill Gang started and, I'll tell you, we were all together. We were all there for the same reason — somebody didn't want us because we were too old.

"We all had the same idea in mind, to win football games. Guys like Pardee, Petitbon, and Pottios, they enjoy playing the game. Jack's the type of guy who may have investments but he's not involved in something that he's going to jump right into after he retires. He's dedicated only to football, like Allen.

"I got a big kick out of Allen, his milk, ice cream, and graham crackers, and how every conversation you got into, no matter what you talked about, always got back to football.

"I never saw anybody work that hard and I always wondered when he got time to, you know, live."

CHAPTER VIII

True Believers

LIKE THE NATIVE AMERICANS whose name they bear, the Redskins traditionally had had very little luck dealing with a bunch of Cowboys from Dallas. The word *massacre* kept popping up in game stories, and it was unenviably appropriate.

Not only had Washington not won any of its last six games with Dallas, it hadn't even come close, giving up a dismaying 35.6 points per game over the span. The teams' last meeting, in the Cotton Bowl at the end of the 1970 season, had resulted in a 34-0 Dallas victory, the first Redskin shutout in nine years.

Now the teams were to face each other again in the Cotton Bowl, but under slightly different circumstances. Both were tied for the lead in the NFC's Eastern Division with 2-0 records, and the Redskins knew, said quarterback Kilmer, "This is the team to beat for the championship. We're ready. We're eager. This will make our whole season if we beat them in Dallas."

The Cowboys, if they were worried, did not indicate it. After all, with a famous multiple offense and a defense anchored by tackle Bob Lilly — "He's a little bit more than great; a man like him comes along once in a lifetime," said his coach, Tom Landry — they had won fifteen of their last sixteen games, dropping only the Super Bowl game against Baltimore. When you play in that league, the Redskins tend to look like very small change, indeed.

"It must not be THAT important a game," said Lilly, not

completely joking, "because I think they plan on only double-teaming me."

Having piled up ninety-one points in their first two league games, the Cowboys were thinking only lofty thoughts. "I don't see anyone stopping us," said middle linebacker Lee Roy Jordan. "I think we're gonna be a great team."

"Did Kilmer ever hurt us as a Saint?" asked cornerback Mel Renfro. "No. He always threw a soft ball, kinda up there hoping someone would run under it."

And the records did show that Kilmer fumbled at the five-yard line the first time he faced Dallas, cracked his ankle the second, and threw an interception when his own man was wide open the third. Impressive he had not been.

Still, as Renfro realized about Kilmer in what would later sound like uncommon prophecy, "Sometimes a change can do wonders. I know I couldn't wait to play against Earl Morrall when he was with the Giants. He's done great with the Colts though. So, it could be the change, not the quarterback."

This was an obviously improved Redskin team from those that had preceded it. It had allowed only twenty points, fewest in the conference to that time, and was number one in total defense, too.

Still, Allen preferred as always to concentrate his public verbiage on building up the opposition for psychological reasons. "The Cowboys," he intoned at his Monday press conference, "do not have a weakness. They have everything; they are probably the best all-around team in the National Football League. They have something else I like in a team: they've been together as a unit for a long time. You can't beat that experience."

Yet two days later, with typical verbal gymnastics, he was saying his own team could do just that, establishing an it-can-be-done, in fact, it-will-be-done mood out among the whispering pines near Dulles. Never mind all those Dallas victories, all that shed Redskin blood, never mind that the Redskins running backs, especially Charley Harraway, had rarely had good days against Dallas. "My answer to that," Allen said in what was to be a constant refrain, "is that's history."

The team members came out with similarly tough statements. Wide receiver Charley Taylor, who celebrated birthday number thirty that Tuesday, said, "I have a thing about Dallas. Man, that's home down there. Grand Prairie is where I'm going when I get to that ripe old age where I don't have to work anymore. Those Dallas boys try to put me down, and that won't do."

The team's resident tough guy, uncommunicative linebacker Chris Hanburger, was equally adamant. "Our defensive system leaves no doubt about what we have to do," he said. "We are better prepared than we've ever been to stop them."

No specifics as to the master plan were to be forthcoming, however. "I'm not going to tell you, I'm not going to tell anybody," Hanburger said. "But we're much more flexible. We can adapt to anything anybody throws at us. We know what we have to do."

Still, some people were yet to be convinced. The Cowboys were made comfortable ten-point favorites by certain cynics in Las Vegas, and even the team's local fans were not so sure. They had heard tub thumpings before, but all that had come of them were losing seasons. Why should things be different now? Why should this Redskin team be the first since 1943 to win its first three games?

The difference, if there was to be one, would be Allen. If his weakness was trying to make every scrimmage seem like the biggest battle since V-E Day, his strength was in getting a team to its highest possible peak when the game involved did have significance, something the Dallas game was brimming with.

In public, however, Allen kept insisting, "The practices this week have not been as good as they were last week. I would like to have seen more enthusiasm, concentration, and fire. Maybe they're saving it for Sunday."

As in most big games involving an Allen team, there was some commotion leading up to it. Out at Dulles, Allen thought he saw a man of dubious repute watching practice from the rooftop of a warehouse across the street, the only building on the horizon. Security man Ed Boynton was assigned to counter-espionage and came back to report the man was a welder taking a lunch break.

There also was an unexpected first-of-the-season appearance at practice by quarterback Jurgensen, his arm in a sling with a mental state to match, a visit that Allen considered ill timed because it distracted the team from the upcoming game.

Out in Texas, Landry, in a less serious mood, said the Cowboys "might scout around a little bit" in respect for Allen's reputation as a master spy.

In fact, when quarterback Steve Goepel was cut by the Cowboys, Washington contacted him and "seemed about equally interested in pumping Steve about the Dallas team as talking to him," his father told a Dallas reporter.

As the game drew closer, all frivolous thoughts ceased, and the Redskins reflected the "surrender hell!" attitude of Diron Talbert. "We must win this game," he said. "We must win to keep the momentum going in this division. When you've got a fire burning, you've got to keep it burning.

"Our theory of success," he continued, "is to win all the games you're supposed to win and then be extra fired up for the games you're not supposed to win. We're extra fired up for this one."

Talbert wasn't kidding. Never behind and not minding an incessant rain, the Redskins scored on their third play from scrimmage, when fullback Harraway took a hand-off from Kilmer and ran fifty-seven yards for a touchdown behind a just-so sequence of blocks by Larry Brown, Walter Rock, and Roy Jefferson.

It was the start of an extraordinary day for Harraway, who accumulated a career-high 111 yards, and the entire Redskin team, which ran for 200 yards while holding the Cowboys, 1970's NFC rushing champions, to only 82. The final score was 20-16, Washington, only the second time ever the Redskins had limited the Cowboys to as little as one touchdown.

And though quarterback Kilmer attempted only ten passes all day, one of them was a maneuver Allen was to call "the big play," a first-down play-action pass to Roy Jefferson that, coming after numerous running series, fooled everyone and went for fifty yards and the Redskins' second touchdown.

In the locker room afterward, Allen could barely be restrained.

"Men," he said to the press, "I know this is an overworked word, but it was a great, great victory — a complete team victory. Nobody gave us a chance, but we thought we could win if we played our game and didn't make mistakes. Why," he added with a nod toward the Redskins locker room, "those guys in there are acting like it was New Year's Eve."

Then, with faultless modesty, the coach disclosed, "I'm proud to say this — the team gave me a game ball. I told them it should be split forty ways."

Finally came the ultimate Allen zinger: "With Texas getting the Washington Senators, we thought we had to come up with a little better effort to make the fans proud of us."

Allen's show of confidence aside, it seemed to at least one of the Redskin players that it was during this particular game, when the Redskins repulsed three Cowboy drives, holding them to three field goals and taking a 14-9 half-time lead, that Allen himself became a believer, and not before.

"At half time, when we came in, we could see that Allen genuinely thought we could win because of the way we had stopped their offense," the player said after the season. "From then on, everything he said really came across. Up until then, there could be detected a doubt in his mind about the team. This was especially true during the exhibition season when we weren't consistent at all.

"He was saying all the time, 'We're good, we're going to win.' But, really, he was still searching. He seemed to be thinking, 'Are we good or aren't we good?' It was only after the first game and the ones after that we were able to tell that George was beginning to feel we really had it.

"One thing that was obvious to me in his feelings was the questioning he had received about his trades. I think there was a question even in his mind concerning the trades. In fact, I think it was heavy on his mind.

"Because after the first game he stressed, 'See what a great game Richie Petitbon had.' Plus his references to the Over the Hill Gang and how well they had played. From that point it was obvious to all of us there was a change in his attitude from a question mark to a positive nature.

"The second game reinforced his feeling that defense wins football games. I heard him make a remark to Edward Bennett Williams, 'See, that's how you win, on defense.'

"But I don't think he was quite convinced going into the Dallas game. I think in his mind it was more a matter of 'Will we do everything right?' "

That they did made the locker room celebration that day all the more effusive and sometimes less coherent.

"We didn't get pushed around today," said a mightily pleased Verlon Biggs. "It's not like reality to me yet. Nobody gave us a chance; we couldn't win our first three games on the road. It couldn't happen but it has happened. I guess the old men beat the kids today."

Most of the attention — and two more game balls, one to guard Ray Schoenke, who handled the mighty Lilly, the other to Assistant Coach Mike McCormack — went to the Redskins offensive line, long thought to be one of the weakest of weak links, which that day had been unusually successful in pushing its runners out and holding Dallas rushers off.

"My God, we're a team!" Schoenke said. "Everyone feels a part of it and cares for everyone else. It's never happened to me before."

The future is now. (*Wally McNamee, Newsweek*)

George Allen, number 37, a 156-pound reserve end for the Alma College varsity of 1943, which had a 1–5 record. (*Courtesy John Rosenkrans*)

Coach Allen with his first team, the 1948 Morningside varsity. (*Courtesy Morningside College*)

Allen's last college job and his first professional one, in 1956 at Whittier College (1.) and in 1957 as end coach for the Los Angeles Rams.
(*Los Angeles Times Photo*) (*Vic Stein*)

(*World Wide Photos*)

Farewell to Chicago. Allen shakes hands with George Halas, Sr. (1.) and George Halas, Jr., after their courtroom confrontation. (*United Press International*)

Head coach at last. (*Los Angeles Rams*)

Always watchful. (*Los Angeles Times Photo*)

Allen with Ram quarterback Roman Gabriel. (*UPI*)

Giving vocal encouragement on the Los Angeles sidelines.

Exhorting. (*UPI*)

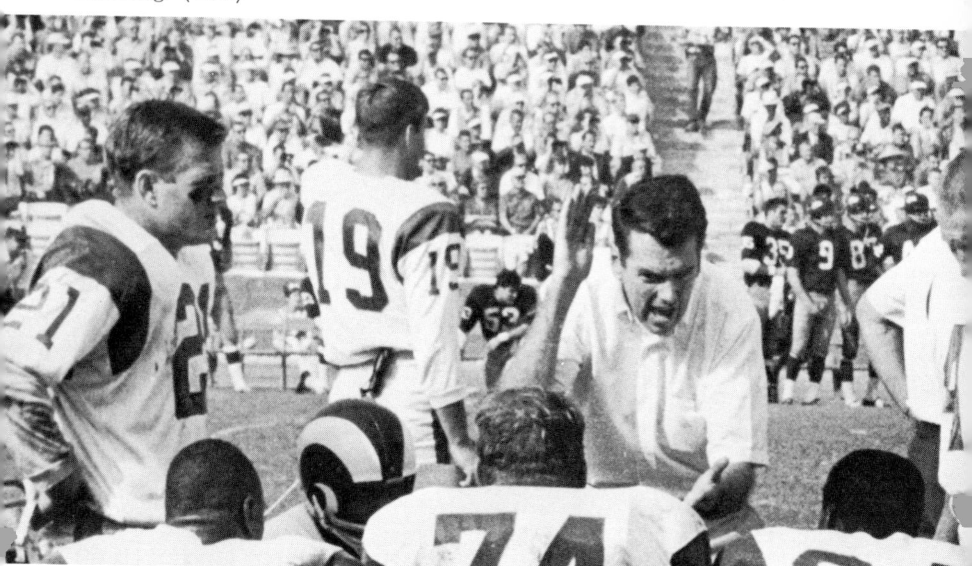

Beseeching. (*UPI*)

Explaining. (*UPI*)

The most dramatic Los Angeles victory. Tony Guillory blocks the punt by Green Bay's Donny Anderson with 34 seconds to go to set up the Rams 27–24 victory in 1967. (*UPI*)

Allen triumphant. Claude Crabb, number 49, and future Redskin Jeff Jordan carry the coach off the field after the victory over Green Bay. (*UPI*)

It's just a game. Grim expressions seeming to foretell their eventual feud, Rams owner Dan Reeves announces he has hired Allen as coach – 1966 (top). (*UPI*) Allen wears sunglasses to hide his tears as co-captain Lamar Lundy protests his coach's firing at an emotion-packed press conference in late 1968. Standing behind Lundy are (l. to r.) Deacon Jones, Charlie Cowan, and Merlin Olsen. (*UPI*)

Happy days are here again. Washington Redskins president Edward Bennett Williams introduces his new coach and general manager.
(*Richard Darcey, The Washington Post*)

Ouch! Quarterback Sonny Jurgensen breaks a shoulder bone in an exhibition game in Miami. (*Paul Fine*)

In a rare happy moment during a personally dismal season, Jurgensen applauds the team during the home opener against Houston. (*Geoffrey Gilbert, Washington Daily News*)

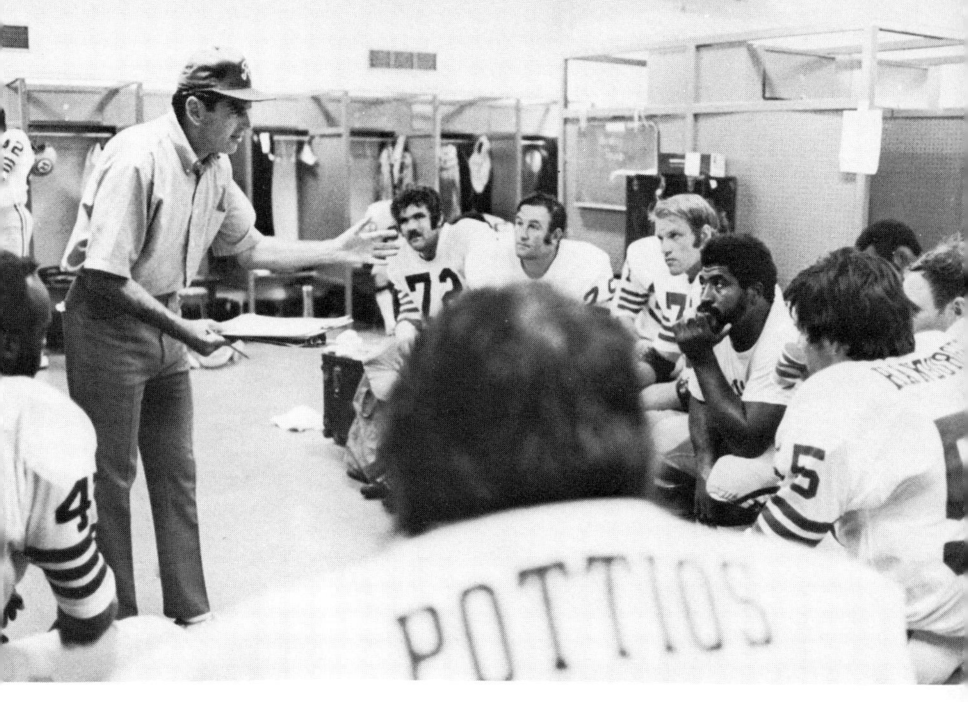

A strategy review for the defense before the season opener in St. Louis, won by the Redskins, 24–17. (*Paul Fine*)

Allen, with disciple Maxie Baughan behind him, congratulates linebacker Chris Hanburger during the Redskins 30–3 victory over the Giants in New York. (*Paul Fine*)

Trailed by Miss National Fire Prevention, Allen is surrounded by fans at an uproarious Dulles Airport reception following a 20–16 victory over the Cowboys in Dallas. (*Geoffrey Gilbert, Washington Daily News*)

Clutching his trusty play books, Allen adjusts a red plastic hat placed on his head by excited fans. (*Harry Naltchayan, The Washington Post*)

Winning is everything. Allen leads the cheers after home victories over Houston (top) and St. Louis. (*Paul Fine*)

The ecstasy and the agony. Charley Taylor strains for a touchdown against Kansas City, only to have his ankle broken as he falls into the end zone. (*Richard Darcey, The Washington Post*)

The perfect catch. With Pat Fischer hanging on, Chief Otis Taylor uses only one hand to score a morale-crushing touchdown. (*John Vawter, Kansas City Star*)

Defeat. Diron Talbert after the 27–20 Kansas City loss, the Redskins' first. (*Paul Fine*)

The comeback. Quarterback Billy Kilmer after the 24–14 victory over New Orleans, the team that had discarded him. (*Paul Fine*)

Allen's final handwritten instructions before meeting the Eagles.
(*Paul Fine*)

R

The impossible play. Chicago linebacker Dick Butkus about to score the winning extra point on a diving catch of a 35-yard conversion play in the 16–15 Bears victory. (*UPI*)

Things don't go right in the 7–7 tie with Philadelphia, and Baughan, Allen, and Jurgensen look appropriately worried. (*Richard Darcey, The Washington Post*)

The Redskins' number one fan pays an unexpected visit to practice and poses with the team. (*Nate Fine*) (*UPI*)

He runs in all weather, including snow. (*Richard Darcey, The Washington Post*)

The Ramskins on the eve of their return to Los Angeles. Front row (l. to r.): George Burman, John Wilbur, Diron Talbert, and Myron Pottios. Back row: Jeff Jordan, Tommy Mason, Boyd Dowler, Richie Petitbon, Jack Pardee, and Maxie Baughan. (*Richard Darcey, The Washington Post*)

Always alone. (*Richard Darcey, The Washington Post*)

Allen with NFL commissioner Pete Rozelle before the Redskins-Rams game in Los Angeles. (*Paul Fine*)

Allen impresses the importance of the George Allen Bowl on quarterback Kilmer. (*UPI*)

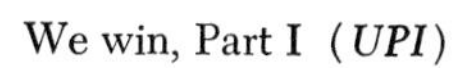

We win, Part I (*UPI*)

We win, Part II (*Paul Fine*)

The beginning of the end. San Francisco's Gene Washington barely beats Pat Fischer on a 78-yard scoring play that tied up the play-off game in Candlestick Park and led eventually to the 49er victory. (*Richard Darcey, The Washington Post*)

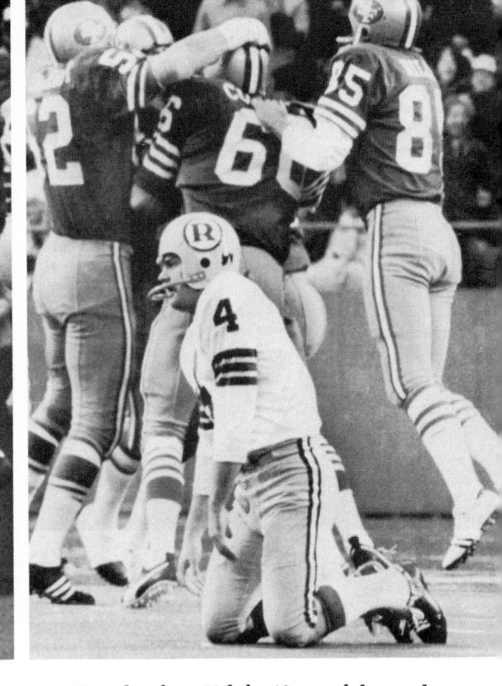

Paradise lost. While 49ers celebrate the recovery of a bad center snap in the Redskins end zone, punter Mike Bragg finds it hard to accept reality. (*World Wide Photos*)

In the season's final minutes, Manny Sistrunk (l.) and Myron Pottios brush aside a few raindrops — and maybe a tear. (*Richard Darcey, The Washington Post*)

The end, for now. (*Paul Fine*)

"Surprised?" said fellow guard John Wilbur of the performance. "No, that's what it means to be a winner. You think positive. You're just confident you can go a long way. Winning this game is sort of a triumph of good over evil."

One of the tackles, Jim Snowden, noted the entire line "got together last night and had a beer together. It helped because it meant we all knew what we'd have to do together. And knowing the extra things we'd have to do, we just went out and did them."

"Maybe this'll make believers out of people," said the other tackle, a drained Walter Rock who slumped in front of his locker. "It was so beautiful, but such an emotional strain. I could stay right here and go to sleep."

Though there was no game ball for him, perhaps the most deeply satisfied of the Redskins was running back Harraway, who had the best day of his career shortly after revealing for the first time that a deep change, a turning toward Christ, had taken place in his life.

A reporter's innocuous greeting, "How are you, Charley?" just two weeks before had brought a totally unexpected, hour-long response. What was on his mind, what he chose to talk about was startling in both its frankness and depth of feeling.

"Things have been happening in the last few days," he began, "deep personal things. Something had been missing in my life. Now I've found a new life. I just let Jesus Christ into my life.

"I've always wanted to lead a Christian life but something was always holding me back, for some reason or other. I'd never been convinced that there is a God. Now I feel very fortunate. I feel very good. I've looked over my life. I haven't had Christ in me. He's been with me. He's been with me my whole life, I just hadn't accepted him."

The dramatic change took place on the afternoon of the Redskins' final exhibition game at a prayer meeting for the players arranged by Maxie Baughan and the Washington chapter of the Fellowship of Christian Athletes.

The guest speaker was Tom Skinner, an evangelist and a black man. "This guy," said Harraway, "was the most dynamic guy I've ever heard. I've heard great speakers before. Maybe this time I was just ripe. For me, it was something. It was what I needed. I'm a new Christian. I feel very personal about it. It makes me feel happy inside, all the time. It makes me feel great."

The reporter had originally approached Harraway to inquire about things physical, not spiritual. The fullback had injured his left knee in the first exhibition game against San Diego and had been out of three games. In addition, his doubtful condition reflected the whole atmosphere of uncertainty surrounding the Redskins four days from the season opener.

The inquiry prompting a torrent of words, Harraway outlined how his new religious beliefs were affecting his entire life, on and off the football field.

"What I have is a belief and a love for God that is sincere. I'm trying to appreciate life, trying to do what you feel is right, trying to do for the next man what you'd want him to do for you.

"It's my whole life that's changed in many different ways, little ways. I've been trying to tell my wife about it this week, about some of the small things that are happening.

"It definitely will affect my football. I have gone into football games with doubt. Now I won't. If for some reason I'm not able to play football, I won't be depressed. I'll know I'm not meant to play anymore.

"Now I have to be honest with everybody. These things that have been happening in the last few days have forced me to be honest with myself and with other people regardless of what might come out of it."

And so, as if he meant to prove what he said that day in one of the empty team meeting rooms at the Dulles complex, Harraway revealed that his knee injury, described by the Redskins as a bruise, was actually "a slight ligament tear," that he had been worried about it but was worried no longer as a result of his new faith.

"I have a knee that's been hurt here and there," he said, "so I've hoped I don't hurt my knee. I guess sometimes maybe this is present in all people, they feel a little insecure about something. Now I can honestly say my insecurities are nil. I can feel happy; God has been with me throughout my life. I feel, with my physical ability and the security I now have, whatever course I should take from here on in will be a good course, wherever it should lead me."

Confessing that he had not been truly happy in years, Harraway said he had finally recaptured the inner peace he experienced as a child: "My father was a career serviceman, so when I was a kid I lived with my grandparents in an all-black town in Oklahoma. We weren't rich by any means. I never wore shoes in the summertime. I had holes in my jeans. I had to walk a block to the rest room. We had no heat or electricity.

"When I was a little older, I went with my father back and forth to Europe. I attended only black schools. I never realized there was racial discrimination. But, looking back, there was.

"But, still, I was a happy kid because I had the love of my grandparents, my mother, and my father. I didn't know love existed then. I took it for granted."

A different story was being told in the Dallas dressing room. Though Coach Landry did say, "We just weren't in the game; it means the Redskins have the jump on us," quarterback Craig Morton was taking a different tack, one that sounded a bit churlish at the time but was eventually to prove as accurate as any Cowboy partisan could wish.

Raising what was to be a season-long Redskin boiling point, Morton succinctly pointed out, "If you'll remember, last year the teams that developed momentum later in the season were the ones that made the play-offs."

Noting that Allen's Ram teams often seemed to peak early

and lose crucial games later on, Morton said, "It's going to be a challenge for him to keep that team — an excellent team this season — together and peaking like this all year."

As for opposite number Kilmer's comments that the just finished sixty minutes was "the championship game for our division," Morton politely demurred. "It's a little early for that," he said without much visible emotion. "What happened today is nothing new for us. Our division was the same last year. You never know what's going to happen. If anything, I would say it comes down to our game in Washington in November."

Back in Washington, no one was thinking nearly that far ahead. As possessors of the league's only certified undefeated, untied team, the citizens of the nation's capital took it into their heads to lose their minds. They went out thousands strong to greet the team when it returned by plane that night and the next day bought out all editions of the local newspapers, which allowed themselves to wonder aloud jingoistically what miracles "Hath George Allen Wrought" and described the coach as elevated to "an estate just short of canonization."

What kind of a team was this, everyone wondered, that had the temerity to win games while wearing the eternally losing burgundy and gold?

"This team has a different personality," answered Jack Pardee. "Once it was Sonny Jurgensen and the bomb. Now it's scrap, cling, hang on, battle. It's like the old Green Bay teams now. We wait patiently and then somebody — it could come from anybody on the offense or defense — makes the big play."

"I was in Baltimore when we won it all," said Roy Jefferson, "and the togetherness on this club cannot compare to the Colts. There has never been anything like this."

Everything was coming up just the way Allen liked it, including the fortune cookie he opened at his Monday press conference that read, "To talk good is not to be good. To do good, that is being good."

Allen tried to be more concerned with the future than the

past, noting as always, "The players have had twenty-four hours to enjoy the victory over the Cowboys. Dallas is history." He did pause, however, to pay tribute to the hordes that greeted him at the airport.

"I only expected a hundred or two. I couldn't believe it when the tower radioed us that there were thousands out there. To see that mass of faces, old people, middle-aged people, young kids. It was like the World Series, the Super Bowl . . ." The coach could barely go on.

"These Washington fans proved to me that they're the best in the country. We never had this kind of experience when I was in Los Angeles. It's coming at a time when the city needs it. The team and I feel we're the only sports team Washington has left and we want everyone to be proud of us."

He then looked resolutely forward, warning, "We will not sneak up on anyone anymore, you will not see us ten-point underdogs anymore," and told everyone who would listen that the 0-2-1 Houston Oilers, the team's next opponent, were the toughest thing since blackstrap molasses and not to be considered casually.

All this was in line with a prediction veteran Allen-watcher Pardee had made in the Dallas locker room. "Coach Allen will do his best job of coaching for the season this week," he'd said.

"There's no way we can be fat and happy. We haven't won enough games yet for that. Coach Allen will have us so scared of the Oilers . . . He'll be a terror this week. This is when he's at his best."

Still, it could not be denied, and Allen would be the last to try, that thoughts of next week notwithstanding, being on top, being the center of attention, being the winner, was the ultimate he coveted for himself and his team. With great relish he told the reporters that the excitement in the city had interfered with his sleep, as had the inundation of telegrams, phone calls, and mail that greeted his unlooked-for success.

"I've been receiving phone calls from Los Angeles, Chicago, New York, everyplace, saying, 'Now you're on the spot,' and I tell them, 'This is a nice spot to be on, it's the way it's supposed to be.' "

If Allen was used to being on that spot, occupying it proved a revelation for some of his players, who had previously come no closer to winning than reading about other teams doing it.

There was, for instance, eight-year-veteran guard Ray Schoenke, a thoughtful, reflective player who had gone through agonies the season before when the Redskins lost five in a row on the way to a fruitless 6-8 season.

"This season," he said at that time, "has been a nightmare. Sometimes I wish I could go someplace else than down to practice. It reminds you of what you went through last Sunday, something you want to forget.

"The physical aspects are always tough, but the mental anxieties you go through are worse. A season like this is an emotional drain on you, frustrating and depressing."

Now, less than half a season later, Schoenke's thinking had undergone a complete revision at the hands of the master psychologist George Allen.

"We all care," he said. "This is the first time we've been a team, really a team. The closeness, the effort, winning and everyone pulling together, this is football. This isn't the same team, I can't even relate it to the old Redskins. It's just an overall team atmosphere, lots of guys who care very much.

"Last year, we'd work out for less than an hour on Tuesdays. Now we sometimes go for more than twice as much, but no one's coming out and saying, 'Oh my God, the sky is falling.' We know now this is the way to do things if you want to win.

"This is what I've been searching for for a long time. This is too hard a business to go through and lose."

Similarly moved was twenty-six-year-old Mike Hull, who, after spending his first three professional years with the Chicago Bears, treated George Allen's ways as the ultimate that football life could offer upon coming to Washington in exchange for less-idealistic tackle Steve Wright.

In contrast to Schoenke, a regular starting lineman, running back Hull was to carry the ball exactly twice all season for a total of eight yards, spending most of his time on the body-crunching special teams, an almost universally despised occupation.

Yet he claimed, "I love playing like I never did before. I never thought I'd find this type of fulfillment on a football team. Playing here is totally invigorating and exciting.

"I never felt I could love being on special teams, but with George you feel you're playing regularly when you're on them. You feel you're contributing significantly to the team's success. I feel like we're all in this together.

"I never felt like that with the Bears. I never found the types of rewards and satisfactions I find here. There's no magic in it, just Allen's approach to football, a positive, well-prepared, aggressive, confident approach to every game. For me, it's a completely new and rewarding type of football."

As excited as some of the players about what Allen had done to the team and the city's morale, public officials of some importance began to take note of the team's success.

First, on the Tuesday morning after the Dallas victory, Walter Washington, the city's appointed mayor, made his way out to the Dulles complex to have a few private words with the team.

The report from inside was that the mayor told the team, quite seriously, "You're the only thing we have left. It's a great thing, thrilling. You've set this city afire with your winning. I need you and the city needs you."

Captain Len Hauss responded in kind for the players, and then everyone sang, "Hail to the Redskins." And Coach Allen, properly appreciative of the visit, noted, magnanimously, "All of us connected with football think we have problems, but compared to the mayor we hardly have any at all."

Later that same day, a man with, if possible, even more problems than Mayor Washington called Allen to say that he too was maintaining a keen interest in the local group.

"President Nixon called me about ten-ten P.M. yesterday," Allen said the next afternoon, "and we talked for about fifteen minutes. He wanted to let us know how proud he is of the team, and reminded me how much winning means to the area. He wished us good luck, but said not to let down."

It was not every day that a President of the United States took his eye off the hot line to phone encouragement to a professional football team, but as far as President Nixon and the Redskins were concerned, the relationship was just starting to get warm.

CHAPTER IX

How He Does It

IT IS A VERB of only three letters, deriving from the Old English meaning "to strive," yet it dominates the life and thought of George Allen with a totality that would boggle another George named Orwell. The word is "win."

If one were to postulate that winning football games was the ultimate good in the world and could construct a human being to fit just that purpose, he would come out a lot like George Allen. Everything in his life, the good and the bad, flows from that single desire. He is so dedicated to winning that even thinking about people who think otherwise tends to make him cranky and out of sorts.

"To be in this league and not be a winner is nothing," he said with emphasis, after the Redskins' first season. "What the heck good is that? To say I'm in the National Football League and walk around and strut, what good is that? It doesn't matter who you play for, the question is, are you a winner, see, and if you're a winner that's something.

"It takes so much out of me to lose, I become irritable, I can't sleep or eat," he said once. "I don't want to lose today even if I can say to myself, 'Well, we'll be better in a couple of years.' I don't believe in spinning my wheels without getting anyplace.

"The achiever is the only individual who is truly alive. There can be no inner satisfaction in simply driving a fine car or eating in a fine restaurant or watching a good movie or television program. Those who think they're enjoying themselves doing any of that are half dead and don't know it. I see no difference between a chair and the man who sits in the chair unless he is accomplishing something.

"Every man was born with the ability to do something well. Every man is a born salesman, accountant, football player, farmer, politician or artist, or something. The individual who uses the ability he was given when he was put on this earth — who works to the very limit of that ability — is doing what the Lord intended him to do. This is what life is all about. This is my religion. My prayer is that each man will be allowed to play to the best of his ability."

In thus making a cult out of winning, Allen has become like an addict in search of a constantly elusive fix. No victory, no matter how climactic, can satiate him for more than a day. After that, any mention of it brings out perhaps his very favorite phrase: "That's history."

Nothing, but nothing, is allowed to defeat him. "Sometimes I'll walk along the beach and pick up rocks and throw them into the ocean," Allen said, while in Los Angeles. "If one of the rocks I try to pick up is stuck in the sand and bigger than I thought, I won't just leave it there and keep walking. I'll stop and dig it out. I'm not going to let that rock defeat me. That same thing applies to my job."

Should anything more substantial get in his way, such as injuries to almost every key member of his offensive team as happened in Washington, Allen refuses to relent. "The more setbacks I have," he said after his first Redskin season, "the more I'm determined to overcome them. I think every setback can be an asset for you, to strengthen you, and bring you closer together and make you more determined to do a better job."

"He keeps a lot inside him," said George Burman, who played for Allen both in Los Angeles and Washington. "The week after the San Francisco play-off game, it was Wednesday and he hadn't been to sleep yet, you could tell. He had replayed that game five times a night. You could tell he was wiped out. Football is it. If we don't win the Super Bowl next year, he'll lie down and think about the two games we didn't win. He carries it with him all the time. That's where the intensity comes from."

This dedication has, of course, brought results. "In the years I've been with Allen," said Jack Pardee, "there has been only one game when we were not playing for money — in nineteen sixty-eight when the Bears beat us in the thirteenth game and made the fourteenth game sort of meaningless. That's the remarkable thing about the man. We're always shooting for something — a title or second-place money."

There is nothing, Allen feels, that winning football games cannot do, including bringing an urban renewal–type revitalization to Washington's bedraggled, low-spirited inner core. "The city needs us" was one of his constant refrains during the season, and he meant it.

"The city needs a successful sports representative for civic pride," he maintained. "With no professional baseball, basketball, or hockey in Washington all the town's energies should be poured into the Redskins. Washington is starved for victories. That is why they appreciate our winning season so much.

"Mayor Walter Washington told me that since we have been winning it has helped him in his job. It probably keeps kids out of trouble. Instead of taking dope or robbing somebody, maybe they're playing touch football, imitating Larry Brown or Charley Taylor. If Washington had a stadium with one hundred thousand seats we could sell one hundred thousand tickets every week."

To make this success possible, Allen has put football in the predominant position in his life. While even as nominally a dedicated man as the late Vince Lombardi put loyalty to church and family ahead of devotion to the team, Allen has always maintained, "Football must come first. Of course, during the off season I tell my players that their church and families should come one-two, with the team third. But during the six months of the season, the competition in the NFL is so tough that we have to put football ahead of everything else."

A believer that "the best leaders don't talk too much, they lead by doing," Allen sets an enviable example in that area. While in Los Angeles, he would regularly sleep at a motel near the team's practice field rather than "waste" the hour and a half it would take to drive home and back, and in Washington he has a full-time chauffeur, not to massage his ego but to eliminate the squandering of possible football time worrying about stoplights. His wife is said to buy all his clothes, right down to his shoes and, in Los Angeles, used to alert the airport barber shop when her husband was coming so he could be trimmed before boarding the Rams' plane. To paraphrase Raymond Chandler, he works hard the way other people think they work hard. In his own words, "I'm just an impatient man, that's all. I don't like to waste time. After all, that's what life's made up of."

Even as a collegiate coach, he put almost every spare moment to work. While most of his colleagues went to coaching conventions to live it up and carouse, sober Allen would be putting the time to good use, volunteering for menial jobs like registering the coaches who were checking in. In that way he accumulated large amounts of useful information on colleges and players and got to meet a lot of coaches, including Sid Gillman. Then at the University of Cincinnati, Gillman later gave Allen his first professional coaching job, as Rams assistant in 1957.

A story out of his Chicago days indicates that Allen made time-consuming efforts to get along with the brusque genius Clark Shaughnessy because he figured he could learn a lot from him. He is said to have carried Shaughnessy's old tin suitcase on the road, apparently thinking it was filled with arcane football information. After four or five weeks of this, Shaughnessy invited Allen up to his room upon arrival at some hotel, and there happened to open the suitcase, whereupon a no doubt chagrined Allen noted it contained the coach's ragged, old overcoat, nothing more.

In Los Angeles, upset because earlier coaches had relaxed to the point of somnolence, Allen cracked down. "Previous Ram coaches, I understand, used to attend every press function," he said. "I just don't have the time. Either we're going to win or we're going to go Hollywood. Last week, I was offered five hundred dollars to speak before a group at a luncheon and I turned it down just like that because it would have kept me away from the football team. We [the Rams coaches] have no speaking engagements during the season. We don't have time for them."

A man who thinks and talks and believes in clichés, Allen has a number of them always at hand to detail the importance of work. "One hundred per cent is not enough," he will say. Or, "You can't win if you're not willing to pay the price." Or, "The tougher the job, the greater the reward." Or, "There are no rewards for an easy job."

When he worked in Chicago, he had a saying by Theodore Roosevelt, "The only man who never makes a mistake is a man who never does anything," posted in his library at home. On his office wall in Los Angeles was yet another motto, "The harder I work, the luckier I get."

"Any coach who worries about the amount of time he's putting in on his job isn't going to be around long," Allen said while in Los Angeles, remembering one who said, "I don't think football should take this much time," and was dismissed shortly thereafter.

"I think if you don't love your job you're in trouble," he continued. "Then it becomes work. If you don't love your job, don't worry about it, because someone else will have it soon.

"You've got to do the job first. You can enjoy yourself after you finish the job."

Looking back on things after the Redskins season, Allen reiterated, "Unless you think about your job when you're not on your job, you're not going to win. I think to be the best at your position you have to be thinking about it all the time.

"I don't think you can win working just nine to five. I think anyone that's nine to five, that type of person, isn't dedicated enough. I think that you have to take work home and that you have to think about your job off the field, and people who say, 'Well, I don't have time to take work home, I don't think about my job,' to me, I don't see how those people can do their jobs."

In his search for people who make Hercules seem like a loafer, Allen has become football's biggest booster of the 110 per cent effort, yet another hoary cliche he treats with absolute seriousness.

"Most people really think they're working hard," he has said. "So it doesn't mean anything to ask for one hundred per cent. You have to demand one hundred and ten.

"Everyone, the head coach especially, must give one hundred and ten per cent. Regardless of how little or how much a head coach works, most of those with whom he is associated will work a little less. It's only natural. I have known head coaches who made it a point never to work at night after dinner and, without exception, their assistants made the same point. More than any other of man's habits, work habits are set by the boss."

There can be no doubt that Allen's underlings got the message. "George is relentless," said Ray Prochaska, one of his assistant coaches with the Rams. "That's the big thing about him. He is the most tenacious man I've ever known. As a football coach he is always on. He never stops."

Joe Sullivan, nominally an assistant coach but really Allen's major-domo in Washington, Los Angeles, and Chicago, was once moved to comment, "Hours don't mean a damn thing to the man. He was the same hard worker with the Bears that he is now. He'd be the only one at the office at night. The only thing that matters is getting things done. If people only knew all the things he did at Chicago. Making trades, heading the personnel and drafting departments, coaching the defense. That's why George Halas fought so hard to keep him."

Even his players have been affected by this lust for work. "George just eats and sleeps football," Ram guard Tom Mack has said. "You'd see the guy working so hard out there you felt you had to put out yourself." And Deacon Jones added, "He'd be a winner if he coached the Tijuana Red Wings. That sonofabitch works harder than anyone I've ever seen. He works so hard he turned me from being a coach."

Redskin reserve center George Burman says it was nothing for the coach to take a film projector with him on his family's annual one-week vacation in Hawaii, and reported on an encounter with Allen at Georgetown Hospital shortly after the 1971 season ended.

"I was in the hospital to have my arm operated on," Burman said, "and when I went downstairs one day I found George in a waiting room. He was in for his annual physical. When I found him he was wearing a smock, waiting to be examined, and reading his notebook. You almost never see him without a notebook. He started telling me about next season and about the functions and responsibilities of the assistant coaches, things like that. Here it was only February and he's planning next season."

As far as Allen is concerned, too much planning is a contradiction in terms. "Winning," he has said, "is the science of being totally prepared. And preparation can be defined in three words: leave nothing undone. No detail can be too small. No task is too small — or too big.

"The difference between success and failure is so tiny it can't be perceived by most of us. Nowadays, there is practically no difference between one team and another in the NFL. And usually the winner is going to be the team that's in better physical condition and better prepared."

To Allen, so much of winning means being organized that he occasionally will use the words interchangeably: "You can walk into a service station and tell whether they're organized or not. You can go into Giant Food and tell whether they're a winner or not. You can go into Capital Savings and Loan and tell whether they're a winner or not. It doesn't take long to analyze, at least it doesn't with me.

"I feel one of my strong points throughout my career has been organization. George Halas has made that statement several times. I can remember the first day that he hired me, he gave me a desk over there in the corner, an old broken-down desk, the middle drawer didn't even come out.

"That night, I stayed late and worked and I had that all rearranged, you see, and then I hit him, I said, 'Say coach, how about that other place over there, that'd be better for our scouting.' I think that if you have an organizational mind and are strong on it you can see things a little quicker and not waste a year or two and lose.

"If you're fairly well organized you can do a lot of things at once. You can have a lot of irons in the oven and they'll all pan out, or if they don't all pan out maybe one or two will."

It has been noted that Allen is involved in more facets of the game than any other coach in the league, and this is true to a staggering extent. Disturbed about the resiliency of the grass at Kennedy Stadium, he brought in his own agronomist — who else would even know where to find one? — who recommended a change to a strain of tall fescue which the building's superintendent was forced to admit "has a hell of a root system."

Disturbed because practices were inefficient simulators of game conditions, he hired a local official, one Bill Dixon, to come out to the Dulles complex every day in full striped regalia to throw flags with impunity.

Disturbed while at Los Angeles that his players were not getting enough rest, he encouraged afternoon naps before road games by offering ten dollars to every player answering bed checks, a bonus system the league declared illegal.

Disturbed at the less-than-successful first-year exhibition season at Washington, the first time he had lost as many as three preseason games, and feeling that part of the cause was extensive travel to faraway places like San Diego and Denver, Allen drastically curtailed the trips to 1972 exhibition games.

He spends hours on the telephone, running up unimaginable bills, finding out what is on the minds of the other league coaches, sometimes talking to as many as nine or ten during one week. Once, so the story goes, he got to Eagles general manager Pete Retzlaff just as tackle Bob Brown walked into Retzlaff's office and asked to be traded, thus picking up a new Ram with a minimum of effort.

Notorious among other NFL coaches for his constant trade proposals, some of them too obviously one-sided to be taken seriously, Allen elicited only laughter one time after whispering a proposed deal to Baltimore coach Don McCafferty. "Sounds like a George Allen trade," McCafferty told Allen himself.

If Allen causes people to shake their heads in amusement and wonder how he can possibly have any more draft choices left to trade, he has made some deals that have been regarded as no laughing matter at NFL headquarters and in other offices around the league.

In the wake of the 1971 season, San Diego and Buffalo charged he had traded each of them the same draft choices and appealed to commissioner Pete Rozelle to expedite a solution. Indeed, Allen had given his number-three and-four choices for 1973 in the deal with the Chargers for Speedy Duncan and the very same picks to Buffalo in the Ron McDole trade.

If that wasn't enough, he also swapped his number two pick to both the Rams, for Rich Petitbon, and the Jets, for Verlon Biggs. Naturally, such a practice has not ingratiated Allen among officials of other teams or the commissioner's office.

Called in by Commissioner Pete Rozelle to explain this duplicity, Allen was penalized his number one choice for 1974 to settle his debt with the Rams. Shortly afterward, he swung a deal with San Francisco in which he gave up high 1974 and 1975 choices to acquire the 1973 draft picks he needed to pay off San Diego.

The manipulations got Allen into still more trouble. Because of the double-dealing, he was fined the league maximum $5000 by Rozelle for conduct detrimental to the National Football League.

In addition, he was brought before a special executive session of club owners and given an unprecedented dressing-down for what Rozelle chose to call "sloppy bookkeeping." It was the first time in his dozen years as commissioner, Rozelle said, that a coach had been reprimanded at such an extraordinary meeting.

The commissioner also disclosed that Allen had mishandled draft choices "a couple of times" as Rams coach but no fines were assessed because Allen and the other teams quickly worked out agreements. This time, however, Rozelle acted, and the Washington *Daily News* emblazoned across the top of its sports page the headline "Flim-Flam Man Burned."

Sometimes Allen gets more players than he can use but, like a small boy and his toys, is loath to part with any of them. In Los Angeles, before the league put a limit on the number of men permitted on the taxi squad, Allen's had as many as eighteen. In Washington, where exceeding the limit was punishable by the league, random daily counts of players wandering around would sometimes exceed the legal quotient, a fact that occasionally made its way into the newspapers, once accidentally, when a reporter wrote that one Willie Germany was seen practicing in an aging jersey bearing the name of long-departed Chuck Mercein, the reporter not realizing that Germany was on the injured reserve list and not eligible to work with the team. After the season was over, the Washington *Post's*

Dave Brady discovered that Allen had been fined by the league for failing to report the activation of receiver Bill Malinchak from the taxi squad.

The coach's devotion to detail extends even past the season's final game. After his opening year in Washington, he inaugurated the first extensive off-season training program in Redskin history. "It's an honor system," he allowed, only to add, "but we'll check 'em out, I'll have my men check 'em out.

"What you do in the season depends on what you do in the off season. You don't use the off season as a vacation or somebody will get ahead of you."

To make sure his message is disseminated to everyone, Allen has propelled the Redskins into the league leadership in assistant coaches with a full nine as well as captains, with five, noting, "We need all the leaders we can get."

Allen even has the relative luxury of allowing one coach, a calm forty-four-year-old Ph.D. named Marv Levy, to concentrate on nothing but the special teams, the units that enter the field only on kickoffs, punts, and field goals. This type of painstaking care paid off most spectacularly in 1967, when Allen's Rams, preparing for their vital game with Green Bay, spent time every day practicing the blocking of kicks by left-footed punters only to win the game on a touchdown coming after Donny Anderson's left-footed punt was blocked with thirty-four seconds to go.

Allen's thoroughness is typified in the manner in which he attacks, some say devours, game films.

"If we win a game," he has said, "I don't spend a lot of time on the film of that game. I look at it just enough so we can try to correct whatever mistakes we made.

"You just can't look at a film once. You've got to look at it three or four times to get everything out of it. I'd say it takes an hour to look at a film properly. I mean an hour on the offense and an hour on the defense. There are five reels on every game. Two offense, two defense, and a kicking reel."

That people are to be regulated with the same exactitude as celluloid is indicated from the following excerpts from the so-called Allen's Law, his rules for conduct at the Rams training camp at Fullerton, California:

"General Conduct — There is to be absolutely no association with the students or working girls at Fullerton College. This is extremely important and any violation will result in immediate suspension from the team . . . Players are not to disgrace themselves on campus by being a loudmouth or a wise guy.

"Curfew — Failure to observe curfew (lights out at 11 P.M.) will be punished by an automatic fine of AT LEAST $100. Last year we had a case of a player sneaking out after bed check. Periodic second checks will be made and any violation will result in harsh action by the head coach. If you think so little of your team, teammates and winning, you'll be the LOSER.

"Gambling — As you well know, gambling is a very serious problem in all sports. Avoid any association with gamblers. In addition, be very careful of strangers who attempt to strike up a conversation and under NO circumstances are you to discuss the physical condition of members of your team or any other subject that might be an aid to gamblers. I cannot completely express how important this is.

"Weight — Each player must weigh in and out every day and a $2 fine will be assessed each time a player fails to do this. A fine of $100 a pound will be assessed if a player is overweight — $25 a quarter-pound.

"Eating — Team members will eat all meals at the prescribed time. It is mandatory that you attend the breakfast. Even if you don't eat breakfast you must report to the cafeteria and be checked in.

"Drinking — Drinking of hard liquor will not be tolerated."

Players are affected in other ways by Allen's completeness of method. "George always thinks about the correctable thing," said Redskin George Burman. "He's willing to accept excellence but not what we did wrong. That's why practices get longer, but not harder, as the season goes on. The extra details. He told me next season we ought to practice bad snaps [a bad one by Burman cost the Redskins a touchdown in the play-off game with San Francisco]. Don't say anything about it, just snap one once in a while so everyone can learn to react to it."

Allen's thoroughness, and the amount of new and usable information it unearths and puts to use, dazzled the once lackadaisical Redskins.

"We use three or four different coverages to handle one situation," said safety Brig Owens before the last regular-season game with Cleveland, "and the coaches sometimes have a hard time telling what defense we're in when they're watching the film.

"We're ready for Sunday's game on Tuesday and we work on defense and offense every day to perfect it. Other coaches usually don't start until later and they only get a couple of days of good work. This way we have time to spot any mistakes and correct them."

As Elroy Hirsch, the former great Ram player later to join the club's executives, noted in Los Angeles, the extra effort Allen demands is accepted because it seems to produce results.

"They [the Rams players] all say they're working a lot harder than they were before," Hirsch said. "George does have long meetings and long practices. But you don't hear a lot of griping. Maybe it's because of the results we're getting. Maybe the players have come to the conclusion this is what it takes to produce a winner.

"George talks about putting out one hundred and ten per cent, which is an old phrase, and about dedication and sacrifice. But, whatever he's done, he's gotten his point across. You look at the results and how do you argue with the guy?"

Allen believes in preparing teams not only with specific nitty-gritty x-and-o type information, but also with talks intended to stimulate the correct mental attitude, something he has indicated is some 90 per cent of the game.

"I've made the statement that you could have the Pro Bowl squad and not win half your games if you don't have the right mental attitude," he said after his season in Washington.

"It's the same way in anything, although sports gets more emphasis. To play good football, to play winning football, you have to have a lot of things. You have to have skill, you have to have teamwork, you have to have, of course, ability to begin with, you have to have the right type of organization to bring it out of you, but if you don't have the attitude to play, the right mental attitude, that you want to go out and play and do a good job regardless of the money you're making and regardless of what's been said about you by the coach or the press or anything, you're not going to do a good job.

"We had that last year, we had the right mental attitude, and this is the reason we were never out of one ball game. I think if you analyzed that aspect right there, you'll find out it's been quite a while since a Washington team had been able to win every game they've played. And this is because of having the correct mental attitude."

To instill that attitude in the Washington players, many of whom had precious little experience with victory, Allen put a happy face on everything and anything. When dealing with Charley Taylor's broken ankle, for example, instead of reporting that the wide receiver would not be ready for the final regular season games, Allen cheerily announced that Taylor would be ready for the play-offs.

"No matter what happened, he always spoke in a positive light, always found something positive," one player said after the season. "Everybody realized he believed what he said. In a sense the fellows developed the attitude, 'We can do it,' rather than 'Maybe we can do it.' And that's the mark of a good coach. He has the ability to transmit his feelings to the ball players. He believes his methods are the correct methods."

Part of the method was trying to instill the type of corny rah-rah feeling, complete with wild-eyed team cheers, that many players hadn't experienced in years. "It's different than any team I ever played on," defensive back Pat Fischer said during the season. "Allen created a gung-ho high school atmosphere in the locker room and it just carried over onto the field."

Other players had their doubts. "I question a lot of the enthusiasm and I ask myself, 'Are these guys cheering because this is what George wants to hear or are they genuinely happy?' " one Redskin said. "I'm not a rah-rah guy, I stand back and take a look. Let's face it, professional football is a business where if the coach likes you you're going to be there. There's guys like that on all teams, guys who get in with the coach. You wonder about it."

As a psychologist, Allen perhaps has no peer in the entire league, knowing how to exploit any and every moment to his advantage. While in Los Angeles, just coming up the steps to work about 8:30 one morning and informed that Vince Lombardi was on the phone, Allen told an aide, "Tell him he got me out of a meeting." He scorned Jimmy the Greek's generally anti-Redskin football odds during the year, at the same time using them to motivate his team, saying in gratitude at one point, "When the season's over I'm going to take him out and buy him a chocolate malted milk with an egg in it." Aware of how useful verbal slips of the opposition could be, he put his own words under lock and key, declaring off limits even the most innocuous statements, such as the obvious comment that the Cowboys had enough talent to field a Super Bowl team, and warning darkly, "They can use something like that against you."

Even away games, usually thought of as bugaboos, were to be turned into pluses under the Allen system. "He would make an advantage out of playing on the road," marveled Jim Snowden. "He'd say let's get the crowd against their quarterback. Let's get them booing him. He'd bring in statistics showing just how our offense compared with their offense."

As games approached, Allen himself would feel the effects of his own mental machinations. On the eve of an exhibition with the Colts, one Redskin reported, he was psyched enough to quake with anger, as if his game plan had been intentionally sabotaged, when running back Tommy Mason, scheduled to play most of the game, came down with a gastric attack and ended up hospitalized.

In arousing his players, Allen sometimes resorted to printed messages, as in the following one attached to a scouting report for a Rams-49ers game in 1967:

"This week we will face a fired-up Forty-niner team coming off a forty-one-seven licking. If anyone lets down this week we are going to be in serious trouble . . .

"Every year the Forty-niners stage an upset. Last year they defeated the Packers . . . This is going to be a rough and tumble game. Make no mistake about it. Are you ready?"

Allen sets greater store, however, in the words he utters at team meetings when, inevitably equipped with the proper statistic about how many years the opposition has been crushing his team's bones, he addresses the multitudes and gets them to disregard the odious past.

Before Washington's game with the Giants in New York, Allen unearthed the fact that the Redskins had won only one game in Yankee Stadium since 1957. "Yeah, Coach Allen mentioned that in one of our meetings," admitted Diron Talbert, an adept pupil. "If George hadn't brought it up, we'd never have realized it.

"But that doesn't make any difference. If you have good personnel, a good coaching staff and sound preparation, the hell with jinxes."

The coach underscored the importance he places in those chats when he made sure to check out a reporter's understanding of one of his statements, explaining, "The reason I ask you that is because if you misinterpret what I'm saying then I think, 'Son of a gun, if I'm talking to my football team will they understand?' Because it's amazing how many times you'll talk to your ball club and I'll say, 'Hey, Talbert, what was the theme of the meeting?' and he says, 'Well, ah, those trees knocked the fence down.' If they miss it, I don't blame them so much as I blame myself because boy, I didn't set 'em on fire, you know."

In general, Allen was especially adept at this type of psychic manipulation. "I gained from him by just listening to him in the meetings and seeing how excited he was," said Charley Harraway. "You could see how serious he was before a game and that had a psyching effect on me, just looking at him. At the team meetings the nights before a game, it'd come across beautifully."

In an ironic aside, however, Harraway noted that private one-on-one attempts by Allen to get him aroused met with less than climactic success.

Before the 20-16 victory over Dallas, the running back recalled, "I remember thinking if I had a good game, and everybody else had their normal game, we could beat Dallas. I became pretty well convinced that we could beat them.

"Then George came up to me and said something like, 'You know, these reporters are saying you never had a good game against Dallas. What do they know?' The next day a reporter came up to me and said the same thing, 'How come you never had a good game against Dallas?'

"So the picture changed for me. I got depressed. I had to build myself back up to where I was. I have my own psyche program. As far as coaches psyching me, it just doesn't work. I really had myself ready, then he comes up and 'Boom.'

"George has a tendency to use bad things that you may have done, like not playing well against Dallas. It always seemed to get me dejected. I appreciated his attempts to psyche up individuals but it just got me down. Most of the time, after talking to him, I'd be trying to psyche myself up again. I never remember coming away and wanting to tear anybody up."

As Harraway noted, perhaps the prime component of Allen's

psychological arsenal was his exploitation of the press. "George was always telling us the press was against us," said Ram guard Tom Mack, while Harraway added, "I could just sit there in the meetings and listen to what he thought about reporters — he did it pretty continuously — and I could leave there hating reporters."

Central here was Allen's famous bulletin board set up in the locker room, off limits to reporters, where he would post clippings he felt belittled the Redskins, hoping these would rouse his charges to wrathful word-eating revenge.

Before the St. Louis opener, Allen displayed a story by Robert Burns of the St. Louis *Globe-Democrat*, suggesting that the new Redskins were ready for Medicare and bitingly calling the former Rams the coach had imported "old favorites who are past their prime" and "old gaffers" who wouldn't be missed in L.A. The Redskins responded as planned, with a 24-17 victory.

Roman Gabriel, a toiler for five years under Allen's system, was especially cautious in his public pronouncements the week before the Rams game with his old coach's new team.

"George probably has a bulletin board in his locker room — he was like that here," the quarterback said warily from Los Angeles. "He tries to find as much information as he can for his bulletin board. He's probably got all kinds of things on the Rams. He didn't get along very well with the organization. He's probably got a whole bedroom full of stuff."

What this massive clipping system was supposed to accomplish was explained by George Burman: "He makes us feel we have something to prove. Sometimes, he'll appeal to a guy who's been traded, that some guys didn't want him and he can prove them wrong. And there's the bulletin board stuff, articles he puts up that knock the Redskins. I think it's an unconscious effort to leave no stone unturned. Because sometimes he'll say, 'Don't believe what you read in the papers.' "

Allen's own explanation for the use of such gimmicks is that "the only gimmicks I use are gimmicks that affect me and will always affect me, and affect others.

"I think that if someone says that we aren't very good or if someone blasts us I want everyone to see it. We had a lot of people blasting us last year, not believing we were any good and critical of us, so we put those up on the bulletin board.

"If they criticize Billy Kilmer, they're criticizing George Allen. If they're criticizing Lenny Hauss, they're criticizing George Allen and the coaching staff. If they criticize Charley Taylor or Speedy Duncan, they're criticizing our whole football team, you see, so we're all in together. If they compliment Billy Kilmer, if he's the player of the week, we all rejoice in that honor. If Jack Pardee's the player of the week, we all are proud of that. So this is the reason I think these things are important.

"These guys are men, but listen, they're still subject to all the whims and emotions of youngsters, just like you are when you're any age. I don't think just because they're pros, you know, it makes any difference. You do as a coach what you believe in, you see."

Most of the players go along with Allen in this, but occasionally a difference will come out. After what proved to be Allen's last game with Los Angeles, a 31-3 rout of the New York Giants, the Rams talked long and loudly about how much their effort had been helped by the fact that one of the Giants had let some anti-L.A. slurs escape from his lips during the week preceding the game. Finally, asked point blank what the score would have been had the errant Giant kept his mouth shut, Deacon Jones had to reply, "Thirty-one-three."

Aside from using them as unwitting motivators, Allen's dealings with the press are strained and strange, largely because he does not seem to understand either a newspaperman's function or how he operates.

The coach's sympathy for reporters on deadline, for example, is limited. The Washington *Post*'s Ken Denlinger discovered this when he had to run around the track with Allen in Los Angeles to get some questions answered, the coach refusing to postpone his daily exercise routine for even a couple of minutes.

If he could, Allen would probably permanently bar reporters from bothering his athletes, but he does the best he can. His locker room is one of the few in the league closed to writers during the course of the week. Reporters wanting to talk to players must wait in a separate room for what can be upwards of two hours while the player of his choice perhaps attends a meeting, enjoys a leisurely shower and finally decides to make himself available.

"George advised me to limit the press' access to me," tennis star Billie Jean King wrote in the *Sporting News* about an in-flight chat she had with the Redskins coach. "Allen told me how his football players were protected from the media, all interviews were approved through him. He would not even consider the possibility of the press interrupting his team practice."

The idea of unbiased reporters searching Joe Friday-like for "Just the facts, ma'am" is anathema to Allen. He expects writers to act like cheerleading auxiliaries to the club, constantly reminding them that "things get better for everyone when we win." He does not recognize objectivity: you are either for the team or against it.

In Los Angeles, he once gave game balls to half a dozen writers whom he felt had cooperated in their stories to the extent of helping the Rams win a game, and even lectured a group of football writers for their lack of enthusiasm, ending with a call for three hip-hip-hooray cheers for the Rams, a request that met with a halfhearted response at best.

Writers, he feels, must stay in their place. When the *Evening Star*'s Tom Dowling wrote some anti-Allen columns, Allen attempted via Joe Sullivan to have him barred from the Redskins locker room following the next game. When his team lost an unbelievable 16-15 game in Chicago, he thought nothing of asking reporters not to disturb his players with questions, noting,

"It's been a tough game for them. We want to get showered, get on the plane, and get out of here." Yet when the *Star*'s Steve Guback blamed a late appearance at practice one day on a faulty automobile, Allen told him in total seriousness, "If it'll help us win, Steve, we'll get you a new car."

Perhaps the most fascinating thing about Allen and his methods are the wild contradictions they encompass. An extremely scientific student of the game, the coach manages to be at one and the same time the most fanatical of superstitious men, believing in a variety of jinxes and good-luck charms of a scope great enough to put voodoo witchmen to shame.

Anything that happens, no matter how trivial, becomes the possible basis for a superstition. When Governor Ronald Reagan visited a Rams practice in 1970, Allen noted, "The last time you visited us, you started us on a winning streak. I hope you'll do the same for us now." Before the third Redskin exhibition game, he made it a point to throw left-handed passes to one of the linebackers, saying "I did that last week and we beat Denver." When he was shown a copy of *Newsweek* with his picture on the cover the Tuesday after the Redskins' first loss to Kansas City, he did a genuine double take and blurted out, "Holy cripes, no wonder we lost, we were jinxed." When someone attempted to point out that the magazine had not seen the light of day when his team was losing, Allen refused to be deterred, grimly maintaining, "Well, it was going through the hopper, anyway."

Many of his superstitions revolve around clothing. He has a set uniform, a California-weight, short-sleeve blue shirt and a lightweight maroon Redskins jacket, known collectively as "the stuff I've been winning with." He wears it no matter what the weather, but not without a sly protestation when considering a game in windy Chicago, "Gee, it's rough to be superstitious."

Any variation from this routine troubles him mightily, and when NFL Films asked if he would wear a microphone to assist in the taping of a documentary, he consented reluctantly, only to rush into the clubhouse right in the midst of a home game with the Eagles and in full view of some 50,000 perplexed fans because he thought the thing was jinxing him and he was determined to get it off at once. The clothing business even came to taint his associates, publicity director Joe Blair switching from his traditional bow tie to a turtleneck when the team started to show signs of being human.

Eager to catch on to a good thing as the winning continued, the entire Redskin team became as superstitious as their leader even to the point of always sitting in the same airplane seats on every trip so as not to offend any celestial powers.

Not even team meeting rooms could be changed once the ball, so to speak, got rolling. There were two of these rooms on the second floor of the Redskins Dulles complex, one larger than the other. After a general meeting with Allen in the big one, the team would break up into offensive and defensive meetings, the defense — Allen being a defensive coach — getting the larger of the two rooms.

Yet when the defenders let everybody down by playing poorly early on, Solomon-like Allen granted the big room to the offense, promising the defense it could get that extra space back by pulling off a shutout. Finally, in the fifth game, they did it, 20-0 against St. Louis. But things were going so well at that point that nobody wanted to change anything, including the defense, which continued to adjourn to cramped quarters for the general good of the team.

"It's like this," explained Diron Talbert, "as long as you keep on winning, you've got to do the same things. You do the same things in practice — chew tobacco on Tuesdays and Thursdays and smoke a ten-cent cigar in the dressing room on Wednesday."

Vowing that he was the type who'd "do anything to win," Talbert hinted that he might make the ultimate sacrifice and go without a haircut as long as the team's good fortune continued, revealing that as a 1970 Ram he had reported to camp with a mustache, continually neglecting to shave it off while the team persevered in winning.

"We won our first six exhibition games and the first three regular-season games," he concluded, "and by that time I began to like the darn thing so much I never did shave it off."

Talbert, in fact, did not get a haircut, and most of the team followed his example. "Nobody wanted to change anything," said John Wilbur. "Even Coach Dowler looked like he had a permanent. When they took a picture of the old Rams before the game in Los Angeles, the only thing missing was me lying down in front with a rugby ball."

For the players, every week in Washington soon became a series of rituals and responsibilities that made Egyptian priests look like carefree playboys.

Every Tuesday night, approximately three quarters of the team would show up at an optional — but naturally well-attended — meeting at a Holiday Inn in Virginia, where beer was drunk, cards were played, and steam let off about Redskin games past and future.

Every pregame Saturday night, the offensive linemen would gather, without Allen, for one beer of their very own, a holdover ritual from the coach's days in Los Angeles. "We'd always do it together," Jim Snowden said. "We'd sit down and talk about the game coming up, about what we could do to get us stronger physically and mentally. If a guy didn't show, they'd go get him. I guess I missed more than anybody and they'd always come knocking at my door."

At that same time, if the game were on the road, or during the afternoon following Saturday practice if the team was in Washington, another tradition would be upheld when Allen, in a further carryover from Los Angeles, would go out and have some ice cream with Maxie Baughan. Should Baughan be a trifle difficult to locate, Allen would get worried, but always broke out a smile when Baughan turned up, asking happily, "Little ice cream, Maxie?" After Baughan forsook him for a coaching job at Georgia Tech, how Allen would manage without his long-time eating partner was a matter of great speculation before the 1972 season.

The most publicized ritual, and the one that went through as many changes as the team's fortunes, involved a large cake sent to the Redskins complex every Thursday starting at the beginning of the season by Washington restaurateur and diehard fan Duke Zeibert.

The cake was coconut and Allen, ever eager to become involved in yet another superstition, made it a point to partake in the ceremony of eating it with the players after practice. Following the Kansas City loss, Zeibert panicked, changed the flavor to chocolate, and was greatly relieved when the Redskins won their sixth game, 24-14, over New Orleans.

Yet despite icing slogans of "Think Seven" gracing his cakes for the next two weeks, the Redskins had the temerity to tie one game and lose another, so a desperate Zeibert changed the wording to "Beat Dallas" the following week, and Allen called it "a championship cake."

That didn't work either, the Redskins falling to the Cowboys, 13-0, and the following Thursday, Thanksgiving Day no less, after three straight nonwinning efforts, there was no cake to be found at Redskin Park for the first time all season. The team responded with a more or less convincing 20-13 victory over Philadelphia and cakes and football players were seen to mix no more.

In addition to everything else, Allen has the quality of a visionary about him, but a visionary who converts his dreams into actuality lickety-split. He imagined the most modern of football complexes to be set in the middle of a virgin forest to aid in concentration and privacy, and less than four months after he announced the scheme the deed was done. "Really," Allen admitted modestly after the season, "it's a form of a miracle. No one could believe it could be done."

Officially called Redskin Park, the seven-acre tract carved

out of a forest became known as Dullesville because of a location two miles east of Dulles International Airport in Virginia's Fairfax County. The official address was 13832 Redskin Drive, but in fact it was in the middle of nowhere, vaguely halfway between the towns of Herndon and Chantilly, surrounded by peaceful farmland complete with red barns, which hid the complex, with its gold goal posts nicely outlined against tall thin trees, until the last minute. If you didn't know where it was, you didn't find it.

Those who did discovered a half-million dollar project, made up of a full-length grass field, a smaller one of artificial surface, parking for seventy cars, and a two-story, 20,000-square-foot building that contained more treasures than King Tut's tomb: handball and basketball courts, sauna and whirlpool baths, a general exercise room bulging with the latest devices, film editing and film review rooms, a locker room, equipment storage facilities, six classrooms, and all the club's executive and coaching offices. Or, in the coach's own finely accurate words, "We have everything under one roof."

No king was ever as happy with his realm as Allen with his little principality. It was a world of his own, a personal fiefdom that he ruled as absolutely as any monarch. Hidden behind secretaries and publicity men, Allen was as inaccessible as Kublai Khan, plotting the complete control, total commitment and attention to detail that marked his success as a coach. The serious hushed tones that characterized all discussions of football made the atmosphere at the complex like nothing so much as a secularized Vatican City.

Allen had been thinking of a similar setup as far back as 1969, when he brought his Rams to Washington to play Vince Lombardi's Redskins.

"I wanted to work out at RFK Stadium and I couldn't," Allen recalled, "so we had to go over to that jailhouse field [so-called because it was used as a detention center during the 1970 May Day demonstrations] and walk across all those parking lots and have everyone staring through the fence, gaping at us like we're in a zoo.

"I was surprised we had to work at a field so far from the dressing room. I told Vince, I said, 'Boy oh boy, you mean to say that you don't have any better facilities than this.' And he said, 'No, I can't even get out on the field there myself when I want to.'

"Now whether he's kidding me or not, that didn't make any difference. The field was in terrible shape the next day, it was all torn up, looked like somebody was ready to plow it for some planting. As you go around the league, you catalogue things, and I thought, well, here's one situation that if anyone comes in here the first thing you gotta do is change these facilities."

Edward Bennett Williams, the team president, found out what his new coach was thinking "the first time he saw our downtown offices, on the night he was introduced as coach.

"That very first time I could tell what he had on his mind, getting us out in the country like he did with the Rams. He considers no distractions to the players important. He thought our offices were really too plush. He felt we didn't need the high-rent district.

"He began talking about moving very very quickly. It became an obsession with him. He would circle the city and circle the city looking for just what he wanted."

How intensive the search was is best described by the searcher himself: "Well, we looked all over. We checked out Episcopal and a lot of other boys' schools. We checked out one of the racetracks, I went out there one day in the rain, to look for space underneath the stands. We checked out military installations. We checked Maryland University, we checked all the golf courses, minor league baseball parks, recreation facilities, schools that dropped football, like Catholic University, junior colleges. There's some reform school in Maryland, and we checked that out. We checked a Jewish boys' school that had good facilities, but they'd be there the same time as football.

"We even had Governor Mandel of Maryland working on it. I met the governor at a banquet and I told him, 'I got a project for you.' He assigned somebody specially to look for us. He had a map and he was going all around the beltway, trying to find us a site in Maryland."

In the end, however, the Free State lost out to the Old Dominion. Originally, Allen was going to work with the Marriott hotel chain and build his complex adjacent to the Dulles Marriott hotel, but discovered, "That's government-owned property there, it'd take too long to get the clearance to buy the fields."

The site Allen eventually chose was located in a largely undeveloped development called Dulles International Aerospace Park, a 500-acre area already served with paved interior roadways, water, sewer and underground power lines, just waiting for some tenants to move in. The Redskins entered into a 20-year-lease with an option to buy the entire site. The rent for the total facility, the team was proud to point out, equaled the rent for the former downtown executive offices alone, and even the large plastic "Redskins" sign would be moved from downtown to the side of the new building to symbolize the completeness of the change.

"The day after Allen was taken to the place he liked, I was out there," Williams said. "Frankly, I had very grave reservations. Knowing how construction moves, I didn't see how it could be accomplished before the season. I felt the Senators were going to move and we could have free practice facilities centralized at the stadium. I really thought of Dulles as a nineteen seventy-two project."

Allen, however, refused to be deterred or discouraged. "His idea for the site was futuristic, like the monorail at Disneyland," said a source close to the team. "He eventually wants to use it to conduct summer camp. Everybody had been talking about something like this for ten years from now. The clubs know sooner or later they all will have to do it. To move an entire organization to summer camp is crazy and eventually will have to be phased out. Clubs are feeling the money pinch, and this is probably the start of a trend. There was a huge initial expense getting Dulles up, but it was cheap considering the long-term prospects. He was really getting it for a steal."

The official announcement of Allen's intentions came on May 12, 1971, with the coach saying in a formal statement he expected his new headquarters to be "a big factor in building the team spirit and organizational cohesion which is so necessary to winning football games.

"Today's brand of winning football requires total commitment, as represented by the unified management and coaching command post which we have designed. We believe that the Redskins facility will be the finest of its kind in the nation.

"This should have been done ten years ago," he said in response to reporters' questions. "This is one of the finest moves the Redskins ever made. We did it in Los Angeles. Everything is based on winning in nineteen seventy-one."

As to the reasons for the move, Allen, thinking of everything as usual, said, "First and foremost, the Dulles location will provide the Redskins with a real home — not just an office building. Our two practice fields will enable us to practice specifically on the type of surface we will be playing on in our next game, plus preserve our field for Sunday games.

"Moreover, the clubhouse will have facilities that our players can use year round to keep in shape. They've been like gypsies when it comes to working out in the off season. Now they have a place.

"Also, we make about twelve round-trip team flights a season. Being next door to Dulles Airport makes it possible to get our gear together and ship it directly across the street and into the plane. Football, like any business, depends on easy access to good transportation facilities, and we feel that this location will greatly simplify and expedite the team's traveling logistics."

Some reporters were amused at the isolation of Allen's proposed promised land and one went out to scout the area and compile a guide to help the players "locate some of the area's watering holes," which turned out to include The Hut, whose bartender promised absolute secrecy to any curfew breakers, the Lake Ann Inn, boasting a team picture of the 1937 Redskins, and the Pleasant Valley Tavern, whose owner, eighty-three-year-old Mollie McAllister, said of football, "I don't like it."

On June 2, less than a month after the announcement, the official groundbreaking ceremonies were held before a couple of hundred people, including eleven Redskins and Virginia governor Linwood Holton, who insisted on calling the team the "Virginia Redskins."

The guest of honor, however, was late. "I was on the telephone," Allen said when he showed up five minutes late. "Someone wants to make a trade. I love that telephone." Then he and the Governor turned the first spadefuls of red clay, watched Larry Brown lay the Virginia redstone cornerstone before commenting with satisfaction, "This will help us to win, and anything that does not help us win does not interest us."

"That building went up in three months," marveled Williams after the season. "It was fortunate the company that owned the land had an idle crew. They poured everything into it. They felt it was a great bonanza, us coming to that area."

As it turned out, everything was ready on the appointed date except the artificial field, only seventy yards of which could be installed. That's just right for a two-minute offensive drill," a never-discouraged Allen said.

In his eagerness to get things finished as soon as possible, Allen took the unusual step of cutting short a late August practice at Herndon High School and brought the entire team back to the complex.

Lining up the nearly sixty uniformed players on the goal line, he pointed to the field and said, "All right, men, let's look for holes in the ground and mark them with sticks for the groundskeepers to fill."

As one reporter noted, "It had to be a first: employees with a salary average of twenty-six thousand dollars moonlighting as landscapers."

After the players had covered the field once and complained they had run out of sticks, Allen requisitioned tongue depressors and had them canvass the field a second time. When those ran out, a third survey with Q-tip cotton swabs was made before Allen was satisfied that the job had been done.

The most noticeable aspect of the completed facility was the very tall, thin trees that surrounded the field on three sides, the fourth being bounded by an eight-foot chain link fence that was useful, as were the trees, for screening the players from casual view.

Above all else, Allen loved those trees, getting upset whenever high winds knocked some of them down, and asking publicity director Joe Blair almost every day when someone from the National Forestry Service was coming out to label his trees. Finally, the day came, and Blair announced with great flourish that the types were Virginia pine, white ash, oak, pignut, hickory, and northern red oak, adding slyly that one pine was of the whispering variety, while Allen winked and called attention to "one dead oak." Still, even this did not prove satisfactory: the identifying tags affixed to the trees, the coach complained, were too small to be read on his daily jogging routines.

"I'd rather have those trees than a wall," he said. "The Lions, for instance, are inside of Tiger Stadium in Detroit. I think this is more aesthetic and it gives us a feeling of being out in the country, which we are, and yet this is ours, you see."

The official explanation for the hidden, parklike atmosphere was that it made for a site free from distractions that might interfere with the players' need to concentrate on preparation for upcoming games.

"It is a wooded area, almost a forest," Allen said with satisfaction on announcing his plan. "We will have seclusion, privacy to have good practices.

"In Los Angeles the practices were usually closed to the public. Once in a while we would have an open one, announced in advance. I think we had five in my five years there. The players think about the people in the stands watching them. To win, you have to have everything under one roof so there are no distractions."

Still, there were certain nontrusting souls who refused to accept Allen as no more than the nature-loving Thoreau of football. Wasn't there that large forbidding fence with its equally standoffish sign, "This Is a Closed Practice. No Admittance. The Redskins Thank You for Your Cooperation." More than that, there was Allen's reputation as the game's master spy, a colossus of chicanery who, the New York *Post's* Larry Merchant wrote, "presumably hires his assistants straight out of the CIA."

The stories of his alleged clandestine exploits were legendary around the league and are said to have specifically led to strict rules against spying in the NFL bylaws. The Lions, for instance, once prepared a new goal line offense for the Rams, but when they trotted it out for what they assumed was the first time in the known world, Maxie Baughan began to shout, "Here it is! Here it is!"

Sometimes Allen is accused of rather conventional tactics. After the Atlanta Falcons cut a player before a 1968 game with the Rams, coach Norb Hecker claimed a member of the Los Angeles staff questioned the ex-Falcon almost immediately.

"They had our offense and our audibles," Hecker was quoted after the game. "They knew our plans and they kept calling our signals to confuse our guys all day."

At other times, more outlandish accusations have been made. As an outgrowth of the Rams-Colts game in Los Angeles in 1967, the story got around that Allen employed a woman to push a baby carriage past the Colts' open practice field in Hollywood, a carriage containing a midget taking films of every one of their formations.

"It sounds like George," Baltimore coach Don McCafferty,

an assistant with the Colts when Allen was in L.A., said with a laugh. "You couldn't close off our practice field out there to the public. We always suspected people were around. So we'd jazz up the formations, put people in motion, things like that that we weren't using at the time, give them something to take home to roost. We were suspicious of George Baby."

Playing on Allen's reputation, columnist Merchant climbed to the roof of an apartment house adjoining Yankee Stadium before a Rams-Giants game, cupped his hands to simulate binoculars, and convinced the Giants that Allen was at work again.

"You change maybe fifteen per cent for a game," a disgusted coach Alex Webster told Merchant, not realizing until his column came out that the writer and the alleged spy were one. "That guy could see everything: what holes we plan to hit, how we changed our blocking. And there's not a damn thing we can do about it now. It's a shame, but some guys just have to have an edge."

Allen's most famous brush with espionage came before a game with Dallas in 1967. Though the Cowboys usually worked out in fence-enclosed privacy, for some five weeks before this game they had practiced in an open area known as Forrester Field.

The Thursday before the game, the Forrester custodian noticed a car parked for the second day along the wire fence bordering the parking lot. The Cowboys usually chased fans from the lot, but this car was cannily parked in the adjoining street, and so had gone unmolested.

The Cowboy aide copied the car's license number, but as he approached to talk to the driver, the car roared away. The Cowboys traced it to a car rental firm, where the vehicle was checked out to one "J. R. Sanders, Los Angeles Rams."

This turned out to be no less than Johnny Sanders, the Rams player personnel director, discovered to be staying in a nearby motel with Norm Pollom, a Los Angeles scout.

The Cowboys were outraged. Team president Tex Schramm lodged an official spying charge with the NFL commissioner's office and told reporters, "I'm shocked that they'd do such a thing and be so blatant about it," while coach Tom Landry said, "My only reaction is I wouldn't do it, but I can't speak for everybody. We don't do it and I don't think it's widespread in the league."

By contrast, Allen was taking the whole thing very very lightly. "We think it's pretty funny," he said once he arrived in Dallas. "All our boys are getting a laugh out of it."

Smiling some more, Allen allowed that "you hear these rumors all the time," then revealed with a twinkle, "Some of our boys saw a guy in a eucalyptus tree at our practice Friday taking notes. A few of them said it was Bucko Kilroy. I said, 'Throw a rock at him,' but the tree was too far away. I wasn't going to mention it until all this came up." Also unmentioned was the fact that Kilroy, weighing in the vicinity of 300 pounds, was in no shape to climb trees of any type.

"It's ridiculous," Allen wemt on. "There would be no reason for it in the first place. You win games with personnel and execution. They have our films, we have their films, we have played each other and know all we need to know about each other. Shoot, I know Bob Hayes can run the hundred in nine-one. Dallas will do Sunday what it does best, and so will we."

This same tack, that there was no reason anymore for anyone to spy, was the one Allen used when asked about the practice after the Redskins season.

"It's a fantasy now," he insisted. "I don't think it's really anything. It's always gone on, it's been a part of the game over the years. George Halas was hooked up in it year after year after year. It used to be a big thing, years and years ago, even before I was in pro football, because everything was open.

"It's really a minor thing right now. You know what everyone's going to do, you know the personnel, you get the film.

Say they got a new play they put in, how're you going to stop it, how do you know what down it's gonna be run on and all that? So I think it's, it's a thing of the past, and we don't even give it a second thought."

Still, Allen is a cautious man, and his suspicious habits extend to his assistants. When a dog ran out on the field during the fourth quarter of the first Redskins-Cowboys game, an ever-vigilant Joe Sullivan, the coach's alter ego, ran out to shoo it away.

"When I saw that dog out there, I figured the Cowboys had sent him out there," a dead-serious Sullivan explained afterward.

"All I know is that Curt Knight came out to kick a field goal and that dog ran out from the Cowboys side of the field. I didn't want Knight standing out there in that rain after he had warmed up.

"That's why I went after the dog. I wouldn't put it past the Cowboys to do something like that. You noticed that nobody from the Dallas side tried to help me out."

Allen's security man, Ed "Double-O" Boynton, says, "I've been around the block a couple of times." Boynton spent twenty-five years on the Long Beach police force, fifteen in the detective bureau, mostly uneventful except for a tangential involvement in one of the most gruesome, bizarre murders in the state's history, the Black Dahlia case of 1947, an extremely sordid affair that involved the torture and butchery of a pretty twenty-two-year-old former movie extra named Elizabeth Short. Hundreds of people were questioned, scores arrested, some even confessing, but the case is still unsolved.

"The damndest thing you ever heard about in your life," said Boynton, who was amazed to discover when pictures of the girl were published that she had once sat down uninvited next to him at a local drugstore lunch counter. And through investigation it was Boynton who turned up the woman who revealed the nickname Miss Short was known by to friends — the Black Dahlia.

Boynton retired from the force in 1964, but chafed at the inaction of being without work. He met Allen through mutual friends and in September of 1966 began his duties with the Rams. "It's been a tremendous boon to me," he said. "I just can't express it in words."

Functioning at times as an odd-job man, for instance helping the Allens move from California, Boynton says the coach is "easy to work for as long as you do your work. He doesn't like to go into a lot of details as to your job. He expects you to know what to do."

As to his duties, "It's kind of a nebulous thing. Basically, the coach feels very strongly about the players concentrating when they're practicing. He'd rather not have people around. When there're a lot of people around they can't concentrate.

"You have to stop it somewhere, he feels, so it might as well be at its inception. When I see people around I just explain to them that we're trying to do a job, and if we let anybody in we'd have to let everybody in and if we let everybody in the place would be surrounded."

What about protecting the team against enemy spies? "That's part of my job all right, but it doesn't amount to very much," Boynton said. "It isn't a very widespread thing, if it happens at all.

"You have to stay alert all the time, though. You never know what's going to happen out there. I don't see, and I don't think Coach Allen does either, the humor in the situation. We've got a job to do out there and we try to do it."

Other people see it differently, even some of the Redskins themselves, especially Diron Talbert, who rains verbal abuse on Boynton as he tirelessly walks around the Dulles compound checking for intruders.

In Los Angeles, the L.A. *Times* even sent a copyboy out to the Rams practice field to climb a wall with a pair of binoculars so a *Times* photographer could get a picture of an alleged spy infiltrating the ranks.

Boynton noticed him because "there wasn't any need for

binoculars, he could have just looked over the wall," and went out to investigate. He found the binocular case and the culprit's shoes on the top of an oil drum, forcing the lad to come down and identify himself in order to get them back on his feet.

Boynton's big problem in Washington was a warehouse across from the Dulles practice field whose roof people insisted on climbing up on to get a view of the Redskins practice. Boynton was equally vigilant in going up after them, occasionally exposing film when the guilty parties were taking pictures.

"People don't usually go to such lengths as climbing warehouses to watch a football team," he explained, "and when they do, you wonder what motivates them. It takes a little effort to go to the lengths of finding a ladder and climbing up, and if there's sufficient reason to motivate people that much maybe there's something behind it. As innocuous as it may seem, you have to play it safe."

If Allen disclaims any interest in spying, there is one type of prevarication he admits he believes in, and that concerns the reporting of injuries. He places no trust in other team's reports, and as far as the Redskins are concerned, would rather not report at all.

"You get reports, you know, about injuries and things like that, or some injury that's supposed to be worse than it is," he said. "Even if you get a report you don't know whether to believe it, and you can't bank on it anyway.

"The worst thing we could do is believe some of the propaganda that comes out. We could get psyched out. Too many players who are supposed to be injured end up playing."

When his own team is involved, Allen acts like a protective she-wolf. Noticing that reporters had noticed that such a relatively minor cog as special-teams member Mike Hull had sprained an ankle in practice, he snapped, "Just because someone leaves the practice field, I don't want you to put him on a stretcher." When more prestigious names are involved, Allen becomes more secretive still.

Though all-pro tight end Jerry Smith suffered what turned out to be an extremely serious groin pull, bad enough to be the cause of dissension on the team's medical staff and allowing Smith to catch only nine passes for nary a touchdown in the team's final twelve regular-season games, Allen consistently tried to minimize the damage when talking to the press, indicating that a little rest would cure it in no time.

And only a chance phone call by an inquisitive reporter turned up what Allen tried to completely hide, that premier running back Larry Brown had been sent to the hospital before the Chicago game.

"I don't necessarily care to report some injury that's gonna hurt my football team, that's the only thing," Allen stated after the season. "All I wanted to do was bring Larry in and out the same day, not even have him, you know, miss practice. Because if another team knows a player's got a bad knee or a bad leg or something, I think it helps 'em.

"If it's a serious injury, naturally you gotta report it, the league has a pretty good rule there," he added, then confessing, "I like to protect my players, put it that way, from injury reports."

Always, in every situation, it was the players. Whatever they wanted, whatever was good for them, was what he wanted. While Vince Lombardi reigned, Allen collaborates. He believes in creating intense personal relationships with his players, converting each of them to buddies, because, "You've got to find out what makes your players tick so you can get the most out of them."

"He has this unusual ability to get along with his players," said Redskin president Williams. "Many of them just won't take the tough, spartan discipline some of the coaches today are handing out. It's true, he doesn't have much in common with them ideologically, but he recognizes that to get one hundred per cent out of his players he has to have a good relationship with them and he strives to get it."

At the most basic level, Allen gets along by refusing to raise his voice. A nonswearer who has made "goldarn it" a byword in the cities he's worked, he feels, "I'd make a fool of myself yelling and swearing. So I have to do it talking quietly to players, respecting their feelings and hoping that humane treatment will get them to do the work."

This lightness of touch was in evidence even during Allen's first coaching job, his one-year stint as end coach for the Rams in 1957.

That was also the last year as a player for Elroy (Crazy Legs) Hirsch, who remembered, "We had a veteran group of ends. Most young coaches are full of fire and want to put in new ideas right away. But George just let us do what we had been doing most of the time. If he did have something he wanted to get in, he brought it up as a suggestion. He'd say, 'Have you ever tried it this way?' He'd never say, 'This is the way we're going to do it.' "

There was more than the milk of human kindness in Allen's method, for he had found equally if not more effective ways of getting his points across.

"The way we're talking right now, I talk to the ball club a lot like this," he explained in a calm, earnest voice. "But then if you just raise your voice, you see, you don't have to yell. I don't know if you people have families or anything but it's just like yelling at your kids. They don't hear you if you yell at them, but you just raise your voice and they hear you, you know, if you aren't yelling at 'em all the time."

"He has ways of letting you know he's disappointed without yelling," assistant Joe Sullivan said once. "You can tell by his voice inflections, the pained look on his face.

"He tells a player, "This is what you did [wrong] on that play; you'd better work on it.' And he expects the player to work on it, right now. You know what he means. He doesn't have to say, 'You dumb so-and-so.'

"George doesn't believe in profanity. He feels it would be a sign of weakness for him to use it. It would be a sign he was letting something get to him, and he doesn't let things get to him."

How Allen's players react to this low-profile system was detailed by George Burman: "We played a terrible game. On Tuesday you get the feeling he's going to rip hell out of us. But no, it's over. Correct the mistakes and get ready for the next game. You're prepared for a tirade, but it doesn't come. Your first reaction is how great that is. I'm twenty-eight and he's not coming on like I'm some grade-schooler. You get the feeling I'm going out there and correct this, not the Pavlovian dog response.

"His attitude is not to get good athletes, whip 'em into shape, rant and rave, bring tears to their eyes, and send 'em out like wild animals. George feels I'm going to get athletes who are going to be prepared to play football. His system among the assistant coaches is, 'We're going to do everything we can to tell you about the opponents, the adjustments you have to make, about what you do right and wrong.' "

"He's not like Lombardi," Larry Brown said during the season. "He doesn't pressure you. He gives you the opportunity and if you don't take it, then it's too bad."

Allen had more concrete ways of showing his feelings than merely holding his tongue. For one thing, there were no end of little gifts for his players, little ways he had of showing that he cared. In Los Angeles, different awards were given out every week, small but seriously taken things like gift certificates for the Ram of the Week and the Big Play Man of the Week, and free dinners for the offensive and defensive players of the week. After the 1969 opener he gave away about sixty game balls to every player and just about everybody connected with the Rams.

In Washington, the trend continued. When a winter storm knocked down some of the Dulles forest trees, Allen had them chopped for free firewood for wood-burning coaches and players. When the team reported for early camp in April of

1971, each player was given a pair of shoes to run in to get into shape. When the team reported in April of 1972, each Redskin found in his locker a box of six heavy drinking glasses, trimmed with gold and bearing the team emblem, with ten team highlights inscribed on the sides. Each player also received a mechanical lead pencil of burgundy and gold, highly appropriate for taking notes in team meetings.

Allen even went so far as to lay a plush bright-red carpet in the team's Kennedy Stadium locker room before the second home game of the season, an effect not lost on, among others, fervent Allen booster Diron Talbert.

"Why, we've got this red carpet now, and that helps us win," he told a pair of slightly incredulous reporters following the game in question. "It sets the right atmosphere. We don't have that old raggedy-assed green thing that was here under Lombardi. It was so bad they had to store it during the summers because Ted Williams wouldn't have it."

Not only in small ways but in large ones, too, was Allen generous. One of his famous tenets is that nothing is too good for those who work for him, an idea that is said to have started way back at Morningside when he demanded and got a salary for his assistant only $400 a year lower than his own. The same applies to those who played for Allen, who soon were able to boast that just about any contract they desired was okay with the coach, including a very high percentage of ones that included incentive bonuses.

Sometimes, other segments of the organization were not as happy as the players with their fancy salaries. Once, wanting to show Rams defensive back Ron Smith that he thought he was doing a hell of a job, he phoned front office honcho Hirsch while Smith was sitting in Allen's office, telling the Ram executive he thought Smith ought to get a $5000 raise for the following season. Smith was delighted, but Hirsch fumed with embarrassment.

Cause of even greater controversy was the personal touch,

the individual meetings with the players, the long talks about problems both personal and professional. Allen's feelings about this were exemplified when he spoke to Buffalo general manager Bob Lustig at a pro football writers' dinner shortly after the Redskins had acquired defensive end Ron McDole from the Bills.

"How do you treat him?" Allen kept asking, with Lustig inevitably replying, "Like any other player," only to have Allen come back and say, "No, no, you know what I mean, what type of guy is he, how do you treat him?" Periodically, the coach would turn to lawyer and club minority stockholder Milton King and say, "This is very important, that he feels at home when he comes into the organization."

"Allen will monkey around with a troublemaker longer than most coaches," McDole himself said after the season. "Lou Saban cut Cookie Gilcrist after one year. Allen will work with a problem player to an extent most won't."

Among the things Allen has done is help one Ram player straighten out a repetitive series of paternity suits. He evinced a tremendous interest in Myron Pottios' prospective baby and the natural childbirth his wife was planning, giving the Redskin linebacker the day off when the baby was due. Still, this was the same coach who didn't tell Tom Mack his wife had a baby until after practice because he wanted the Rams guard to concentrate on his workouts.

To some players, the Allen method is the only one worth playing football under. "This is the way George is, he treats you like a man, he allows us to be people," said George Burman. "This is not by design but almost by default. Because of his dedication to certain technical aspects, because he's so busy with other things — knowledge of the opponent, the game plan, conditioning, practice and meetings — he allows me to be myself, do what I want to do, as long as I perform on the field.

"Perhaps there is just no time left to get into discipline. I don't think that he's ever sat down and thought, 'What do I do with guys who deviate from the norm?' You know, some coaches have an image of an athlete and any variation from that is open to attack to make you conform to that image. George has discovered — maybe not necessarily consciously because he's so busy with other things — one way to be a winner, treating the athletes as men."

Yet even Burman had to admit that dealing with Allen on a personal basis could be difficult. "Sometimes you can tell you're communicating on a different wavelength," he said. "You can tell his mind is on the third quarter of some game and the down-and-yard situation. He might answer 'yes' or 'no' but you have the feeling he hasn't really heard you."

"You know, he never looks you in the eye," one Redskin said. "He always has his hand up to his forehead or on the back of his head. He's always kind of looking down," while a teammate noted, "He's really weird, there's no other word for it. I think he's basically an insecure person. It probably stems from something in his youth, maybe not being big enough to play football."

"There's something kind of mechanical about George," Rams guard Tom Mack has said, while a Washington player who prefers to avoid identification has the following evaluation of the coach and his methods:

"There's no feeling for George Allen on my part. He's like any other coach, when there's a need, when there's a deal that comes along, you can count on going. He's very personable with me, very friendly with me. But it would be stupid to think he wouldn't trade me, especially George Allen. If he could trade me for Duane Thomas or get two good players for me, he'd do it. This is how I've always looked at the game. He's probably most convincing to younger players, the ones who don't yet realize this is a business, the ones who still have that college spirit.

"I have a lot of respect for George Allen as a football coach. I respect his coaching. Without a doubt, he is one of the best.

But there is that lack of a personal touch with me that makes me hesitate to say George Allen is my man and I'd follow him to the end. If I had a bad game I'd better watch the papers, especially in the off season, because he'd trade me in the off season. That's why I find it difficult to believe in this forty for sixty crap and this family crap. It only works when you're winning."

Is Allen genuinely dedicated to his players? His wife thinks so, saying during one Los Angeles crisis with Dan Reeves, "You have no idea how he loves those forty players of his. He goes around the house talking about Merlin Olsen and Lamar Lundy and Roman Gabriel as if they were his own children."

Others doubted. Especially harsh on Allen were the players he traded, who looked askance at the good words the coach had previously lavished on them.

The highly iconoclastic Steve Wright, traded to the Chicago Bears, said, "As a man, Allen didn't impress me. I thought he was mealy-mouthed. He couldn't motivate an amoeba, but he knows it and has surrounded himself with exceptional assistants.

"People try and compare him to Lombardi, that's like comparing a fish and a horse, it ain't the same kind of animal. He's too surfacy, he can't motivate real people, the only people he tends to motivate are superficial and are motivated for superficial reasons. He's got a good football mind as far as being a tactician, but he doesn't have any idea of what a professional football player is really like or what makes him tick, because he didn't play football. He only knows how to run a team. He thinks every pro player doesn't smoke, never chases chicks, and goes to bed at eight P.M. Now that's not very realistic, is it?

"I know for a fact he lies to your face, which was one thing Vince didn't do. He told John Hoffman to bring his family out to Washington, that he'd be on the team. When he came up to tell me I'd been traded, he couldn't say it. 'Spit it out, George,' I said. 'I don't care.'"

Most revealing of all the anti-Allen anecdotes came from his old team, the Rams, whom the *Evening Star*'s Tom Dowling went out to talk to early in the season, ending up with a couple of columns that almost got him barred from the Washington locker room.

"George is a player's coach," defensive tackle Olsen told him. "He makes you feel like he's doing it for you. His strength is in organizing and unifying a team in its defensive strategy. He works hard to establish trust between himself and the players.

"Then after a while you find that George just doesn't tell the straight story. He's always got some gimmick. After a while you get so you just sigh and say, 'Well, George wants to get us up for another game.'

"The man will pay any price to win. But after a while the unfortunate, negative influences started to come out. George would say one thing, the front office another. It was hard to pin down. All you could think was that it was just a shame.

"But the pressure, from within and without, became continuous and the stimulus of caring about winning just became mechanical. A team gets to where it just wears out."

Why does Allen provoke such strong animosities? "His extreme dedication won't let you take him indifferently and he doesn't want you to take him indifferently," said Burman. "The single-minded operation George goes through could make him difficult to get along with. He's hard to work for because you have to work hard. He's so incessant toward a goal that other people might feel vulnerable psychologically, that they're not as dedicated. Some people cannot accept a man like that who has that kind of dedication. It's not comfortable in his presence, not knowing how to communicate. And if he does make a mistake with that dedication, people jump on him all the more.

"I would find it difficult to say that he is less than excellent in his chosen field. Some people find it hard to operate in that atmosphere. Other people are vitalized in that atmosphere.

Others look for every fault they can find and try to bring him down to their hustling, beer-drinking level. Probably the fact that George is not seen participating in the normal vices we all have probably bugs people."

It was the Ram who was closest to Allen who gave, the week before the Rams-Redskins game, perhaps the most incisive analysis of how Allen operates and why.

"I have a lot of respect for Allen as a coach," quarterback Roman Gabriel said, speaking slowly, choosing his words with care. "I used to as a man.

"Personally, he and I don't see eye to eye the way we used to. It's just something that happens whenever a football coach leaves. There's always a little bit of bitterness.

"I felt he was insincere as a person. He's not aware of this. I'm sure he doesn't do it personally. He's so tied up in football he's not aware he hurts people sometimes. Like maybe telling two ballplayers both of them will start."

Allen's own analysis of the strong emotions he arouses in people closely parallels Burman's. "I think it's because, first of all, I know what I want to do and I'm not going to change too much," the coach said. "And, secondly, I put an awful lot of myself into things, so much that some people can't believe that you put that much of yourself into it. Some people don't want to put forth that type of effort. Maybe they don't think it's worth it.

"I'm an emotional person myself, I feel very close to my players, and I would do anything to help them. But I don't, I don't want to let down. I think that five and a half months of the season I just want to work people and drive 'em and get the most out of 'em. Sometimes they don't respond to that, you see, sometimes they don't want to work that hard, they want to have more fun, you know, and they react differently. Yet those who realize it and stay with me and win know that this is the way you have to do it. I like dedicated people. Usually those who go against me aren't quite as dedicated."

Of all the almost endless anecdotes surrounding Allen and his ways, there is one, related by Mel Durslag of the Los Angeles *Herald-Examiner*, that says it all best:

"George Herbert Allen worries like no other coach in football. This isn't to say that other coaches don't worry.

"But George even worries about the fact that he worries.

" 'I worry too much,' he once confessed. 'This worries me.'

"Now he reflected on the matter and he added, defensively,

" 'But goshdarn it, I have a lot to worry about. There is so much to be done.' "

CHAPTER X

Hail to the Redskins

IN THE GEORGE ALLEN SYSTEM, where even writers are expected to get behind the team, there is not a particle of doubt as to where the fans' allegiance should lie. They pays their money and they takes their choice — the Redskins, of course. Could it be any other way?

Thus it was that early in the exhibition season, when the Redskins had shown very little different from their seamy past, that Allen seized on the possibility of boosting their sagging morale by calling for a clamorous homecoming at the first game in Washington.

Noting that he would like to see the Redskins get a standing ovation before every home game, Allen added, "Kings, queens, and presidents do not always get such an ovation," and called it his "biggest thrill" when the Los Angeles fans gave just such an acclamation in what proved to be the Rams' last home game under Allen.

The fans, however, chose to respond to Allen's request in their own good time. Hardly responsive after two lackluster exhibitions, occasions they had long grown accustomed to, they remained stolidly fixed in their seats when the new Redskins ran out on the field for the very first time.

But after three surprise victories on the road to start the regular season, almost everyone in Washington was prepared to believe on the day of the home opener. Sensing a welcome even beyond his expectations, Allen took the opportunity to make every squad member feel important by having all forty players introduced.

With the appreciative Washington fans on their feet bestowing a staggering four-and-a-half-minute ovation, each Redskin in numerical order trotted onto the field for an individual introduction, as the Houston Oilers stood around bewilderedly in the rain and watched the game-delaying celebration.

Without question, it was the Redskins' finest moment since Sammy Baugh was a youngster. With RFK Stadium festooned with such banners as "Hail to the Over the Hill Gang" and "Deadskins Come Alive," Washington was the perfect example of a city gone temporarily berserk over a pro football team.

Having suffered endless frustrations, the Washington faithful had pined for this day. Over the years, the Redskins could be remembered mainly for their egregious blundering ever since they fumbled the first kickoff on the day the stadium opened in 1961 and went on to lose to the New York Giants.

From that day forward, the Redskins managed to remain as error-prone as any team in football. In his first game as coach, a 35-0 exhibition defeat by Baltimore in 1966, Otto Graham suggested, to the acute embarrassment of the team president and others, that President Johnson, who had chosen to attend, stay home the next time, which he gladly did.

In Graham's first league game, fullback A. D. Whitfield set the unofficial record for the highest fumble in Redskin history, the ball squirting straight upward to unprecedented heights, Whitfield recovering after two Cleveland Browns had taken swipes at the ball on its descent. No matter, the Redskins lost, 38-14.

Even in victory, the Redskins had a knack for the bizarre, the most outrageous incident of all coming the day Graham unthinkingly sent in Charley Gogolak to kick a last-minute field goal in a 72-41 rout of the Giants, whose disbelief was supplanted by outrage as the extraneous points were rung up on the board.

Having endured more than their fair share of grief, Washingtonians greeted a winner with a uniform hysteria that affected almost everyone from the lowest-grade government worker to the White House. The extent of the city's emotional state could be measured by a supposedly staid congressman, Frank Thompson, New Jersey Democrat, who reported excitedly to constituents in his newsletter:

". . . For years I have been an unreconstructed fan of the New York Football Giants. But two things have happened of late to strain my allegiance. First, there was the announcement that my Giants were to be moved to the Hackensack Meadowlands. Hackensack Giants? Ridiculous!

"A second source of strain on my old allegiance is the coming to Washington of George Allen and the remarkable resurgence of the Washington Redskins under his direction.

"The town is, of course, delirious. To my amazement I found myself last Sunday sitting in the rain watching the local heroes claw and fight their way to a 22-13 victory over the Houston Oilers. I can report with absolute accuracy that there were in excess of 50,000 certified lunatics in the stadium.

"The fans gave the players a standing, screaming, shouting, stomping ovation when the Redskins took the field and maintained themselves in a continuous state of hysteria until the final whistle. At times they chanted, 'Defense! . . . Defense! . . .' much as Giant fans of other years did when Sam Huff and company were performing their exploits.

"This sort of enthusiasm is contagious. The front pages and the editorial pages are full of copy and comment on Mr. Nixon's proposed and potential nominees to the Supreme Court, George Meany's latest blast at the President, Henry Kissinger's new China policy. But the real topic of conversation is the Redskins. And whatever happened to Martha Mitchell?"

Climbing rapidly in the pecking order of Washington demigods to the point where he could even orchestrate crowd reaction at the stadium, Allen commented with satisfaction on the fans' behavior.

"I'd like to see a replay of that four-and-a-half-minute standing ovation," he said. "We've never seen anything like that. That was the difference in the game. The fans. The players and I may never have that kind of experience again.

"And the fantastic thing about it was that I understand not everyone had arrived for the ovation. Afterwards, I asked Mrs. Allen what she thought of it all and she said the traffic was so bad even she missed it.

"Why, we didn't even get a reception like that when we won the world's championship in Chicago. They have got to be the greatest fans in the world. Too bad one hundred thousand people couldn't see that game."

And so, to further impress upon his charges, particularly the holdover Redskins long accustomed to defeat, the special joys of winning, Allen contacted a local television station and had the tape of the ovation played the following morning for the players' edification.

Declaring that the ovation "put us over the top emotionally," quarterback Kilmer said, "Last week was so emotional because we had gone down and beaten the best at Dallas. We were drained, very drained. We didn't come out of it until Wednesday."

The object of almost everyone's affections, the Redskins had been lauded the previous week in a full-page newspaper advertisement taken by one of the Washington area food chains. In an open letter "to every member of the Redskins' family," it said:

"For years we have needed something in our community to provide us with a feeling of oneness, a unifying catalyst to make us so very proud.

"You have given us this, not just for ambushing the Cowboys but for providing the warmth that comes from a feeling of togetherness.

"By your great accomplishments in St. Louis, New York, and most recently in Cowboy country you have shown us the eloquent rewards of working and playing together.

"Your accomplishments transcend the standing in the National Football League. They are best reflected in the spirit of our great Washington neighborhood where, at long last, we all have something to cheer about as one.

"The magnetism of your efforts makes us all feel so much better and so much prouder.

"Thousands greeted you ecstatically at the airport Sunday night on your triumphant return. The rest of us were there in spirit.

"We of the Giant Food Family know that we echo the sentiments of every family in Washington, in suburban Maryland, and Virginia when we say . . . Redskins, you are beautiful and we love each and every bloomin' one of you!"

Most players were significantly moved by the city's emotional outpouring, particularly long-time Redskins such as tackle Jim Snowden, playing for his fifth coach in his seven years in Washington.

"It felt good," he said after the season, "to be treated like professional football players instead of guys just playing football.

"Each year you wonder if you're going to be around, and you really wonder now when things are getting good. It's something I'd like to go through again. Everybody's kind of old, but, like Allen says, you can't beat that experience."

As it had been for other old-line Redskins, football for Snowden was a tabulation of might-have-beens.

"The year before Allen came," he said, "we almost had a good season under Bill Austin. We went all out against Minnesota and just barely lost. Had we won that one, I don't think we would have blown that nineteen-point lead the next week in New York."

Then there was the one year under Lombardi. "Lombardi was like Allen, only they're different personalities," said fullback Charley Harraway. "Lombardi smiled once in a while and looked like he wasn't thinking about football. But I think he always was.

"George is just so obvious about it. He doesn't seem to enjoy anything else."

"With Lombardi," said Snowden, "we had the idea that we were going to have a winner here soon. It was a season of promise, really, of getting to know him and what he wanted, and everybody had the feeling that things eventually would work out.

"With Allen," he continued, "it was the feeling of 'immediately.' You're expected to win. He talked about winning the first day I met him, at the Redskins office. He told me I had a good season the year before and he expected another one. He said he had tried to make a trade for me for Charlie Cowan when he was with the Rams and he was glad now it didn't happen.

"Then when he rearranged the defense, that's when I started thinking Super Bowl. That's what we always needed. Sonny could put 'em down, but we couldn't keep 'em down.

"When Sonny got hurt, everything was up in the air. Would he be back in time? But Kilmer took over, in a way. We had good practices. Sometimes Billy would have a tough time in the games but the defense would come up.

"By the fifth game, there was no doubt in my mind we were going to be in the money."

The newcomers, to a man, felt the same way. "Welcomed" to town at a Touchdown Club luncheon after the fourth game — formerly, the affair had been held for rookies, but in Allen's first season there weren't any — they got up individually and professed their gratitude for being part of Washington's latest New Deal program.

"I'm happy to be here," said Ron McDole, "especially if you've been watching the scores coming out of Buffalo." Added Tommy Mason: "If Larry Brown and Charley Harraway stay healthy, I'll probably play until I'm fifty."

One of the more serious speakers was John Wilbur, who, as much as anybody, epitomized the new breed of Redskin.

Unlike some others who had previously worn the burgundy and gold, he would throw a cross-body block on his own flesh and blood if they stood between a Redskin runner and the goal line.

After the second game of the season, against New York, Wilbur bared his teeth to a reporter who dared bring up the subject of three holding penalties charged against him in the game. "You didn't see anybody get in there, did you?" he growled.

Actually, as gentle as an old-fashioned bedside practitioner off the field, ready to offer a friendly handshake, pleasant smile, and light conversation about his move from the West Coast into a 1790-vintage townhouse in Georgetown, Wilbur nevertheless could get highly emotional about the Redskins.

Taking his turn at the Touchdown Club podium, wide-eyed and ferocious enough to make the audience choke on its cobblers, he said, "You've heard that Coach Hughes of Houston says we're overrated and Craig Morton says we're going to peak out at the middle of the season.

"Well, they can all go to hell."

In the living room of his home, drinking coffee from the solid side of a broken and jagged mug, Wilbur, staunchly loyal to Allen, allowed there weren't many teams in the league he'd play for because, not having Allen's personal touch, most organizations "objectify" the players.

"They treat you like property," he said, acutely aware of player-management relationships as a prime mover in the Players Association. A fierce supporter of players' causes, he even took his practice-ending striders on the grass alongside the Astro-Turf field at Redskin Park at a time when the Players Association objected to the owners' installation of artificial turf in stadiums.

"The Rams," said Wilbur, "are a Dallas-type organization. They don't like to think so, but they are. They wanted us coached like Landry does. Coach Allen is more personal. He makes you feel like part of a family. I'm too old and too well educated to be fooling around with a bunch of idiot owners."

Rebutting the charge that Allen buys much of his loyalty with the generous salaries he pays, Wilbur says, "You saw what happened to St. Louis when St. Louis was the highest paid club in the league.

"You can't buy allegiance. It's the whole thing, the facilities, going first-class. A lot of coaches waste so much energy. They just don't have their thinking clear. It's knowing what you want and what you have to do to get it.

"The way to enjoy football is get with a winning team with good management. I spent too many unhappy years in Dallas. At the time I thought it was great but you learn. I had a coach who coming in on Monday thought every game was a crisis. Here, the owners let George float and do his thing. You're treated like a human being."

Though a restaurant partner with Roman Gabriel, Wilbur, calling the Ram quarterback "goddamn impulsive," blamed him for the Ram-Redskin uproar, centered on the pros and cons of Allen as a coach and person, that lasted the entire season.

"He started it. We kept it going back and forth. It seemed like when there was nothing to do we'd shit on each other. It was sort of ugly. There was no value in it."

For the Redskins, the controversy served to sweeten Washington's early successes at a time when the Rams were struggling. To Wilbur, the Redskins' opening-game victory in St. Louis was a once-in-a-lifetime thing.

"It was a great coincidence, coming together on the first day of the season," he said. "It was really beautiful, something that doesn't happen often in your playing career. From that point, the snowball just rolled and rolled."

Arriving back at Dulles Airport after the third-game victory over Dallas, Wilbur was quite ready to be bathed in fan adulation. "Some of the other guys ducked off to the side and missed most of the crowd," he said. "I decided I was going to enjoy it."

So he marched triumphantly into the hordes only to discover the excitement even more than he bargained for.

"I found Edward Bennett Williams, Double O, and Coach Allen surrounded," he said. "I became part of a phalanx to protect the coach. There were guys trying to tear off his clothes. They were mad."

Refilling his coffee cup and settling again into his living room sofa, Wilbur reflected on all the improbable happenings of the season: Nixon going to practice, all the presidential phone calls, presidential candidate George McGovern buying Wilbur's wife a hot dog at the stadium (Wilbur later campaigned for McGovern), the airport crowds.

Even death: a young man in his early twenties died while trying to get to the airport to welcome the Redskins back from Kansas City. Evidently impatient from waiting in the interminable lines of traffic, he drove up the shoulder of the road, struck a bridge abutment, and careened over a steep bank to his death. Allen later wrote a letter of condolence to the young man's mother.

"When you stop to think about it," said Wilbur, his face contorting as he did so, "that should never happen, a guy dying because of the Redskins."

But the fan fervor almost knew no bounds. Scores of fans, no longer satisfied seeing the Redskins on a weekly basis, or unable to get into the park, began trekking to the distant Dulles encampment to watch practice. Often accompanied by small children, they would line up against the wire fence at the edge of the woods to get glimpses of their heroes.

Being one of the capacity of 53,041 that filled RFK Stadium on Redskin Sundays became a status symbol without price, with Senators and presidential possibilities Edmund Muskie of Maine and Ted Kennedy of Massachusetts appearing regularly with Supreme Court Justice William O. Douglas, diplomat and former governor Averell Harriman, humorist Art Buchwald, and numerous others.

President Nixon became a relentless fan, and when a big game approached, the Redskins office spent half its time turning down ticket requests from legislators. Finally, when wide receiver Clifton McNeil was added to the team in midseason, there was despair that even seats for his immediate family might not be available.

The team found itself the subject of effervescent editorials in all three local papers. Columnist Buchwald wrote of them often in his nationally syndicated column. The players themselves were much in demand everywhere, from talk shows to car lots to restaurants featuring barely clad waitresses. There was also talk that the euphoria generated by a winning season raised spirits so high that even the federal government was, heaven forfend, performing more efficiently.

Most people, who never got closer to the team than the television set, turned to other forms of adulation. One group made personalized frog-shaped beanbags for each of the forty players, with a giant-sized one for George Allen. Posters, signs, stickers, and large cakes flowed constantly into the team's headquarters, and the letters were unending.

They came from all over, from Washington, Brooklyn, and Los Angeles and a lot of small places in between, hamlets like Laurel, Mississippi; Sullivan, Missouri; Pepper Pike, Ohio; Emporia, Kansas; and Wytheville, Virginia.

They asked for autographs, gave advice on plays, sought to start fan clubs, and offered congratulations to the team in general and some players in particular, like the ailing Sonny Jurgensen, told by one tyke, "You're still my favorite quarterback, Sonny. My hair is red, too." Typical was a note from Missouri, saying, "I think you have the best team there is in the world. I watch every one of your games on TV if I can. If there were more, I'd watch them."

Sometimes, parents would send in works of their offspring

not originally meant for public showing. A Virginia man mailed two posters done by his small son with peace symbols in one corner and a Redskins helmet in the other. The first read, "I love you Redskins. I know you will cream Houston tomorrow. Please do it for me." The second, "The Redskins creamed the Houston Oilers 22 to 13. I knew they would do it."

The father's note read, "Attached you will find two notes I found taped to my boy's bedroom door Sunday and Monday mornings. I think they speak for all of us."

As the celebration mounted with every victory, Allen became, if possible, even more serious because, as Wilbur said, "Being a coach is like being a general. You've got to win every battle. There are very few who can meet that type of challenge consistently."

Among the players, there was no doubting Allen's commitment to that goal. "He's got an ulcer out of it," said Wilbur. "And his wife is French and a great cook, too."

Charley Harraway also could testify to Allen's undeviating mind: "One night before the season we had a little get-together at a hotel. We brought our wives and Gail met George and the other coaches for the first time. The next day, I'm in the Redskin office and all the people who met Gail, the coaches and everybody, are saying, 'What a really beautiful wife you have.' Every one of them is saying the same thing. Here I am going along saying, 'Thank you, thank you, thank you.'

"Then I meet George and he says, 'I was just thinking about you.' That kind of stopped me. Then I figured he was going to tell me how beautiful my wife was, like everybody else.

"But no. He says, 'I was just telling the coaches how really good you looked last night; you really looked like you're in good shape and ready to play.' "

Viewing Allen's intensity far more seriously, yet another Redskin suggested, "I can't see a happy ending for anybody who works that hard. I just hope he keeps winning. I'm not sure what he would do if he lost. He might put a gun to his head."

Dire conjecture notwithstanding, Allen remained riveted in his pursuit of still more victories after the Redskins had built a winning streak of three games. Having lost the built-in advantage of being underdogs, he felt impelled to find new psychological weapons.

Though the odds makers had come to regard the Redskins with new respect, Allen still could remind the team there were others, real or imaginary, who were putting them down. Diron Talbert went so far as to say, "I think a lot of people are envious of the Redskins' being so successful."

Going into the home opener as ten-point favorites over Houston, Allen harped all week on the dangers of "letting down." Especially anxious on the eve of the game, he told reporters, "I hope they're ready. I really don't know."

Wary though he might have been, Allen watched the Redskins document his faith in veterans, the defense rising up to insure a 22-13 victory on a day the offense failed to score a touchdown. Five field goals and an interception and eighteen-yard run by Ron McDole for the first touchdown of his long career were all the Redskins needed.

Stressing that experience counts, the burly McDole, pinned down by Lilliput-sized reporters, said, "We've been through the war many, many times. When things go wrong, we won't head for the sideline."

Playing on the notion the following week that it would be next to impossible to beat St. Louis yet a third time in eight weeks, Allen stressed the Cardinals, on the verge of elimination from the title race, would be a "desperate team."

Echoing the coach's psych-up speech of the week, Jack Pardee said, "It's going to be difficult to get ready. We're going to see the two previous films, see ourselves beating them, so we'll have to concentrate even more to keep from being complacent."

Inadvertent as the remark might have been, Allen nevertheless attracted suspicion of having already counted another victory over St. Louis before the game when he said the previous Wednesday, "Five games don't make a season, that's the goshdarn thing." By everybody else's mathematics, the Redskins had only played four games.

Sure enough, they had no trouble with St. Louis, winning handily, 20-0. Throwing the ball as recklessly as they had in the first game, the Cardinals, who had watched Rich Petitbon intercept three passes in the opening-day meeting, saw Pardee take a turn at intercepting three, as the crowd chanted, "Par-DEE, Par-DEE, Par-DEE."

Having a 5-0 record and the league's last undefeated team, Allen actually enjoyed a rare evening out in public, taking his wife to celebrate with a dinner at Duke Zeibert's, a downtown Washington restaurant that likes to consider itself a localized version of the old Toots Shor's of New York.

His arrival, marked by a red carpet, was the signal for a four-minute standing ovation, no small accomplishment in a city where people pride themselves on ignoring the entrances of the mighty.

Allen made a brief speech, noting that the players always gave three cheers in the locker room after a victory. Despite the changed surroundings, he suggested the diners put down their forks and give out with three cheers for the Redskins right then and there.

Not a person refused.

Reinvigorated as much by thoughts of the next opponent as the evening out, Allen proceeded to get the Redskins primed like never before for their game with Kansas City. In psyching the team that week, he even got unexpected help from Oakland boss Al Davis, who, wanting nothing more than a defeat for his division-rival Chiefs, said, "The Chiefs look like they're too strong for anybody. The Redskins don't have the overall physical ability."

In fact, Davis was striking at the heart of the matter. Said tackle Snowden, "They were so much bigger than we were, so huge, so overpowering; their receivers were larger than our offensive line."

Describing a tackle by middle linebacker Willie Lanier, Charley Harraway recalled, "I had just jumped over a defensive back near the sideline and I was about to land and keep on running when, just before I hit, he knocked all the wind out of me. That's the hardest I'd been hit in a long time. I was watching out for him the rest of the game."

Getting in the proper frame of mind to take on the likes of 6-7, 275-pound Buck Buchanan and friends, several of the Redskins began throwing punches at one another on the Wednesday before the game, as portly assistant coach LaVern (Torgy) Torgeson, his cap getting knocked askew, rushed in with others as peacemakers.

Delighting in what he called a "spirited" practice, Allen further commented, when queried about the many insects that had invaded the campsite and pestered just about everybody, "They don't bother me as long as we're winning."

With tension mounting as the big game neared, Double O cracked down harder in his campaign to oust spies, approaching a man on the loading platform of the warehouse across the street from the field. Peacefully submitting his drivers' permit, the man proved to be a power company official supervising the installation of electricity in the Redskins' own building.

One of Allen's final concerns was the size of the crowd expected to see the Redskins off at the airport. "It isn't often that a team is so honored," he told reporters. "Just as long as it doesn't interfere with our flight schedule." Fans were thus advised not to seek autographs as that might delay the takeoff.

At high noon that Saturday, a crowd estimated between 3000 and 4500 assembled in the rain at Dulles Airport. Led by then D.C. City Council chairman Gilbert Hahn, who was joined by the vice chairman and other city officials, the crowd sang "Hail to the Redskins." A high school band played, Allen introduced his five captains (the more captains the more channels of communication to the other players), and the team boarded the plane, to chants and the waving of placards and umbrellas.

The sendoff, however, went for naught. Opening a 17-6 lead at half time, the Redskins failed to hold back the Chiefs after Charley Taylor, who had caught seven passes for 125 yards, had his left ankle broken on a tackle by Emmitt Thomas as he fell over the goal line at the end of a thirty-six-yard scoring play with only forty-three seconds left in the half.

Generally acknowledged as the turning point in Washington's season, the Taylor injury enabled defenses to tighten up on the now much less dangerous Redskin attack. Going nowhere in a hurry in the second half, the Redskins watched Kansas City become the first to capitalize on their crippled offense. Playing with less favorable field position, the defense also weakened for the first time and was finished off four minutes from the end of the game by a remarkable one-handed touchdown catch by Otis Taylor. The score: Kansas City 27, Washington 20.

"I think they felt it like we did; when Charley went out that was it," Snowden recalled. "After that, they started coming and wearing us down and took control and that was it."

Allen took the defeat like a Paradise Lost. Backed up by a crush of reporters in a cubicle next to the Redskins dressing room, a grim Allen could not disguise his disappointment, nor did he try.

"I just want to go through this once and get back to my team," he said sternly.

Though he said, "We have no excuses, no alibis," he had a ready-made one in Taylor's injury and, before long, could not resist a mention of it: "Charley Taylor is a great receiver. It hurt us not to have Charley in there in the second half. But that's part of the game."

Then, motioning toward the reporters' note pads, Allen, his voice rising, said, "We'll bounce back. Put that down and underline it."

Finishing his remarks, he drained his cup of milk, threw it

angrily into a nearby barrel, and walked back into the almost silent dressing room.

Recalling that bleak day after the season, Allen said, "I knew Charley Taylor was going to be out for most of the season if not all the season. To lose is bad enough but then to lose your captain and star receiver . . .

"Then the other thing that made it tough to lose was that we had a two-game lead going into that game and I felt that this was one game that Dallas was counting on us to lose, that by beating Kansas City we would have discouraged Dallas a little more and eventually opened it up to three games."

Defeated though they were, the Redskins were to receive their grandest welcome of all from the fans. One, two, even two and a half hours before the appointed time, long winding lines of twin red taillights could be seen rolling along the access road to suburban Dulles Airport, car after car after car heading out to meet the very same plane.

Normally as deserted as the cow pastures that adjoin it, on this Sunday night in late October the road to Dulles was to be the scene of a traffic jam a solid ten miles long. Cab drivers would curse, people would miss their planes, cars would have accidents, get stuck in mud, run off the road, while many folk, despairing of reaching the destination, would simply pull over to the side wherever they were and drink a beer.

Those who got through were numbered from 8000 to 12,000, a crowd that would have done credit to the departed Washington Senators. Yet they were at the airport not to see a game but simply to welcome home a team and its coach.

And not a victorious group either, but one that had just lost a key game. This was the measure of the madness that George Allen and his Redskins had created in a normally unconcerned capital city.

Horns honking, cries of "We're still number one" coming out of windows, the cars followed specially erected signs and the waving flashlights of nearly 150 policemen on overtime to a fenced-off and barricaded area between a mail depot and a repair shop. There they waited, but hardly in silence.

The cross section of people present, from gray-haired retired couples to drunks to toddlers in tiny football uniforms who wondered why they were still awake to more drunks, would have done even George Gallup proud. They climbed trees and lampposts, gave out with massive roars when the most innocuous planes were sighted, and put on such a crush that two young women fainted dead away.

To keep them happy the Redskins band, complete with the requisite burgundy and gold wool hats, stood on a trailer providently provided by the U.S. army and played "Hail to the Redskins" until their spit valves clogged. Even some of the team's official cheerleaders, the Redskinettes, including one girl who came out despite a bandaged eye, were crowded onto the same platform. Their waving pompons kept getting caught in the long part of the band's trombones, but everyone pretended not to care.

For the Redskins were coming home and churlishness was not the order of the day. True, they had lost for the first time in six games, but the pugnacious feeling in the crowd was "What's one game, anyway, buddy?" Any doubters of the team's omnipotence had the good sense not to be present.

The signs displayed, betraying in uncertain lettering the haste that went into their production, reflected this mood of Nevermore.

There were the simple "So What? Welcome Home, We Still Love You" to the finely metered "Kings Have Fallen Before, But Superskins Will Fall No More." And naturally there were the political ones, "Nixon Got Beat One Time But No More" and the inevitable "George Allen For President."

When the plane finally came, it was almost anticlimactic, for the players, if not the fans, looked decidedly subdued by the loss as they were introduced individually, coming off a mobile lounge into waiting buses.

The biggest cheers were reserved for Allen, the master builder, but he too was at a loss for even his usual homilies when facing the convulsive throng, saying only, "It's unbelievable, unbelievable."

Then the team was gone, but the fans refused to let go. They marched into the terminal's main building only to be greeted by thousands of handbills advertising "Go With The Redskins To The Super Bowl." All night long and most of the morning optimistic groups who figured the team would win it all chanted, "Sixteen-one, sixteen-one," and sung bleary choruses of "Hail to the Redskins" as they wobbled down glass-lined corridors. Finally, even the staid public address system was affected, and the voice that usually announced Flight 505 to London broke out into that sainted song.

But the outpouring of emotion that Allen's Redskins had caused did not please everyone, notably R. Dan Mahaney, the airport's manager, who was so taken aback by the disorderly throng that night that he reached an agreement with Allen that "personal contact between the public and the Redskins just isn't going to happen. It's protection of the players we're after. The safety of the players comes before anything.

"That Sunday, we had one fatality, one man broke his arm, and there were two heart attacks reported. Several women fainted and had to be hand-carried through the body-tight crowd. The ambulances couldn't get through and after the players departed people couldn't get their cars out. Traffic was backed up for miles.

"Most of the people went into the main terminal and quite a few into the bar. Some got rowdy so we closed the bar. The drinking, we noticed, was extremely heavy.

"There must have been a ton of debris, mostly beer cans, whiskey and wine bottles, and the usual litter. I never saw so many beer cans in my life.

"A lot of young people like to whoop and holler and raise hell on any pretext — and greeting the Redskins is a good one."

So when eager hordes came out to meet the team after a November loss in Chicago, they were refused information as to the time and landing spot of the Redskins' plane and told with varying degrees of politeness to go home.

Undaunted, some 500 came out again and waited all of a December night for the team's 6:45 A.M. charter to arrive from the West Coast after a nationally televised victory over Allen's old team, the Rams.

Drinking beer and for the most part wearing topcoats over pajamas, the fans themselves seemed surprised at their tenacity. A Hilda Kurth of Hyattsville, who told a reporter she knew nothing at all about football a month before, added, "If somebody had told me a week ago that I'd get out of bed at four A.M. to see a football team, I'd have said they were nuts." But there she was.

Yet except for one man who drove his truck right onto the very landing ramp itself and found himself one of four persons arrested that morning on drunk and disorderly charges for his trouble, the faithful got no closer than half a mile to the objects of their affection. Spurned though they were, they understood, for these were, after all, the Redskins, and accusing them of anything uncharitable was simply not done.

If that airport reception after Kansas City was the capstone of it all, it was another Dulles reception, three weeks earlier, that first signaled the presence of something extraordinary, something that would eventually be celebrated in a cover story in *Newsweek*, a feature in *Life*, extensive, three-network television coverage, a filmed special, and more, all detailing what George Allen did to a football team and its city.

That reception came at the end of an October week which saw Washington's baseball team move to Texas and at the end of a day which saw the city's football team beat the Dallas Cowboys after six straight losses to them and take over first place in the National Football Conference's Eastern Division.

While the Kansas City reception had been as carefully orchestrated as a political rally, with fans exhorted to come out and meet the team, this one had the swirling spontaneity of Lindbergh's landing in Paris. Only the city's newspapers, buried in calls demanding to know the team's arrival time, had even a hint of what was going to happen.

What happened was no policemen and 5000 fans, complete with tambourines, cowbells, Indian headdresses and effigies, descending on a Dulles freight hangar in such a mad Bacchic frenzy that airline officials feared for the team's safety and called Coach Allen in the air and asked his advice. Having mildly suggested a few days earlier that an airport welcome might be nice, he had no choice but to agree to come on down.

While waiting for the team's arrival, the enthusiasts remained behind metal doors on which they pounded ferociously like the waves of a sea, alternately roaring, "We're number one, We're number one" and "Defense, Defense, Defense."

"I've been a Redskins fan all of my life," said one man, wearing the appropriate cap and carrying the appropriate blanket. "But I've never had anything to root for before. George says he hoped for more people out here, and he's got it."

When the plane did land, 200 or so influential well-wishers, including Miss National Fire Prevention, complete with tiara and looking for some free publicity, joined the wives of players who had managed to get onto the field, not even waiting for the doors to open but rushing full-speed across the runway to surround the plane, yelling "We're number one" and waving V signs.

As the players descended, bathed in TV lights, they seemed slightly dazed by the orgiastic emotion of the throng. Attorney and Redskins president Williams could hardly speak for a change, but managed to call it "the happiest day of my life in sports."

"I've been fourteen years in Los Angeles and never seen anything like this," said Mrs. Jack Pardee, the linebacker's wife, with another wife adding, "If they make it to the Super Bowl, I won't. I'll have an absolute heart attack." As it turned out, she didn't have to worry.

The biggest roar came, as always, for Allen. Wearing a ridiculously huge red plastic Redskins cap, placed on his head by persons unknown, his grin appearing to split his face, fending off fans who kept pummeling him and yelling, "Hey Georgie Boy," "Big George," "You're number one, baby" at his face, all he could say about the welcome was "Great, great, great."

Typically, when questioned a few days later about the ferocity of the reception, Allen said physical fear was the last thing on his mind. "I was concerned with getting those play books knocked out of my hands," he said. "I would've hated to see those papers come loose."

Though Allen and Williams had a limousine waiting at the runway, the players had to wade through the main crowd where they all but disappeared inside clusters of autograph seekers. Defensive back Mike Bass was signing his name in Magic Marker on kids' T-shirts and immense defensive end Verlon Biggs looked things over and said, "It's together."

"Is it real?" one man asked his wife, who responded with "Kiss me, it's real."

Also for real was the genuine concern for the coach and his team at the highest level of government in the land. The day after the Kansas City loss, Allen received a specially delivered, hand-written message, now framed in his office, which said:

Dear George,

I saw the game on TV yesterday.

A truly great team must prove that it can be great in defeat as well as in victory.

The Redskins proved they were a *great* team yesterday.

You are still going to win ten.

RMN

CHAPTER XI

Crisis and Controversy

As they stepped off the plane from Kansas City, the returning Washington Redskins could have been confused with a charter flight from Death Valley, so woebegone were the looks on their collective faces. Expressions sad as any funeral testified that something, the feeling perhaps of God being on their side, had expired along with the team victory streak at that first losing experience in the Show-Me State.

Coach Allen showed nothing more than his usual preoccupied look. Though he didn't like to have it nosed about, he had lost games before and already was thinking of ways to take the sag out of the team's lumpish morale.

The first thing he did was cancel Tuesday practice for the first time that season. "It shows I have confidence in them," he explained when asked the reason why, pleased to have the opportunity to expound on his trust.

"Other coaches would have had them out hitting the sled after a loss, but I thought a change of pace would benefit the team. They had a hard physical game and we have some bumps and bruises."

And when the well-rested players turned on the news that night, they were further elated to learn that their tireless coach had consummated a trade that seemed at one stroke to heal the team's major bruise, the loss of wide receiver Charley Taylor. While they had spent the day presumably napping, Allen had acquired former all-pro Clifton McNeil in the merest wink of an eye. Who would have thunk it?

The unexpected day off and the even more unexpected trade resulted in perhaps the world's most spirited practice when the team returned Wednesday to prepare for visiting New Orleans, good enough for Allen to use his highest accolade, "a winning practice," to describe it.

Even much-traveled Richmond Flowers, former Cowboy, twenty-four-hour Redskin, and already on his way to New York, was impressed. "If Dallas had the same enthusiasm they have in Washington," he said, "Dallas would be fourteen and o."

What impressed the Redskins most was the facility with which Allen had managed a trade, and a good one, with a team inside Washington's very own division.

"He does some amazing things," quarterback Kilmer said of his coach. "He doesn't let anything pass him by. He knows who's up for trade and who's unhappy."

Ironically, the first such player Allen had nosed out as Redskins coach was Kilmer himself, who was disturbed that the Saints had placed their trust in rookie college legend Archie Manning. Now with his old teammates coming back to see what they had been missing, Kilmer preferred to take a gentlemanly approach.

"I've got no ax to grind" is the way he put it. "It's just the seventh game in our path, another game we've got to win."

Not so placid was Dave Kopay, a former Redskin running back now wearing Saints colors. Like a surprising number of former Allen players, a number that would increase as the season lengthened, Kopay was less than impressed with his old coach.

He remembered a victory party after the Redskins' final preseason game when Allen walked over to his third-best running back and fourth-best pass catcher, put his arm around his shoulder, and said, "You've made the team, Dave. You'll be our fourth running back." Five days later, Kopay was cut.

"I'm not bitter at George," he said after recounting the story. "I was disappointed. Especially after that speech in front of my wife and me. He didn't have to do that. It came as a complete shock. I didn't know what to do. It was really weird. I felt like dropping out or something.

"I felt I had earned a spot. I had played capably and professionally, I thought, while a lot of people were hurt. I guess there's a lot of things you can't control in football. A lot of things, I guess, you can't control in life."

Though no one else, not even Kopay, seemed to be able to generate any excitement about the coming meeting between the spotty, 2-3-1 Saints and the Redskins, Allen could be counted on to treat it as a veritable milestone in human events.

The coach actually went so far as to claim, "This game has become the biggest goldarn game of the year for us. Everyone thinks we're going to win, but there's no guarantee. It's a very important game for us; we've got to regain momentum."

Not even the possible nonavailability of the Saints' injury-prone Manning, who had engineered the team's upset victories over Dallas and Los Angeles, could calm Allen's nervous stomach.

"I think he's going to start and play the whole game," the coach said. "That injury-report stuff is a lot of propaganda every week. The worst thing you can do is believe some of that propaganda."

Actually, Manning did start the game, but was sacked four times by the Redskins defense before leaving midway in the second quarter of a game Washington won with relative simplicity, 24-14, after blowing a 17-0 lead. As a banner hung from Kennedy Stadium's upper deck put it, "Saints Have Fallen Archies."

There seemed to be no end of things to celebrate that last afternoon in the month of October: Larry Brown gaining more than 100 yards for the second time in three games, Billy Kilmer completing nine consecutive passes and leaping to the top of the league's quarterback statistics, Pat Fischer returning an interception fifty-three yards for another score, and the team boasting its finest midseason record in eighteen years.

But best of all was the news from Chicago. The pesky Bears had dropped Dallas, 23-19, leaving the Cowboys two full games behind the conference-leading Redskins, cause enough, it seemed, for the heady talk of magic numbers and sites of championship games that filled the newspapers the very next day.

Even Virginia governor Linwood Holton, wearing a "Virginia Is For Lovers" button, was down in the dressing room congratulating the troops like he'd known them for years, even though he had to ask help in identifying Kilmer and persisted in calling the team, "The Virginia Redskins."

As for Allen, he looked slightly relieved but not completely. "It's good to win after you've lost a football game," he admitted. "I was worried, extremely worried, that even though we were in first place we might have a letdown."

A concern, it turned out, that was extremely well founded. For of the next three games the Redskins played, they would win not a single one, morale would slide, and the team, the public, the coach, and the newspapers would become involved in an increasingly evil-tempered debate over the starting quarterback position.

At this point, however, even the upcoming game with the Philadelphia Eagles was not on Allen's mind, as the unyielding perfectionist in him insisted on spending almost his entire Monday press conference discussing the state of the Kennedy Stadium field. As one newspaper headlined, "Low Grade Grass Has Allen Smoking."

"That football field upset me so much I don't want to talk about anything else," the coach began before he even got to his chair.

"The players were slipping all over the place. You don't realize it until you look at every play on film and someone is falling down every time. On some plays on the film, four guys are falling down. That could cost us a championship, not having that field in shape. A field like that can cause hamstring pulls and groin pulls; our players could fall down on a play that could result in a touchdown.

"Whoever has a job to do for me, I expect them to do a professional job. They originally told me the reason the field never was in good shape was that the Redskins practiced on it. When the Rams played here in nineteen sixty-nine it was terrible and I asked Vince, 'How do you allow this?'

"His comment was, 'Well, we practice on it.' But that's not true anymore. We not only don't practice on it, we didn't even let the Saints practice on it Saturday.

"It should have been aired. It probably should be rolled. It was so wet that when we were just walking on it, it squished. I said to an official once, 'Hey, replace that divot.' Our lives depend on that field."

As usual, most other mortals were not able to get as upset as Allen. Arthur "Dutch" Bergman, manager of the stadium-controlling D.C. Armory Board and himself a former Redskin coach of eons past, responded, "If the Redskins have a complaint it will be the first we've had in ten years. If the field is a little heavy, it's because of the weather. We have to go by weather reports. We cannot control what God is going to do. And you can tell Mr. Allen that."

Presumably so informed, Allen returned his mind to the soon-to-be-upon-him Eagles and tirelessly tried to convince the world that even that 2-5 group would be more than a worthy match for his own 6-1 team.

"Nobody believed me when I said Archie Manning would start for the Saints," Allen reminded the cynical doubters he assumed were always surrounding and belittling him. "The Eagles are capable of winning a lot of games this season. They are playing up to their potential. New coach Ed Khayat has them all hustling, they are more dangerous now."

The coach concluded with a bit of prophecy that turned out to be more accurate than he intended: "If anyone thinks that all we have to do is show up, they're in for a big surprise. Dallas could now bounce around and never lose another game; the Cowboys are that good."

Still, the only interest anyone could arouse about the low-trajectory Eagles had to do with the hygienic philosophy of new coach Khayat, who had taken over an 0-5 team in midseason and immediately put some unusual regulations into effect.

"Good grooming is one of the many facets of good discipline," the new man said, and consequently ordered everyone, including thirty-year-old Nate Ramsey, a mustache wearer since the seventh grade, to get rid of unsightly, i.e., all, facial hair or face the consequences. The Eagles trimmed and easily won their next two games.

"I know we won twice, but I hope people are intelligent enough to realize it had nothing to do with hair," said Tim Rossovich, the Eagles' disgruntled middle linebacker. "If you could have been around the week it happened you'd have seen how bad it was.

"When a guy's on the field the only thing that should be on his mind is football; he shouldn't be thinking or talking about his hair. A team that's lost five in a row doesn't need that type of distraction.

"I think a coach's main objective is to teach his players to win instead of worrying about hair and mustaches. We had enough trouble as it was; everyone was pretty upset with not winning games, and it probably hurt us more than it helped."

The Redskins, allowed the luxury of hair long as they could grow it, looked on the Eagles' anguish as a regrettable side effect of being one of football's have-nots.

"When you're losing, a lot of things happen that wouldn't ordinarily happen," said linebacker Harold McLinton, his sideburns almost long enough to meet under his chin. "Everyone's relaxed around here. There are no types of hang-ups about clothes or hair or anything."

Myron Pottios, his own hair edging farther and farther down the back of his neck, was eager to agree.

"If that were true, we'd all shave our heads and play bald and have a fantastic team. If I could be all-pro every year I'd shave it off, but it's just not that way. Hair is definitely irrelevant to football."

The fount of this thought, though not previously known as a Consciousness Three spokesman, was none other than Coach Allen, who voiced no objections at all to hair at any length.

"Short hair is not going to make anyone a good citizen," he said. "We have a lot of solid citizens here. I respect the player more than his sideburns."

Turning then to a particularly shaggy reporter, Allen said: "I believe that a shave and a haircut aren't going to make you a better writer, and I don't think they'd make my team better football players. Besides, I have enough trouble getting my kids to cut their hair."

As the week went on, that was not to be all the trouble Allen had, for, as in the previous game with New Orleans, he experienced increasing difficulty getting anyone to take Philadelphia as seriously as he did.

"I know I won't convince you guys," he said finally, "but the Eagles are a fine team. Maybe you'll believe after Sunday's game."

What most observers chose to believe instead was that there was something wrong with the Redskins. They turned the ball over seven times, gained only sixty-one yards on the ground while Larry Brown, the league's leading rusher, was held to forty-three yards and two fumbles on twenty-two attempts against the worst rushing defense in the conference.

Fourteen-point favorites, the Redskins never so much as led and needed a blocked field goal followed by a thirty-eight-yard runback followed by a personal foul against the Eagles followed by a thirty-two-yard pass from Kilmer to Clifton Mc-Neil with only four minutes, nine seconds left in the game to salvage even a 7-7 tie with the Philadelphians.

At that, the Eagles almost won as they tried to set up a field goal attempt from the Washington twenty-five with three seconds remaining. However, a pair of Allen's canny veterans, Diron Talbert and Jack Pardee, chose to spend those three seconds ambling around in the Eagles backfield, and Philadelphia, out of time-outs, never got off the play.

"I saw the field goal team running on the field; I knew they had to get on in a hurry," Talbert said with a fond smile. "I was watching the referee; I could see in his eyes he wanted me to hurry it up a little bit.

"He was just fixin' to call time. I pointed to the scoreboard. There were all zeroes. I said to him, 'Hey, the game's over.' He said, 'The game's over,' and I hauled ass out of there."

Not everyone in the Washington locker room felt like grinning. Quarterback Kilmer, who tasted boos for the first time in his Redskin career as the fans became restless at the conservative nature of the team's offense, admitted, "I guess my play-calling wasn't so hot after all. We were lucky to get a tie."

A subdued Allen also had an explanation for the lack of offensive flair. "The big thing, the message I wanted to get across in that last series, was that we didn't want to give them anything cheap," he patiently explained.

"We weren't going to take any chances, do anything desperate and lose the football game. A tie won't hurt us in the standings."

What might, though, was the team's sudden generosity with the ball, thirteen turnovers in the last two games compared to ten in the first six. "We'll have to play better than we've played in our last two games," Allen said, not realizing that things would immediately proceed to get a whole lot worse.

Charley Taylor's humor did nothing to lighten the growing gloom as the Redskins prepared for their next chore, the Chicago Bears. "My condition is improving," he said on the sideline at Redskin Park. "I'm only using one crutch now."

The source of concern was the physical condition of Larry Brown, who had been laboring all season with a damaged knee and had looked his worst against Philadelphia.

Brown was nowhere to be seen as the Redskins resumed work

on Wednesday, having been given two days off following the Eagles debacle. Announcing that Brown was "under the care of" the team physician, Allen admitted that his best running back had played "in pain" against the Eagles, adding, "We want him to take it easy for a couple of days. We want him to have a couple days' rest. There's probably some fluid there. The best thing is to take it easy on him."

That there was more to Brown's injury than the coach cared to divulge became more apparent when one of the players said he had seen Brown in the building that morning walking noticeably stiff-legged and Assistant Coach Ted Marchibroda admitted that Tommy Mason would start Sunday's game against the Bears in place of Brown.

With Allen's penchant for secrecy rivaling such familiar Washington institutions as the FBI and CIA, the Case of the Fly-By-Night Fullback proved a cloak-and-dagger episode to rival anything out of Erle Stanley Gardner.

First, a call to Brown's apartment confirmed the seriousness of the injury.

"Larry's in the hospital," his roommate said.

"Which one?" the caller asked.

"I can't say," he replied. "I've probably said too much already."

Then, a call to Georgetown turned up Brown, hospitalized but saying nothing except, "Talk to George Allen."

A hospital source, however, revealed that Brown had first been there as early as Sunday night after complaining of pain following the Eagle game, that he had been x-rayed and released, but was admitted Wednesday afternoon. Two of the entries on his medical record upon admission were "possible thrombophlebitis" and "venous obstruction" in his left calf, public knowledge of which, Allen seemed to feel, would provide unholy aid and comfort to the expectant Bears.

Nevertheless, the Redskins denied there was any blood clot and said he was "put in the hospital for medical supervision and more rest than he would get at home."

Not only had his initial hospitalization been kept secret, but a Georgetown spokesman said that no official information about Brown's admittance or the nature of his ailment could be disclosed now that he was in. And after the reporter's phone call to Brown, all incoming calls to the room were screened. Local reporters reacted by charging Allen with attempting to manage the news.

While the Redskins doctor echoed Allen's on-the-record view of the case — "It is not certain that he will not play; there will be a re-evaluation made Friday and Saturday" — it was apparent to most that Brown would be watching the Bears game on television in the hospital.

Losing Brown for that game was crucial for, despite his gimpy knee and a pulled thigh muscle, he still ranked as the league's second leading runner and held out hope for a second straight league rushing title.

Moreover, the Bears seemed perfectly vulnerable to Brown's darting, slashing runs. They had the third worst rushing defense in the conference and the week before Green Bay rookie John Brockington had added additional embarrassment with 142 yards on the ground.

In Las Vegas, the odds, favoring the Redskins by three earlier in the week, fluctuated sharply as Brown's condition was revealed, dropping first to "pick-'em," then to two-and-a-half points favoring the Bears. And just about the grimmest-looking man to be found on the eve of the game in Chicago was the august Edward Bennett Williams, club president.

To Williams, that evening at the Redskins' hotel appeared all the darker because he viewed the team, stripped as it was of almost every phase of its attack, on the verge of total collapse. The list of injuries on the offense read like an all-star line-up: Sonny Jurgensen, Larry Brown, Charley Taylor, and Jerry Smith. Had Williams known that Charley Harraway was to get knocked out and miss the second half of the Bears game he likely would have stayed home.

"Without Jurgensen, we were primarily a running team,"

Williams recalled after the season. "Then with Brown and Harraway hurting, our running game was badly damaged. On top of that, the injuries to Taylor and Smith hurt the running game still more.

"Nobody grasped what fine blockers they are until we had to rely on the Jeffersons, the McNeils, and the Dowlers. They just couldn't make the sweeps go. We were reduced to running inside. And without Taylor and Smith, our passing game, for whatever it was worth, was badly damaged.

"In retrospect," he said of Allen, "it's remarkable how he was able to hold them together."

In fact, not only had Brown been ailing badly since before the Eagles game, so, too, had Harraway, a better-kept secret. On the Thursday before that game, Harraway revealed, he tore ligaments in his left knee playing handball at Redskin Park with Harold McLinton.

"I really messed up the leg; I couldn't bend it," Harraway said. "I hopped up on the training table and they packed it with ice for a long time, but I still couldn't bend it. It wouldn't move, or anything.

"I sat there wondering why it was happening to me. That was just a couple of months after I accepted Christ. I remember, just when I got in a car so they could take me to the doctor's, I remember praying, asking God whatever he wanted me to do in life I would understand. But, at that moment, I wanted to play football badly.

"I went into the doctor's office on crutches and Charley Taylor was there — he still had the cast on his foot. Charley told me there was nothing wrong with me. When I went to show him, my leg stretched right out. I couldn't believe it. I kept stretching it out and it didn't hurt. Charley laughed. He said, 'I told you there was nothing wrong.'

"I sat up on the table with my knee bent, and I was just relaxed and leaning on it and the doctor started examining the right knee. 'No, this one,' I said. I think my prayers were answered. It was like I threw away my crutches.

"The ligament had been torn before and was still loose and that time it was torn some more. It hurt after that, but I played anyway. I prayed that I would be able to finish the season."

Wanting a victory in his first return to Chicago as Redskin coach more than anything except perhaps a win later in his return to Los Angeles, Allen stressed his frequent theme, the greater the obstacles, the more satisfying the victory. In Los Angeles, Allen had beaten the Bears three out of five, and Rich Petitbon predicted yet another success, voiced less on logic than the need for a morale-boosting positive stance, as he recounted his days as Allen's disciple, beginning in Chicago.

"Looking back, I like to think I've had three of the most interesting coaches: Halas, Allen, and Clark Shaughnessy," Petitbon said. "Two things made Halas. He was a good judge of players, the best in the league for decades. And he was consistently tough, but fair.

"Allen is the better coach. Years ago when he was just an assistant in Chicago it was obvious to those who played for him that he was the best coach in the country.

"Nothing is beyond him, nothing too big for him to handle. Last winter, he even knew how to handle it when they fired him in Los Angeles. And nothing is too small for him. He takes the time to be thorough on every little detail.

"I'm sure it was Shaughnessy who created the T formation in Chicago, and one thing Allen learned from his association with Shaughnessy was not to be afraid to try new things. From Halas, I think Allen got some of his take-no-foolishness concept. You must abide by Halas' interpretation of strict club rules — and by Allen's."

The stage thus set, Papa Bear versus his former unruly cub, the Redskins, and Allen in particular, were positively numbed by one bizarre play that seemed the essence of the Redskins' plight of dwindling luck.

With the score tied 15-15, Bears center Gene Hamlin, ironically a former Redskin cut by Allen, put the thrill back into the extra-point play with a high, over-the-head snap from center.

Holder Bobby Douglass chased the ball frantically as a group of Redskins chased him, then got off a wobbly desperation thirty-five-yard pass that bulky linebacker Dick Butkus, of all people, clutched with a diving catch in the end zone for the winning point. If awards were given for the year's most outrageous play, nothing else would have come close.

Compounding the Redskins' misery was a barely missed forty-five-yard field goal by Curt Knight that would have been his sixth success of the game. It came in the last fifteen seconds after Sonny Jurgensen made his season's debut in the game's last two minutes and directed a desperation drive of forty-one yards, one of the team's few successful ones, across midfield. More would be heard about Mr. Jurgensen at a not-so-later date.

Simply stunned, they sat there in the Soldier Field dressing room, silent and mournful. Allen's aide-de-camp, Joe Sullivan, staggered toward a corner, looking as though there were a death in the family. The team doctor stared at the floor as if he himself had let Butkus get away.

The bitter tone of his voice revealing his feelings, Allen told reporters, "I don't have anything to say. You saw it. You ask the questions." He also lit into a New York writer, who dared to wonder what were the "bad breaks" Allen had referred to.

"Who are you?" Allen roared. "How long have you been watching football? You haven't been paying much attention.

"Look, we got Charley Harraway hurt today. We've already lost Larry Brown, Jerry Smith, Jurgensen, and Charley Taylor, but I'm not really talking about them now.

"Did you really see today's game? How many times have you seen a linebacker catch a pass for the winning extra point? That was a ten-thousand-to-one play. Did you see Clifton McNeil open when Jurgensen's pass was knocked down? Did you notice that on Knight's last field goal try there was absolutely no wind until the ball was snapped? Even from forty-five yards it would have been squarely through the uprights. But just before he kicked, the wind kicked up again."

What Allen did not know was that former Redskin humorist Steve Wright was shouting from the Bears bench at the moment of Knight's kick, invoking the Viking god in control of the elements: "Odin, Odin, where are you now that we need you? Blow, Odin, blow."

Perhaps sensing imminent disaster, another natural force, Richard Nixon, booster extraordinaire, had a phone call waiting for Allen when the coach returned home from Chicago.

Allen said the President told him he'd watched the entire game on television and wanted the coach to know all of Washington was behind the team, himself included. Mr. Nixon also asked about the physical condition of many of the injured players, and seemed especially interested in the return of a formerly injured quarterback, one Christian Adolph Jurgensen, more familiarly known as just plain Sonny.

In this the President was far from the loneliest man in town. For spurred by Jurgensen's success in moving the team in Chicago, albeit against an acquiescent prevent defense, an entire city would soon forget poverty, busing, Vietnam, and other less pressing issues to concentrate on picking a quarterback for its football team.

For though he had completely missed the first eight weeks of the season, no one in Washington had forgotten Jurgensen. How could they? For years all the team had had was his bulging, red-topped figure, the statistics that paired him with Johnny Unitas as one of the greatest quarterbacks of all time, his reputation as a pure passer without peer.

For years he had thrown for countless touchdowns, only to have a callous and porous Washington defense give them all back and more. If he could somehow be united with the current bunch of stifling defenders, the world had better clear out. Even club president Williams shared this feeling, saying after the season was over, "If we could get the Jurgensen of nineteen sixty-nine, or better, the Jurgensen of nineteen sixty-seven, for nineteen seventy-two, then we could go to the Super Bowl. I really believe that."

While the question of whether he should be returned to the starting line-up seemed to explode without warning in Allen's face after the loss to Chicago, the pressure behind the blast had in fact been slowly festering since the season began. Even if he wasn't in the line-up, he had never been out of anyone's mind.

The first mention of Jurgensen after his exhibition injury and operation had faded from the news came the week before the season opener, when the *Evening Star*'s Steve Guback thought to call the ailing quarterback at home and see how he was doing.

What Guback got for his trouble was a small-scale dressing-down about a story suggesting that thirty-seven was too old to recover from a serious setback.

"I see where you wrote I couldn't come back," Jurgensen said over the phone, sounding annoyed. "Age has nothing to do with it, it's a matter of how quickly it heals and mends. Johnny Unitas is coming back. I intend to do it."

This was the side of Jurgensen the press had come to know over the years, snappish and ill at ease with reporters, a legend not only for his playing but for the speed with which he showered and left the locker room ahead of their panting questions.

Three weeks into the season, however, on the Tuesday before the first Dallas game, a new Jurgensen would emerge. Appearing at Redskin headquarters for the first time since the injury was a pipe-smoking man with his left arm in an expansive white sling, the picture of affability and relaxation as he laughed and exchanged small talk with amazed reporters. This was Sonny Jurgensen, for the first time in his life no longer number one.

"This is just about my first time out of the house," he said, peeking out of a second-story window to watch the huffing players below. "I've been kind of bored; I've just been sitting around, so I thought I'd come down and read my mail."

Painfully eager to see action of any sort, Jurgensen nevertheless downplayed any potential rivalry with fellow quarterback Kilmer. "I just want to get back and make a contribution," he said. "As long as Billy's doing the job, it's great. This is a team, not a one-man effort."

Still, there was no denying his envy at not being able to play with as snappy a team as the Redskins had become in his absence. "First in defense?" he asked, not believing the statistics he was reading. "Now that's some difference. Let me tell you, an effective defense makes all the difference in the world. The offense only complements what the defense does. Now there's not the pressure to score every time we get the ball," a pressure he was very familiar with.

George Allen was feeling pressure of a different sort, the pressure of getting his team ready for the seemingly unbeatable Cowboys. Only the day before, he had commented with scorn on Dallas' inability to decide between Roger Staubach and Craig Morton, declaring flatly, "I'm a one-quarterback man.

"I don't think two quarterbacks, two general managers, two presidents, or two business managers are any good. You've got to have one man and let everybody believe in him.

"You've got to let the ball club know this is the guy, and that you're going to stick with him rain or shine. Even if you pick the wrong guy you can still win sometimes because the club knows he's the man in charge.

"Actually, that was a problem we had first in Los Angeles. We had Bill Munson and Roman Gabriel, and the crowd was always booing and asking for the other guy. The way to answer that was to name Gabriel as our quarterback. They booed and sent a lot of mail to me, but then we started to win and that ended it."

In Washington, though, it was just beginning. Emboldened by Jurgensen's presence, reporters hastened to ask Allen what his eventual plans for the quarterback were, eliciting for their pains a miniloss of coaching temper.

"That's the least of our concerns; the least said about that the better," Allen said, literally turning around where he stood in his impatience at the question. "That's too damn far in the future when we've got the biggest game of our lives this Sunday. We've got something going. Why lose it?

"I can't answer questions on something that might happen; it's bad for the football team. Three or four weeks from now, when Sonny's ready, it's a nice problem." Usually quite astute, that was to be Allen's worst prediction of the season. The closer Jurgensen got to being ready, the nastier the predicament became.

During that week and the one following, Jurgensen slowly began working out. First with his injured left arm in a sling, then without it, he threw increasingly harder. At the end of the second week, Dr. Pat Palumbo, the team physician, said that previous estimates of the quarterback's readiness for the sixth regular-season game had been overly optimistic. More accurate would be plans to see him in action somewhere between the seventh and eleventh weeks of the fourteen-game schedule. For the rest of the month, Jurgensen's name once again dropped from sight, only to return later in greater force.

During team practices, he was a strangely sad figure, jogging alone to keep his weight down, doing menial chores like throwing to the defensive backs to warm them up, trying to balance the intricate mental necessities of wanting to come back but not wanting to disturb the team's pattern of success, of getting ready for an opening that might never materialize.

The week before the seventh game, against New Orleans, he worked out in pads for the first time, and on that Friday declared himself physically capable of returning to action. "I could play in a limited capacity in an emergency right now," he said, jolting his once-injured shoulder several times with the heel of his right hand to demonstrate its strength.

Jurgensen spent that Sunday, like many others, upstairs on the stadium phones, communicating ideas to healthier athletes below. "It's been a very difficult period," he had said about similar chores. "I don't feel like part of the team."

Ostensibly, things were going to get better, at least according to Dr. Palumbo, who, apparently without consulting Allen first, said in the locker room after the Saints game that he was giving Jurgensen the medical okay to practice full-tilt during the coming week and be activated to appear against the Eagles if necessary on the following Sunday.

Informed of this during his Monday press conference, Allen flipped. "I will make that decision; it's my decision, not the doctor's decision," he said tartly. "He's got a long way to go yet. We'll activate him when I think he's ready. If Doc made that statement, he didn't talk to me about it.

"Billy Kilmer has done a great job," the coach continued, still snappish. "Pretty soon if we're not careful we'll have a division there [between the quarterbacks] like some of the other clubs have."

As the week progressed, with newspapers trumpeting, "Decision on Sonny Due," it became obvious that Allen, no matter if he said, "Bill Kilmer's our quarterback, he's done a great job," until his throat ran dry, was going to activate Jurgensen, the better to be prepared should unforeseen emergency strike.

When the fateful Friday turned up, Allen was amused to see a horde of newsmen, five microphones, and three cameramen out to greet him. "You'd think we were making some sort of announcement or something," he laughed.

Then he admitted the expected, that he had reactivated Jurgensen. "It's nice to have Sonny back," he said. "I think he's about ready to go. It's been a difficult time for him — like being in prison."

The quarterback agreed. "It's been a very long, frustrating seven or eight weeks," he said. "I'm just starting back, but I'm glad to be part of the team again. When the time comes that I'll be needed, I'll be ready to play."

After the season, Allen revealed additional sympathy for the plight of number nine. "Sonny had a very frustrating, disappointing season," he said. "I used the expression that it must have been like being in jail, and he agreed. I guess you could say that being in jail and getting paid like he was, that probably isn't a very good expression.

"But after a while the money doesn't mean that much. Since this was the first time the Redskins had a decent defense, he could just feel it, that if he were in there, you know, he'd be threading needles. He was real anxious to play."

As for Kilmer, the number one designate maintained, "Sonny will be a help. I'm glad to have him. You always know there will be somebody there. If you can't handle the pressure, you don't deserve to be in there."

Jurgensen saw no action in the Eagles game, and though Kilmer was not outstanding, Allen maintained in the dressing room, "I never considered using Jurgensen," adding in heat as reporters persisted, "Never, not at all. You're not listening. I just said Bill Kilmer is my quarterback. He had some bad breaks, but he's done a great job."

This message was repeated the Monday before Chicago. "Kilmer is our quarterback," Allen said tirelessly. "He brought us where we are. Because we didn't win we can't blame him. Sonny will be brought along slowly. He is not ready to play. We activated Sonny to get him ready, not to play him at once."

Pausing for effect, the coach continued with emphasis, "I'm not going to let anybody dictate to me who should play. I've never had any problem at quarterback and I'm not going to have one here. When we look at the films, Bill Kilmer had very little help."

Apparently, no one was listening. After Jurgensen's Chicago appearance, everyone was asking the same old question, and the coach was still giving what the *Evening Star,* referring to the salary he was paid to decide such weighty matters, headlined as "Allen's $125,000 Answer": "Kilmer's still our quarterback. He came through when we needed him."

The Jurgensen faction felt differently. The team was floundering, they said, and here was the greatest right arm in the history of mankind ready and willing to take over, getting better just as the team was getting worse. What could be more logical than giving him a shot?

Keeping Kilmer in was the reply. Hadn't he done so well with the team, better than anyone had expected? He was Allen's type of quarterback, it was said, conservative and ball-controlish. He was also, more than Jurgensen, the selfless leader whom the players were devoted to, whereas Jurgensen's promotion might only bring more problems than plenty, upsetting the delicate balance of the first winning Redskins team in generations.

Allen, the one-quarterback middleman entangled in the type of controversy he most detested, was quite upset. Though he told newsmen, "Nothing in the press disturbs me," the anxious atmosphere at the team's headquarters made the opposite seem true.

"I never, never want to be in a position where it's 'Should you play this guy or this guy?' " he admitted after the season. "I like to make a decision and give the man the benefit of the doubt that he's better than the other guy. This is one of the reasons I think we've won, that very seldom in my coaching career have I been on a teeter-totter. The players know that; they like it too."

Though some players said privately that the team had not been overly disturbed by the two-quarterback dilemma, Allen insisted that at the very least it was "distracting. I felt that I owed Billy Kilmer the job, he had led that far, and I wanted to give him every opportunity to keep the job.

"I was disappointed that there was so much attention given to changing quarterbacks on radio shows, television shows, and I even understand there was a poll. I don't remember seeing it, but I was told about a poll on which quarterback to use. None of that helped our football team. In fact, it ended up hurting it."

Indeed, there was a poll, and when it appeared in the self-proclaimed "small, nervy and idealistic" Washington *Daily*

News, the word from Redskin Park was more on the order of "You're trying to destroy the team."

It started innocently enough when *News* columnist George Solomon, amused by the fuss and "because George Allen has so much on his mind we decided to help him," asked a number of people, including his mother — "Whoever you want, George Allen should play" — his mother-in-law — "Whoever you want, George Allen should play the other guy" — and even his two-year-old son — "I want cookie" — about their quarterback preferences.

The *News* sports editor liked the story, and in the manner of editors everywhere, decided to improve on it by running in the space above it an "Official QB Ballot," with pictures of both Kilmer and Jurgensen, explaining, "The Washington *Daily News* feels the fans should voice their opinions."

Voice them they did, and with a size and ferocity that was amazing. In the next couple of days, close to 2000 pieces of mail responded to that simple request, with everyone from pre-teen newsboys to Sammy Baugh-remembering fans of thirty years' duration to one particularly nasty congressman getting their opinions in. They sent little notes on parts of paper bags and four-page letters handsomely written on engraved letter-heads. Scrawled, typed, illegible, and poetic, the opinions rushed in.

They voted for everyone they could think of, Howard Cosell, President Nixon, Eddie LeBaron, Sonny Sixkiller, even Solomon himself. One wanted Kilmer at halfback, another wanted Jurgensen and Kilmer to alternate quarters, a third called Jurgensen, "my idle."

Indicative of the deathless seriousness with which the team was taken in Washington, a surprisingly large number of people viewed the poll as the most heinous act since the kiss of Judas. "The hell with you, fellow," one man wrote, while another complained in a rage, "Bums! Drum up support and not try to kill the spirit. Who the hell do you think you are? Lay off trying to involve the team in your bush and amateurish fight to sell newspapers." Even a dozen or so Xeroxed "Official Coach Ballots" showed up, with Allen picked over Solomon, who was warned, "Stick to your job of second-guessing His Decisions on Monday morning."

Those who managed to address themselves to the question at hand revealed mixed emotions, often as much against one man as for another. "We were a winning team till *Jerky* moved down on the bench," read one unsigned square of paper. "Kilmer was and is great without *Jerky*."

Most respondents, while expressing warm feelings for "Billy the Kid," felt, as one man wrote, "anyone that can walk and chew gum at the same time can hand the ball off." What the Redskins needed at this dire junction was nothing less than "The King of the Quarterbacks."

" 'Super Gut' is right on," exclaimed one note, adding, "Jelly Belly Forever," while another writer made a barely literate attempt at poetry:

> I vote for old Number *Nine*
> For most of the time,
> When he played, the points
> Were there on *time*.
> He puts it on the Money
> And we call him Honey.
> How Sweet it is!
> There is no ifs, ands and Buts,
> We here in D.C. want Jurgy as our Q.B.!

In a more familiar tone, another writer asked, "Solomon, if you were sick for eight weeks but came back healthy, how would you feel if the editor said your temporary replacement did a fine job and you were on call so to speak until he really wrote some bad stuff?"

The final tally, not surprisingly, showed 1225 for Jurgensen, 594 for Kilmer. The old ways die hard.

One of the strange facets of this particular embroglio was that while in a similar situation in Dallas the respective quarterbacks were barely speaking, Kilmer and Jurgensen remained, as well as could be determined, rather close friends.

They had come together at training camp, where writers had labeled them "Paunch One" and "Paunch Two." And even while the controversy supposedly raged, early arrivals at Redskins practices could watch them playing catch with each other, running and laughing for all the world like grown men involved in a careless kids' game.

When approached for official statements, however, both men took on mantles of glumness. The word had come down from on high that the press was fomenting dissension and was to be looked upon as the enemy. An extra effort was suddenly required to interview the pair: they were busy preparing for Dallas, it would be best not to disturb them, were the ploys reporters who wanted to talk to the two quarterbacks had to cope with.

Kilmer, usually the most affable of men, displayed increasing shortness of temper as the cries for his head continued.

"That's George's decision," he said with brisk annoyance. "You can play one quarterback at a time. That's all I have to say about it. It's quite natural for people to be concerned about it, but the team is thinking about beating the Cowboys. We don't care who's the quarterback, who's the tight end, who's the tackle, we just want to win."

Would the shade of Sonny Jurgensen peeking over his shoulder make things more difficult for him on Sunday?

"Not at all," the quarterback said, once again annoyed. "Every game I play I'm nervous. I've always said I thrive on competition. It'll just make me play better."

As the corker, Kilmer added that Jurgensen's presence had if anything made things easier for him in the past hectic weeks: "The only thing that would make me nervous would be not being prepared. Sonny's been helping me a lot with film work. We stay late at night and do more film work than we've ever done. I actually feel more relaxed." So there.

If Kilmer managed to be relaxed, Allen did not. Pathological in his fear of distractions, he could only hope that the quarterback fracas would not deflect his team's attention from what he, and everyone else, began referring to simply as "the championship game."

The last time the two teams met, the Redskins had been only the third club in eight seasons to gain more than 200 yards rushing against the Cowboys, but things had changed somewhat in the ensuing seven weeks.

For one thing, the Cowboys had established themselves as the NFC's top offensive team, as well as its top defensively against the rush. They had settled on Roger Staubach as a quarterback, won two straight with him, and were only half a game behind the mini-slumping Redskins in the race for the Eastern Division lead.

Plus Washington was in what Allen glumly described as "the worst physical shape we've been in all year. It's impossible to answer what line-up we'll have or who is going to play." Some half a dozen starters were far from full strength, including running back Larry Brown, released from Georgetown Hospital that Monday. "You don't regain your strength in five days," the coach noted, further depressed.

Despite Allen's professed gloom, the team tried to keep up a stern front. "Little ol' injuries won't even count," said Diron Talbert, who had a couple but wasn't saying where. "You've got to be strong. That's the way you win championships. It wouldn't matter to me if they closed down the training room."

The early line on the game was pick-'em, and the ticket demand was astounding. The telephone number at the Redskins office was dialed by what seemed like every single member of the House and the Senate as even congressmen had to scrape for ways to get in. And newspaper advertisers were asking, and apparently getting, as much as seventy-five dollars for single seats.

The atmosphere began getting to the players, making them

a bit on edge. "We want it badly, everybody does," said Sonny Jurgensen, while reserve center George Burman even shaved his mustache for the occasion.

"It's for a clean slate," he explained. "You can't stay constant doing the same things. I guarantee everybody is excited. You could feel it in the huddle. By Sunday we'll be emotionally higher than for the first Dallas game."

Even Allen began to get the fever, running around in short pants despite the near freezing weather. "When you're alive, you're warm," he reasoned with his inimitable logic. "When you have a big game to play, you're alive. It's win or else. That's the way to live, that's the way we want it."

As everyone except participants in the *Daily News* poll expected, Allen refused to tamper with what he considered a good thing and opted to start Kilmer at quarterback, as he had the previous nine weeks.

"He's the guy who brought us this far," the coach said, "and he's been totally prepared every week. Sonny isn't ready yet. He'll be available if needed."

The quarterback designate, prophetically as it turned out, was preparing himself for all eventualities. "It'll be nothing new to me if I hear boos," Kilmer said. "I've heard them before. I just go out and do the best I can with what I have."

On the Sunday in question, that turned out to be not enough. Things took a bad turn early in the first quarter, when Dallas quarterback Roger Staubach, apparently caught for a loss behind the line of scrimmage by an ankle-tackling Diron Talbert, managed to get away — "He just snatched his little ol' foot out of there," the defender reported later — and ran twenty-nine yards on a diagonal to a corner of the end zone to score the game's first and only touchdown.

The capacity RFK Stadium crowd of 53,041 didn't like that. They didn't like the paltry Redskin running attack, good for but sixty-five yards and two first downs, either, nor the way Larry Brown, just out of the hospital and obviously hurting, took eleven attempts to gain only twenty-seven yards, two less than Staubach managed on just one run. And they didn't like the two field goals the Cowboys added on the way to an eventual 13-0 victory. And so they booed.

First timidly, then with greater strength, the same Washington fans who had given their team an incredible four-and-a-half-minute standing ovation little more than a month before gave way to their frustrations on this chilly Sunday by booing their sunshine heroes.

Most of all, they booed the quarterbacking. Not that Bill Kilmer was doing a bad job — he finished the game with a quite creditable ten completions out of sixteen attempts for 118 yards — but he wasn't being spectacular, the way you-know-who used to be. Though as Dallas coach Tom Landry would cogently point out after the game, "You don't just lay off half a year and go in and just fire the ball in a big game," the fans were adamant. When the second half began and it became obvious Kilmer was going to start it, the roars of "We want Sonny! We want Sonny!" became louder and louder still.

With the Cowboys driving for a score late in the third quarter, Allen told Jurgensen to warm up. The crowd began to stir, and then, when he momentarily flipped off his jacket to reveal that much-loved number nine the crowd ignited, their dreams seemingly fulfilled. But when the Redskins returned to the field after Dallas registered a field goal, it was with Kilmer still at quarterback. The fans, at a peak of rage, booed outrageously, so much so that even the players on the bench, who like to pretend the crowd isn't there, turned to the stands and yelled for silence, waving their arms in angry frustration.

"I probably handled that wrong," Allen admitted after the season. "When I talked to Sonny, I just said, 'Warm up.' I didn't put him in right away because I wanted to give Bill another shot. I was hoping he'd lead us and I wouldn't have to take him out of there. But the crowd thought he was gonna go in the next series and then they started to boo. It was all because I didn't want to knock a guy out of a starting position who had done a great job for us, you see."

Kilmer did no better on his last chance than on the ones that had come before, and with 2:14 left in the quarter Sonny Jurgensen walked out on the field to overwhelming cheers. But the euphoria was to end almost as soon as it began, as Jurgensen's first play turned into an interception for Dallas' Cliff Harris. Jurgensen was to throw another before the afternoon was over, and the Redskins lost not only the game and the Eastern Division lead but also their hopes for a miracle savior.

"I was just trying to go in and do what I could," Jurgensen said afterward. "I was rusty, no doubt about it. We had the chances, but we didn't make the plays offensively."

After watching one of his teams get shut out for the first time since 1969, Allen was inordinately late in meeting with the press. His usually well-groomed hair slightly mussed, he was, as always after a loss, more than a bit testy with questions not to his liking.

"I don't have much to say. We played good and hard and we lost but we're still in the race" was the coach's initial comment. When pressed about the team's mental state, he retorted, "If everyone here was as ready to write as we were to play, you'd all do a great job writing."

Unsurprisingly, questions about the quarterback situation irritated Allen the most. "That's the least of our problems," he said. "Billy was doing a good job, but we weren't scoring. We needed to throw. Sonny needs a lot of work. That's obvious. A man doesn't become a quarterback in one week. Just because he's been playing the position for years doesn't mean he's ready after a long layoff. It's like a baseball player laying out for a long while — his timing is off.

"You fellows who've been writing that we should have started Jurgensen did not help the situation. That hurts the team. There's nothing wrong that a couple of injured players couldn't mend."

When a newcomer had the temerity to ask about the quarterback situation once again, Allen became irritated anew. "Christ Almighty," he said. "We got behind, and needed scores in a hurry and I'm asked a question like that. We had to throw and Sonny is a better thrower. That had nothing to do with winning or losing."

Although they obviously displeased him, Allen refused to comment either that day or the next on the boos that had echoed and re-echoed across the Stadium. His players were less delicate.

"I hope you're satisfied," Charley Harraway snapped at the first reporter who approached him, looking for a quick way to vent his disgust. "It was very ugly.

"It didn't help any when you're playing at home where you're supposed to have the favor of the crowd. It definitely didn't make you feel welcome."

"I think it's terrible," seven-year veteran tackle Jim Snowden said. "They call themselves Redskins fans. They say they'll back us all the way, and then they turned on us the minute we needed them. We needed the fans to believe in us. We needed the spark. Anything would have helped. We've tried to bring a winning season to Washington. But, hey, when they turn on you that fast . . . If we had turned on each other that way it would have been a disgrace."

"What gets me is the hypocrisy," complained defensive tackle Bill Brundige. "They've said all along they'd do anything to have a winner here. That's how they show it. That's what really upsets me.

"Those fans don't know what they're booing. They don't know if a receiver runs a bad pattern, they don't know if he falls down. They say they'd do anything for the Redskins, they're so glad to have a winning team at last. Then this . . ."

"When I came here I thought they were the greatest fans in the world," George Burman said. "I didn't think there was any reason for this today. Bill called a good game, he executed well. But the fans have the right. They pay their seven bucks. We've got to get untracked. We've got to deserve the cheers."

Equally understanding was the target of all the ill favor, quarterback Kilmer. "I don't blame them for wanting Sonny," he said, forcing a smile that failed to erase the disappointment in his face. "He's a real fine quarterback. That's about all I can say."

Usually one of the last to leave, Kilmer turned and walked out of the dressing room door, that day the first to go, driven away by disappointment as much as anything else. Though tackle Talbert was to say, "Don't count us out yet," most of the team was thinking the thought Allen had expressed best, "Boy, it's been a long time since we won a game."

CHAPTER XII

Presidential Pardon

A LITTLE BEFORE 2 P.M. on a wind-blown thirty-degree Tuesday near the end of November, the gates of the Redskins' country hideaway, usually as implacable toward interlopers as the Great Wall of China, suddenly swung open just as the players were swinging into early calisthenics.

Into the compound strode an ordinary, perhaps shortish fellow wearing a topcoat as a concession to the weather, followed, like Moses splitting the Red Sea, by a surging group of humanity. The man was Richard Milhous Nixon, President of the United States, who had taken time out of surely the world's most hectic schedule to make a visit that wanted words stronger than unprecedented to describe it, a visit whose sole purpose was to offer personal encouragement to his favorite team and George Allen, his favorite coach.

Always the consummate politician, Nixon could not have chosen a time when the Redskins were more in need of inspiration. The loss to Dallas had dropped them out of first place in the Eastern Division for the first time all season and, after taking their first five games, they had won only one of the following five and were due to face the suddenly resurgent Philadelphia Eagles, losers of only one of their last five games, on the coming Sunday.

At the time of Nixon's coming, the team had scored only one touchdown offensively in the last fourteen quarters and sportswriters weren't the only ones claiming that "the magic is gone." But Allen for one resolutely refused to bend.

"It's easy to be negative," he said, upset by the very thought, at his post-Dallas Monday press conference. "We're still in a very advantageous position. We are a half a game out of first place with four games to play. A ten-three-and-one record will put us in the play-offs regardless of what the Cowboys do, and I think we can win every game remaining on our schedule.

"This case is in our hands. Everybody should be rarin' to go with what's at stake."

But when a reporter with a long memory asked if critics might recall that his Los Angeles teams also lost big games late in the season, Allen had heard enough.

"That's asinine," he said curtly. "We were six and one for the first half of this season. I'll take that. Should we lose early? People who say that don't know what they're talking about."

Allen's rhetoric notwithstanding, the team's massive slump bore a strong resemblance to the one that hit the Rams in the 1970 season when, after sweeping their first three games, they won only two of their next six. Even Allen's reaction then sounded appropriate to the Redskins' current predicament.

"I'm not very proud of the way we've been playing," he had said, "but we're going to come back. There isn't anything we can't correct.

"Age has nothing to do with it. This is a game of state of the mind. How badly do you want to win? That's the question that takes precedence over everything else.

"The test of a football team is how it reacts when it loses. It's easy to smile when you win. The test is what you do now — and we're going to lick the problem."

In 1971, however, Allen was to have more than mere hopeful words to help him over the hump, he was to have the aid and comfort of the nation's President. The two had first met nearly twenty years before, in 1952, when Nixon was a senator from California and Allen the coach of the future President's alma mater, Whittier College. Both men liked what they saw.

"He spoke at an NCAA banquet when I was coaching at

Whittier," Allen recalled. "We had a nine and one season that year and won a championship, and he commented on it. I went up and spoke to him after that, and so I got to know him. He's a very knowledgeable football man, by the way. He follows all football very closely, not only tactics but personnel, and you can converse with him very intelligently."

That was not all the two discovered they had in common, for both saw life and football as interchangeable metaphors of the utmost significance.

"The President thinks football is a way of life," said Allen, hardly the one to argue the point. "He played football at Whittier. He is a competitor. That's it. He is a competitor.

"One of the things I admire in the President is not that he came back and won but came back after being beaten twice. The determination to come back shows he is a competitor and that is why he likes football.

"He is a very dedicated man. I really appreciate dedication. That's really what I look for most in my football players. I look for it more than anything else. We have players with less ability but more dedication and the dedication often makes the difference."

Once ensconced in the White House, the President naturally became the Allen-coached Redskins' most fervent supporter, staying up late to hear games played on the coast, sometimes catching home games by going to Camp David, Maryland, where the Baltimore TV channel comes in clearly, listening on the radio if he had to, even keeping an open phone at the Florida White House to get the play-by-play of the first Cowboy-Redskins game in Texas. Allen became a more-than-occasional guest at White House state dinners and after the season ended would drop over to the place to say a personal goodby before Mr. Nixon left for Peking.

Now, with his favorite team floundering as he himself had so often floundered in the past, the President knew it was time to act. He phoned Allen an hour ahead of time to make sure his visit wouldn't get in the way of any essential push-ups and, after discarding the idea of a helicopter trip because of excessive winds, drove out to the camp with such eager speed that the White House press corps was lost in the dust and showed up ten minutes behind. The visit was such a surprise that Joe Blair, the team's publicity man, had left the compound to go to Philadelphia only minutes before the President's arrival.

Once inside the gates, the President walked over to Allen standing, quite appropriately, underneath a goal post. The coach blew his whistle and the team, noticing who it was, gave out with whoops and hollers and literally ran over to get a closer look.

Clearly in his element, the President proceeded to personally greet nearly half the team. "How're the bruises, Larry, Charley?" he asked running backs Brown and Harraway. "Bill Kilmer," he said, extending a hand. "UCLA. My wife used to watch you."

Greeted next was another quarterback, Sonny Jurgensen. "Old Red, from Duke, you're a little after my time but just a little," the President, a graduate of Duke's Law School, said, causing the oldster to turn an even deeper shade of red.

The President even remembered a fellow former Californian, punt returner Speedy Duncan. "You're an old Charger; I saw you play against the Rams," he said, causing Duncan to smile and recall, "Yeah, they beat us, fifty-one to ten."

A top priority, the President noted, was to encourage the offensive line. "One thing I want to get across is that I think the unsung heroes are the offensive linemen. I think they should get more recognition," adding after the appropriate pause, "and more money," a sentiment greeted with roars.

One of the linemen he so boosted was Ray Schoenke, chairman of a Maryland citizens' group pushing liberal Democrat George McGovern for President. Nixon only smiled when introduced and informed of this, but Schoenke and John Wilbur, another McGovern supporter, chose not to be present in the wire service pictures taken of the President surrounded by hulking players. Still, the next day, after one of the papers had incorrectly transferred the executive praise to the defensive linemen, Schoenke was disturbed enough to bring the matter up with the appropriate newsman, saying, "Even when the President praises us it doesn't come out right."

When the Chief Executive got down to the encouraging talk that was to be the brunt of his visit, he claimed to have no doubts that the team would not only beat Philadelphia but take three of their last four games and earn a niche in the NFL play-offs, telling Allen as a measure of his confidence he'd like "a reservation for a seat" for that postseason game.

"I came out to tell you that the whole city is proud," he began. "Win or lose, you've already been great for the city."

Referring to the booing the team received the previous Sunday in RFK Stadium, he noted he had heard "plenty of boos myself in my lifetime. Don't let it bother you. A great majority of people in this town back the team.

"I saw the loss to Kansas City and I watched this last game on television, too. You took a physical beating and you gave a beating, too. But the important thing is that the spirit was there; from the standpoint of spirit you still had it at the end of the game. I'm just as proud of you when you lose as when you win. I wouldn't have to say that but, of course, the press always believes I just congratulate winners.

"I think you'll win three of your last four games, which will be good enough to make it into the play-offs. Maybe it'll be a wild card, but you'll be there. You have the experience, you have the physical ability and, most importantly, you have the spirit. You have a lot of old pros on this team. You know, I'm sort of an old pro in my business, too.

"I hope you win all four, but I'm not suggesting that you will win your division. Remember, I'm going out on a limb. There aren't any votes in Washington but there are in Texas.

"I've always said that in life, as well as in sports, politics, and business, what really makes a team or a country is when it has lost one, it doesn't lose its spirit. I think this team has the spirit it takes. I think this government has it. You're going to go on and win."

The President added he followed the progress of Allen closely because "he used to coach at my alma mater, Whittier. You must think that I sound like him talking. But when one of his teams is down, it comes back. Spirit is the reason. Win or lose, you've never lost your spirit. In sports, it makes a big difference."

Then, after more introductions and more pictures and even three "Hip Hip Hooray" cheers suggested by Allen, the coach told quarterback Kilmer to run a play in the Chief Executive's honor.

"Let me call it," Nixon said, asking for a screen play to Harraway. Against no opposition, it was executed perfectly, bringing a smile to the President's face. "That play will beat Philadelphia," he said, with Allen adding, "You can call them anytime for us." The final word, however, went to Jurgensen, who smiled and asked, "Where were you when we needed you on Sunday?"

Unwilling to use up more of the team's invaluable practice time, the President passed up an invitation to tour the sacrosanct locker room, but did pause to chat with reporters about the team's problems, at times sounding and looking more like Allen than the coach himself.

"The team had had more than its share of injuries lately," was his primary diagnosis. "As the team gets better, it is going to be stronger. When Brown and Harraway are limping, they gain sixty yards. When they are healthy, it means one hundred and sixty yards.

"If they get Jerry Smith back and Brown and Harraway as well and Petitbon is healthy, they will be tough for the playoffs. These are a bunch of pros who have won some and lost some. As long as they have the proper spirit, they will do all right."

The President was also asked how he had managed to find the time to make the unusual visit. "I take my work with me," he confessed, again sounding just like Allen. "It was between one and one-thirty this afternoon when I decided to come. I have a three o'clock appointment but I figured I could come back here for a while and still get back.

"I sit in the car and work, I work in airplanes, wherever I go it's there. I get it done. But I just thought it would help the team to know someone was behind them. To help their spirit."

Then some churlish soul wondered why Mr. Nixon hadn't extended the same helping hand to the defunct Washington Senators, sorely in need of assistance as they had been.

"The Senators?" the President responded with a laugh. "It wouldn't have helped. In baseball you can't say to Harmon Killebrew, 'Come on, go out there and hit the ball.' He's already trying to hit the ball. It's more an individual effort than football.

"In football, it's more of a team effort; morale is everything. In baseball, spirit and morale are not as important. The Redskins have the right spirit."

Finally, after nearly three quarters of an hour with the team that would bear his stamp for the rest of the season, at the very least, Nixon and his entourage went back to their cars, the President first pausing for a final wave to his boys, saying, "Any time you need a play, just call me."

If anyone was happier than the President with his new toy, it was Allen, who knew just how to convert the visit into much-needed team spirit. "It was one of the greatest honors I've ever had," he said after practice. "With all the problems he has [remember Mayor Washington?] it is remarkable he could take time out to visit us. It's just the lift we needed."

And so it proved to be, with the Redskins righting themselves sufficiently to win their next two games against a pair of the also-rans in their division, first beating the Eagles at Philadelphia, 20-13, and then taking the Giants at RFK, 23-7. Both games, however, turned out to be memorable not for the scores or even who won but rather for the effects they had on the team's pair of quarterbacks.

As the week before Philadelphia unfolded, the balance of power seemed to be shifting toward pure passer Sonny Jurgensen, whom Allen gradually conceded had the attributes necessary to rouse the team from its offensive somnolence.

On Sunday, after the Dallas loss, Allen had said, "Kilmer is still my number one quarterback." Commenting on Jurgensen's ineffective relief performance at his Monday press conference, he noted, "I have been in football a long time and I think I know when a player is ready. I don't think Jurgensen is ready yet to go full time."

Yet starting on Thursday, Thanksgiving Day, Jurgensen began working at the number one quarterback position in place of Kilmer for the first time since the regular season began, getting up to twice as much work in deference to his nearly two months of rust-inducing inactivity.

Jurgensen confessed to feeling a bit awkward, albeit strong-armed, in his new position. "He's giving me more work," the quarterback said. "Sure I'd like to start, but that's his decision. There's not a guy in the dressing room who doesn't want to play."

On Friday, Jurgensen got his most work thus far and the ambivalent Allen, who started the day by saying, "Quarterback is the least of our problems, the situation's the same as it's always been," ended with a boost for the old professional.

"Jurgensen looked better this week. It is really one of those things — he's like Joe Namath, you don't know when he's going to be ready." He finished on a decidedly ominous note, claiming, "We are running out of time . . . It's about time we won a football game. We need this one bad."

Just getting the team to Philadelphia proved as difficult as finding a quarterback to lead it, as the Redskins' train had a slight accident, which was followed by a ride on a bus with a broken transmission. By this time, the feeling that Jurgensen would get his first start of the season was unanimous, but Allen would claim after the contest that he delayed the actual decision until only two hours before game time. And it was for Jurgensen he did decide, giving the quarterback, now thirty-seven, a pin in his left shoulder, another chance in the city that had witnessed, not always with equanimity, the beginnings of his professional career.

It was not to be the most auspicious of homecomings and much later, after the final regular season game against Cleveland, Jurgensen — admitting he had "kicked around" the notion of retirement, adding, "I don't want to go out a bag of bones" — was to explain what went wrong.

"The opportunity to play again was something I had looked forward to," he said. "But I was too impatient. I tried to do things too quickly and I made some mistakes. I did things I don't ordinarily do."

What he did was run, something he had previously done with perhaps the most reticence of any quarterback in the league, and he did it not once but twice. On the initial attempt in the first quarter, he did go for eight yards but his boldness resulted in a destructive gang tackle and a fumble, the Eagles recovering.

With the game still scoreless on the fourth play of the second period and no receivers available, Jurgensen elected to run again. On a third-and-twenty-five situation on the Eagle forty-two, he took the ball up the middle, gaining ten yards, giving half a thought to lateraling off, as tacklers closed in, finally keeping the ball, landing on his left shoulder, and landing hard.

The run led to the game's first score, a forty-yard field goal by Curt Knight, but the repercussions were to be more serious. For Jurgensen was slow to get up and those who watched him as he left the field with bowed head noticed he held his left arm limply out and away from him like a useless and evil presence he no longer wanted to be associated with.

Jurgensen took some center snaps near the bench while the Eagles had the ball and, when the Redskins regained possession, came back in the game for one more play.

"I wanted to see if I could hand off and if I could throw," he said. "What I wanted to do was lateral off to Charley Harraway, but Charley was busy throwing a block. I handed off to Larry Brown instead, and right then I knew I'd had it for the day. I'd tried to hand off with my left hand, but I couldn't lift it. It pained. I hollered for Billy to come in."

Kilmer did more than just walk on the field. On his first play he threw a thirty-yard pass to Clifton McNeil to set up a field goal, and before the half was over he added the Redskins' first offensive touchdown in ten quarters, a twenty-seven-yard pass to Roy Jefferson, as Washington preserved its first victory in four games.

In the locker room afterward, Kilmer was close to ecstasy, happy to have won a game, any game, after the long unproductive spell. "Geez, I'm glad to get that seventh victory," he said. "It's been a long time coming. Number seven is harder to come by than rolling one in Las Vegas."

Temporarily being number two had only been a temporary setback, as it turned out, and Kilmer said he was "just glad I got a second chance. I couldn't begrudge the coaching staff the change. The offense was sputtering and the coach wanted to give Sonny a chance to see how he could do. I can understand and respect his position."

Kilmer added he had "no animosity against the fans either. I got hundreds of letters last week, a jillion of them, and not one of them was negative. People said they were booing the situation, not me. They were just getting uptight.

"I've been through a lot of things in my life, almost getting killed in a car accident included. Getting taken out of a game is not the worst thing that ever happened to me."

Not everyone was in a position to share this joy. There was still the question of the status of the superseded Jurgensen to be resolved. Allen, for once, came right to the point. "It is very doubtful that Sonny will play next week," he said when questioned. "I don't know yet the extent of the injury, but his arm was kind of numb when he went back in and tried to hand off. I would think that Kilmer will start next week."

The man in question, usually a rapid dresser, would this day be the last man out of the locker room. He couldn't raise his left hand, he said, and dressing with the use of only the right was a slow process. His face was a sad one, accentuated by grimaces when he bent to pull on his socks and zip-on half boots.

"I guess I'm just snake-bit," the quarterback said, summing it up nicely. "I know one thing, I'm damned sick and tired of getting hurt."

Why, he was asked, had he chosen the unlikely alternative of running the ball. "We needed to get on the scoreboard," he explained. "Football is something you feel. You've got to have a feeling for what you can do. That run was an instinctive thing; you go where you can. It was just a freak accident, that's all.

"I had anticipated starting today," he went on as reporters stood by in respectful silence. "I was really looking forward to playing full time again. I was enjoying it while I was in there. We were moving the ball. A quarterback gets into a rhythm. At first I was feeling my way. I was just beginning to get going. I felt it coming. I was doing what I wanted to do.

"It's a real big disappointment. I was just getting back to starting, and I end up back being injured. I'm at the same place again."

Technically, things were better than Jurgensen expected. X-rays were negative, revealing a bruise to the left shoulder's soft tissue, nothing more, an injury unrelated to the fracture of the same shoulder that had kept him out for ten weeks.

Still, Allen did not sound like he was about to try any more noble experiments with his brittle quarterback. "We'll just have to re-evaluate his condition as the week progresses," he said after confirming the x-ray results on Monday and calling them "encouraging."

"We'd like to keep him on the active roster," Allen went on, "but if he's unable to play we cannot take a chance in that situation. If Jurgensen has to stand around and cannot contribute, he will not be on the active roster."

After the first day of practice, he sounded equally grim, calling Jurgensen "very doubtful as of today" for the upcoming game against the visiting New York Giants. "He tried to throw a little bit and hand off, but it was too painful. Being satisfactory from a medical standpoint is one thing, from a playing standpoint another."

As it turned out, while Jurgensen was not deactivated, neither did he see any more on-the-field action that season except for holding on kicking situations, demeaning work for one of the superior quarterbacks in league history. Still, though he could never admit it, one part of Allen's complex mind must have been relieved at this, for nothing in the entire season had or would disturb him like the controversy he couldn't control, the public's uncertainty and division about who the starting quarterback should be. That this point still festered in the coach's psyche became once again apparent on the Monday following Jurgensen's new injury, when Allen became mightily irritated about persistent questions on the quarterback situation and finally let the anger out.

"If you guys want to foul up the whole goddamned thing — a winning team — with polls and writing about one position, go ahead," he steamed.

"Forty guys are busting their guts. That's the whole story, and we spend a half hour talking about one guy. Why don't you write about the others," he continued, reeling off a massive list of previously unacclaimed heroes, concluding, "let's talk about things like that."

In point of fact, the days that followed provided precious little to talk about. Allen tried to juice up interest in the

Giants by calling their quarterback, Fran Tarkenton, "the original scrambler" and pointing out with a wounded look that the Redskins hadn't beaten the New Yorkers twice in one season since 1953, but no one seemed interested.

"We have got to win our game, we have just got to win it, it's a very very important game," the coach would say almost every day, but the message never reached the ears it was aimed for. Allen was reduced to calling the practices, "very average. There seems to be a lack of concentration. I can't understand with all we have at stake not having a better practice."

If the Redskins, doubtless thinking ahead to next week's "Revenge Bowl" with the Rams in Los Angeles, were not at what Allen would consider an emotional pinnacle for the New York game, the New Yorkers were lower still. Going nowhere at an uncertain speed, they easily became 23-7 losers in a game uninteresting enough to allow Allen, who gloated to reporters, "a lot of you guys were in grammar school the last time the Redskins beat the Giants twice," to present Clifton McNeil with a sentimental game ball just for being a former Giant who tried hard.

About the only person the game made any impression on was losing quarterback Tarkenton, who had three of his first seven passes intercepted, four on the day, and looked just plain worn out in the Giants locker room afterward.

"George Allen understands what this game is all about," he offered in a completely unsolicited testimonial. "He's taken a defense that was possibly the worst in the league and made it one of the two or three best. They have four quality defensive linemen who play as well as any defensive line in the league except Minnesota.

"No one has done much against that defense all year. You saw what Dallas' offense did yesterday [fifty-two points against the Jets, the NFL high for the year]. You should have seen that offense against this team."

On the dark side of thirty himself, Tarkenton riled at

the much-publicized notion that the Redskins were some kind of home for the aged and infirm.

"This is a fine, experienced team," he said. "Thinking it's old is ridiculous. It's not an ancient, decrepit team by any means. He's got a good blend of young players in there, too.

"Give the man credit. If there is any genius in stopping a scrambler, let 'em gloat. I think Allen deserves a tremendous amount of credit. He's done a hell of a job. In fact, he's done an incredible job."

There was to be more excitement later on, for if Tarkenton was down, his opposite number, Washington's Kilmer, was up, so up in fact that the story of his early hours' exploits was to drive the India-Pakistan war right off the Monday afternoon front page of the city's tabloid *Daily News*.

In the predawn hours of that morning, the *News* had been tipped off that the William Orland Kilmer, Jr., thirty-two, who had listed his occupation as "professional football" after being arrested and charged with being drunk in public at a coffee shop of small distinction, was none other than the Redskins' illustrious quarterback.

Hardly inclined to bury its find, the *News* splashed the story all over its front page, in massive type headlining "Arlington Cop Nabs Kilmer after Row in Sandwich Shop," followed by a smaller "Redskin Quarterback Faces Drunk Charge," and the resulting "Tempest in a Toddle House" was on. For it was to a Toddle House in Arlington, Virginia, one of a chain of unassuming places, that the Redskins quarterback had repaired with a female companion around 2 A.M. Monday.

"It was my only night to go out, and I was hurting," he explained later. "My neck was jammed down my throat the first time I was sacked by the Giants. I was with some of the fellows earlier. I had a few drinks but I wasn't drunk. I just wanted some breakfast."

Breakfast he got, $4 worth or thereabouts, but when it came time to pay up, Kilmer discovered he had nothing smaller than a $100 bill to hand over to Mrs. Bessie (Mom) Levan, the matronly redhead who functioned as the place's chief cook and cashier.

"The waitress gave me some trouble," Kilmer reported. "She said she didn't have any change. I asked 'What else can I do?' I didn't have anything else on me. I told her to keep the one hundred dollar bill until I came back later.

"She came back and gave me about eighty dollars in change. While we were discussing the situation, a policeman came over and asked me if I was a smart aleck. 'Hey,' he said, 'don't get so belligerent.' And I said to him, 'It's none of your business.'

"I said, 'If she needs a hundred dollars that badly, she can have it.' And I threw the money at her."

Where the money landed is unclear to this day, but the *News*, in a classic irresistible dig, noted in its story that "there was no immediate report on whether Mr. Kilmer, who yesterday completed only four of the 14 passes he threw at Kennedy Stadium, hit the woman with the money."

At this point the policeman, an off-duty Arlington officer who was having an early morning cup of coffee and later admitted he didn't recognize the great man, asked Kilmer to step outside. He suggested Kilmer go to his car and calm down, but the quarterback balked. "I told him, 'If you think I'm wrong, put me in jail.' He did, right in the cooler. Then I kept quiet. I was not violent. There was no assault and battery, or anything like that."

After the police report was filled out, Kilmer was taken before Special Justice Walter Johnson—presumably no relation to the late baseball celebrity of the same name—of the Arlington violations bureau. After being informed by the officer of the alcohol on Kilmer's breath, the judge told the quarterback he had to pay $15.25 — $10 collateral and $5.25 in court costs — before he could go home.

Kilmer used a $100 bill to cover this expense too, telling the judge, "The cause of all this trouble is because they wouldn't change a one hundred dollar bill at the Toddle House." For his part, the judge confessed to having trouble changing one himself, and told Kilmer he would forfeit the fine unless he showed up the following morning to contest the charge. Properly apologetic, Kilmer felt there was nothing to contest.

"I have never been grabbed before," he said the next day. "I was drinking and disorderly. I was not in a car. I did not go out before the game but after. The main thing now is to get ready for the L.A. Rams."

As far as the now famous big bill went, Kilmer allowed that Bessie "can keep the one hundred dollars and have a Merry Christmas. She can spend it on the kids. The best Christmas I can have will be to get the Redskins into the play-offs."

"They were the most expensive eggs I ever had," the quarterback added on a wry note. "Pete Rozelle will probably put the Toddle House off limits now."

In a town that made big deals out of even the smallest Redskin doings, the Kilmer caper was all anyone wanted to talk about for days. Tom Dowling, the *Evening Star*'s sports columnist, wondered if it was a black mark for the city that Kilmer had been caught in a short-order house rather than a stately French restaurant, the *Daily News* published a lead editorial defending its play of the story, and Matt Kane, an enterprising bartender-restaurateur, put a big sign in his window reading, "Kilmer . . . you can eat Breakfast *free* in my place anytime! Matt." Even *Pro Football Weekly* got involved, heading a Washington story, "Kilmer Leaves Jail to Rally Skins."

Also profiting was the Toddle House, where things all began and which was now enjoying enough visitors to qualify for status as a national monument.

"People come in here and ask for our one hundred dollar cup of coffee," said Elaine Thompson, a day-shift worker. "They want to know where Kilmer sat and they want to sit there, too."

They also want to see the famous $100 bill, unfortunately

cashed by a cab driver later that fateful morning. And as for Bessie, she will apparently remain Kilmer-struck for life.

"He's my man," she said. "I took his order, cooked his food, and served it. And he ate every bit of it — eggs, sausage, toast. I hope he comes back."

Kilmer's boss, George Allen, who had fined the quarterback and three teammates $500 apiece for violating curfew during the exhibition season, chose to take a light view of the current situation.

"I'm not going to make a big thing out of it; I'm not going to change any plans," he said. "My only concern is getting ready for the Rams. I haven't seen the newspapers, but if someone else did that nobody would even know about it."

After the season, Allen reiterated that his casual brush-off of the affair was hardly accidental. "That's the way it was handled; it could have been the other way," he said. "I could have called him in and given him a big fine and maybe, maybe benched him, you see.

"You go out after a game, you have a couple of drinks, and you get in some minor, well, altercation isn't quite the word for it, I guess, but that's all right, and as a result you speak too loudly.

"This is what Billy did, when he has a few drinks he raises his voice. I didn't think it was that major an issue and I wanted to get ready for whoever we were playing next, I've forgotten who it was."

An admission of high irony, for that next game was against the team that had turned Allen out in the cold, a revenge game with the Los Angeles Rams that Allen was later to call the biggest of his entire career.

CHAPTER XIII

The George Allen Bowl

IT WAS MONDAY MORNING, one week before the most important Redskin game in twenty-five years and the most important in George Allen's life, when Billy Kilmer reported to work at Redskin Park.

His first stop was the second-floor office of one Joe Blair, the thin, highly strung, chain-smoking man who is regarded as the George Allen of NFL publicists because he gives 110 per cent, or more, to his job.

Standing in front of Blair's desk, an unusually anxious Kilmer confided, as Redskin players are wont to do in the compassionate Blair's presence, "I got arrested last night, Joe."

"I know," Blair said. "It's all over the afternoon paper. It's on the street already."

Stunned by the development, Kilmer managed only to repeat "Already?" before slumping into a chair. It was hardly the way to begin the most important week of that or almost any season.

Perhaps more than any Redskin who hadn't played for the Rams, Kilmer knew what this game meant to Allen and the players he brought with him. Kilmer shared an apartment with an ex-Ram, Tommy Mason, roomed with him on the road, and knew how badly the running back wanted to win this particular game.

"It all started the April before when we had our early camp," Kilmer said. "That's all I heard. George and Jack Pardee and Myron Pottios, all the old Rams, would say, 'I just can't wait for that Ram game.'

"It wasn't a public thing, but it was a continuous thing. In July, when training camp opened, it would come up. It would always pop up if the Rams were on TV or if one of them said something in the paper. If Roman Gabriel said something, there was always some comment, 'Wait till we play 'em.'

"It started building way back then and I said after we beat Dallas and were three-nothing, 'We're going to come down to the Ram game and some way, somehow, the whole season is going to lay on that game.' "

There were other thoughts, too, that ran through Kilmer's mind that morning in Joe Blair's office. Grudges aside, the Redskins needed a victory to make the play-offs for the first time since the 1945 title game — also against the Rams but so long ago the Rams were still in Cleveland.

And, finally, Billy Kilmer thought, this was to be the biggest game of his life. Discarded by two teams and now thirty-two years old and nearing the end of his ninth pro season, he would be returning to the Coliseum, the site of some personally memorable games he played as UCLA tailback but a place where he had never won as a pro, and he would be there in front of an immense Monday-night national television audience.

Kilmer swallowed hard and walked down the hall to George Allen's office to tell him the news.

"The worst thing we can do," Allen told him, "is let this thing affect all of us and you personally. I want you to think L.A. and nothing else."

"And that's what I did," Kilmer said after the season. "I worked harder than I ever have before. Every morning that week I was in the office at eight-thirty and I engrossed myself in movies. I never read a paper. I kept my mind strictly on the game.

"We'd have a quarterback meeting at ten and after that it was practice. After practice, I'd look at more movies until six at night and then I'd take movies home with me. I never went out any night that week, so nobody could bug me. I didn't go out to eat, anything. I went through every day that way.

"I figured if I didn't win that game people would say, 'Oh, he's out drinking all the time' and 'He's not the right type.' I felt I had to vindicate myself.

"I don't believe I'd ever gotten myself in such a position. I created a lot more pressure for myself, having this thing over my head. Here it is the biggest game of my life, to beat L.A. and to get to the play-offs, and I create more pressure for myself than I should.

"I decided I wasn't going to let anything affect that one goal of beating the Rams. It meant too much to too many guys on the team. That incident, money, anything else, they didn't mean anything. The only thing that mattered was beating the Rams."

If that wasn't obvious all season, the Redskins began talking openly of beating them in the dressing room immediately after they had defeated the Giants the week before.

"It's been bothering me for some time, just trying to keep it out of my mind," Pottios admitted. "I was thinking about it last night and this morning. I'm glad it's here. I think we're going in with a little momentum.

"It's really something. I've asked for twenty tickets although we're only allotted six. I called some old friends of mine, Ram ballplayers, but tickets are scarce. Besides the ex-Rams, it's a big game for others. Like Roy Jefferson lives there and Larry Brown lived there for a while and Mike Taylor and Mike Hull went to USC.

"The thing that gets me is the curiosity. I know so many Rams so well. We're dying of curiosity to see what happens when we play against each other."

"I wished all along this season that we would still be in contention when we went out there," Jack Pardee confessed. "The game has been in the back of my mind all year and I have plenty of friends out there who have been reminding me."

Other ex-Rams seemed equally anxious. "It's kind of ironic," said guard John Wilbur, dressed in his street clothes but sitting in front of his locker thinking of Los Angeles, "that this is our big game of the season." Added Rich Petitbon, "We're in the stretch and we're getting stronger."

For the original Redskins, it was no secret what was on the minds of the so-called Ramskins. "I can't help but think George was thinking about it a little this week," said Jim Snowden. "We know how he feels about it. We'll all be caught up in it once he gets to layin' it on us this week."

Outside the locker room, Etty Allen was every bit as excited as her husband or any of the Redskins. "Let's beat those Rams now," she said. "It's great, isn't it? In fact, that's the reason George and I married each other. We both like challenges.

"You can't imagine what it's like going back there. We've asked for eighty-five tickets. We have so many friends there. And the seats we got are probably in the screeching end zone.

"Have you been to Palos Verdes? That's where our residence is. We live in Washington but our residence is there. It's so beautiful, the olive trees and the sea."

Although the Redskins had slightly the better record, 8-3-1 to 7-4-1, unsympathetic Las Vegas odds makers installed the Rams seven-point favorites, and the spread was to hold right up to game time. At his customary Monday press conference, Allen remained his cautious self, in no way anxious to incite the Rams.

"They will have an advantage playing at home," he said. "We'll have to play better offense and I'm sure we will. The big thing we have going for us is that we are a team. Everybody is happy for everyone else's success. We are not one or two individuals."

Allen's mention of "better offense" was significant. The Rams attack having been noticeably productive the previous two games, Allen was banking heavily on Kilmer to get the Redskins offense untracked as never before during the season.

Recalling still more pressure, Kilmer said, "I felt I had to have a big game. We felt their outside linebackers would play to stop our running game, that they would try to pinch the run, pinch Larry Brown in and contain him inside.

"I felt they believed if they stopped Larry they stopped the team. I don't think they respected me as a deep passer. I felt I had to throw deep to loosen 'em up. And I felt I could throw on 'em. I knew I had to, I had to have a good night."

Far more than Kilmer, the focus of attention early in the week was Willie Ellison, the Rams running back who was largely a reserve for Allen but had been elevated to the first unit by Allen's successor, Tommy Prothro.

Against New Orleans the week before, Ellison had run for a league-record 247 yards in a 45-28 Rams victory and needed only 71 more yards to surpass 1000. Adding still another dimension to the Rams-Redskins rivalry, Ellison made it plain that it would be happily apropos to achieve that plateau against Allen.

Among all the Allen-Ellison lore that surfaced during the week was a Ram version of how Ellison came to score three touchdowns in a 1970 game against the 49ers in San Francisco. Ignored most of the season by Allen, Ellison, it was said, substituted himself for a shaken-up Larry Smith and scored a touchdown. Later in the game, noticing that the defense-preoccupied Allen hadn't observed his deception, Ellison substituted himself two more times when Smith wasn't hurt and scored two more touchdowns.

Reaching Roman Gabriel, another Ram with controversial ties to Allen, before the game was no small chore either, with the quarterback having all his calls screened by a lawyer. Once getting to Gabriel, a secretary's voice could be heard on the line requesting a copy of whatever was written.

Recognizing with everyone else that Allen's return to Los Angeles would not be for the typical football game — "It's like when Nero burnt down Rome" — Gabriel insisted, "I'm better off down-playing it. If I let my emotions carry me I'll be ready to play tomorrow and that's too soon."

Ignoring all bounds of a pro football player's usual propriety before a big game, however, Deacon Jones told the Washington *Evening Star*'s Jim Bethea, "We're going to blow Washington right out of the Coliseum, that's what we're going to do. There is no way they're going to beat us. They just can't handle us."

Adding some thoughts about Allen, Jones said, for good measure, "He taught me how to be a winner. I respect him for it. But Monday night I'm going to shove it right down his throat."

Making Allen's bulletin board almost immediately after finding its way into print, Jones' words provided Allen still another psychological weapon with which to prepare the Redskins. Except, according to Kilmer, they didn't need much in the way of Allen's unique stimulation.

"There wasn't any pressure on us from him," Kilmer said. "We all knew he wanted to win badly and we went through the week motivated. I believe he felt he didn't need to get us psyched up anymore.

"Usually, he fed on newspaper articles. He'd talk to us at the general meeting every day at eleven-thirty. Like before the season opener, he brought up the articles about Alex Karras and how we couldn't win as a team without Sonny. Before the second game against New York, he fed on the idea that the Redskins hadn't won in New York in so many years. But going to L.A. seemed to be incentive enough."

In Washington, the weather was overcast, damp, and foggy as Allen worked the team daily in two-hour-plus practices. "Everything was loose," Kilmer recalled. "They were good practices. I wasn't throwing the ball over anybody's head or into the ground. Everything fell into place all week. I think it was because I had so engrossed myself in their team.

"Even in the seven-on-seven skeleton drill, everything was run perfectly. There was a lot of clapping and shouting. There was some joking, too, about me. Ron McDole's and Petitbon's wives said I could come to their houses for breakfast any time if I left one hundred dollars.

"If they could laugh about it, I knew it wasn't going to upset their play. So I knew it was up to me. I could feel the pressure myself."

Following Wednesday's practice, Allen, out of character but apparently unable to camouflage his feelings any longer, suggested the Rams were no longer the fundamentally sound team they had been under him, downgrading Prothro's use of surprise plays and calling them "gadgets."

"The Rams are a great gadget team. They use every type of gadget that's ever been used. They're not new, they're used, they're just passed on down over the years," he said, surrounded by reporters furiously scribbling every word of this rare outburst that seemed directly contrary to the coach's doctrine of never giving psychological ammunition to the enemy.

"They use the double reverse, the pass off the reverse, the fake punt and pass, the fake punt and run. That's what I mean by gadgets.

"They use more than the whole league combined. Dallas is not a gadget team. Dallas doesn't punt on third down and things like that. Over the years I've found gadgets can hurt you more than they help you. For every touchdown you make with them, one will backfire and the other team will get a score."

The following day, Tommy Prothro, sitting behind the desk that was once Allen's, offered a stark contrast in personality. Unlike the almost feverish Allen, the former UCLA coach was a portrait of relaxation, a big man, 6-3, 250 pounds, who wore a white dress shirt open at the collar and leaned back in his chair while he talked.

That very day, a Thursday, Prothro had given his team a day off from practice, another contrast with Allen's style. "We've done most of the things we want to do," he said, in the pronounced drawl he has retained from his early days in Memphis. "No two coaches work exactly the same.

"The Redskins play the same kind of football you were used to watching here for five years. They force you into mistakes which they don't make themselves. I'm not as worried about Washington stopping us as I am of Washington creating mistakes. In other words, making the big defensive play against us."

Just the opposite, Prothro strove for the big offensive play, quite often the kind of surprise play Allen decried as "gadgetry." Unorthodox as his strategy might be among the pros, Prothro calmly cited what he believed to be the benefits of his style when told of Allen's comments.

"We've tried two fake field goals, failed once and scored one touchdown," he said, lighting another cigarette. "We've faked a punt three times and gained five, thirty-nine, and forty-two yards, getting the first down each time. We've made one onside kick and recovered it.

"We've run some reverses, gained some yards and lost some yards. We've run some influence plays, by that I mean blocking in the direction the play is going, and it's worked sometimes and sometimes it hasn't.

"It's my feeling, rightly or wrongly, that if you break the percentage enough people aren't going to know what you're going to do. If we just break even on these plays, we'll have a better chance to execute our bread and butter."

Also unlike Allen, the veteran of the college campus showed no inclination to stock his team with veterans. "When I took over the job I found that the Rams had the oldest team in the history of pro football. I didn't have to do anything to have a good team this year. But I didn't want everybody to grow too old at once. I wanted to have a good team three or four years from now and at the same time not do anything that would prevent us from having a good team this year, too."

Even with eight rookies, the Rams were pro football's second oldest team, second to, of course, Allen's Redskins. Like anyone else even vaguely aware of the upcoming game, Prothro expected an "emotional" one, adding succinctly, "There are a great number of players here with a great feeling for George Allen, and I'm sure he offended a few while he was here, which you can do when you coach a team. Also, I think you want to beat your friends and enemies more than you do your acquaintances."

All the differences between Allen and Prothro having been examined — Prothro had never been called by the President; Allen's favorite food was vanilla ice cream, Prothro, obviously more flamboyant, preferred chocolate; Allen thrived on hard work, Prothro hated it — the war of words continued to escalate.

Rich Petitbon, Redskin and ex-Ram: "Tommy Prothro said I could not do the job in the newspapers after I was in camp for about six weeks and one exhibition game. When he told me I had been traded to the Redskins I couldn't have been happier. I would like to ram the ball down the Rams' throats. If you would talk to Roman Gabriel he would say he would rather be with Allen."

Roman Gabriel, Rams: "When Washington comes here, Mr. Allen is liable to leave the Coliseum with a football in his mouth. But I never said I'd throw it. Allen gave me an opportunity to play. My opinion of him professionally is that he's a good coach. And he did a great deal for me and the Rams. But I have to think he's a selfish man. He tried to give the impression that we were unhappy here after he left."

Diron Talbert, Redskin and ex-Ram: "I have as much respect for George Allen as I have for my mother and father. The Redskins gave me just what I wanted in the way of financial terms. If you play for the Rams you about have to get into the play-offs to get a salary that's on an average with other teams."

Marlin McKeever, Ram and ex-Redskin: "Now that I'm back here, thanks to being traded by Allen, I'm so glad and happy it's ridiculous. I'm in Coach Allen's debt."

Jack Pardee, Redskin and ex-Ram: "I retired once. I think

about it every year. But I'm not thinking about it now. I wouldn't have played with the Rams again. I broke in enough new coaches. I wouldn't have played if they hadn't traded me. I told them so."

Tommy Prothro, Rams: "I like ability first, then experience. It would be great to get ability with youth and experience but really all I want are the best football players."

George Allen, Redskin and ex-Ram: "Give me those old geezers every time."

And so, on Saturday afternoon — President Nixon having called Allen on Friday night to wish him luck as usual — the Redskins headed out west to a sequestered Redondo Beach hotel that Allen favored. From the balconies offering the best views, players could look out at the blue sea with sailboats dotting the horizon or to the mountains above where Allen's Palos Verdes mansion overlooked the entire idyllic setting.

The excitement surrounding the game mounted geometrically. Reporters from Los Angeles had even taken the unusual step of crossing the country to sample the pregame air in Washington, and requests for press tickets were as great as for any league championship. "I don't care how many years you guys write, or what sport," Allen said after the season, "you'll never see anything like that as long as you write."

Practically forgotten in the tumult was Kilmer, who was to look back and remember, "I had my own little incentives — going back to L.A. and going back to the Coliseum. I grew up in Azusa and had tons of friends in L.A. Once we got to the hotel I kept getting calls for tickets. There were eighty thousand seats and there still weren't any tickets to be had.

"Playing in the Coliseum always meant something to me, more than playing in the Rose Bowl. As a kid, my father took me there and to me it was everything. That's all I wanted to do, grow up and play there. I was like the little kid who goes to Yankee Stadium and sees Babe Ruth and imagines himself at home plate some day. That's what the Coliseum means to me. Every time I go there I get a chill up my back."

Though Kilmer had sensed early in the season, as he said, that the Redskins' future would come down to this game, he had no idea when he was traded to Washington, nor for that matter did Allen, that he would end up the crucial figure in the struggle.

"At the time I thought I would be on the bench," he said. "I didn't see how I could move Sonny out. He was always in good shape, he played hurt well, nobody moves him out. Jim Ninowski and Frank Ryan had been behind him for years. I didn't think I'd get a chance.

"I asked George as soon as he got me to get me with another team. All I could think about were the teams that needed a quarterback. I wanted him to get me out of it. In his way, he just didn't do anything about it. I'm not the type to cause trouble so I went along, except I had one alternative, to play out my option. I figured I wouldn't sign, I'd just let it slide, then get out after a year and go off somewhere else.

"So going into camp, I didn't have that good an attitude. Then I got a chance to play in the first exhibition, at San Diego. I wasn't really in good shape and I didn't play well. That embarrassed me. I decided then to get in shape and I tried to resolve things with myself, do the right thing, go along with the program. I looked around at the other guys and I decided to work with them.

"There was Ron McDole and Jack Pardee and Len Hauss and Walter Rock, all my type ballplayers and I thought, 'This is better than being in New Orleans.' We were all looking for the same thing, a championship team to play on.

"When Sonny got hurt, I knew I was going to have to make my mark now. I had been talking a lot, I wanted to go somewhere else, now I had the opportunity, if I don't produce I can go back home. That's when I began doing all the right things, study, take movies home, go along with George's program.

"I believe the first three games were the key to our whole season. They were all against teams in our division and they were all on the road. Every one of those teams — St. Louis, New York, and Dallas — had been ranked ahead of us before the season.

"When we won them all, that set the tone for us. We weren't afraid to play anybody, and that's a big psychological factor for any team. We felt if we could beat Kansas City we would go undefeated the rest of the year. When Charley Taylor got hurt right before the half of that game, it cut our season right in half. Before that, everything had been smooth, but after that we had our problems.

"When Sonny started to come back, there were pressures on me. I admit it, but I met them. There were pressures from all over and naturally you're aware of them. You go into a place and you can hear them talking, 'Sonny should be playing, he can do this and he can do that.' And I imagine it was the same for Sonny.

"Both of us had pressures on us but there was no animosity and we tried to make it the best we could for each other. But there's no use in not facing reality. I face it and try to wade through it and I think we both did well.

"We socialized together, we talked a lot, we realized we had a defense that could hold and that we didn't have to take chances. He felt bad because he couldn't play, and I'd have felt the same way if I had been in his shoes.

"He helped me, though, especially in setting up to throw. That's the worst part of my game. I get a little lackadaisical in the mechanics of quarterbacking. And sitting and watching movies he was a big help. He's good at picking on defenses and he'd relate his ideas to me. I've been on teams before where the two quarterbacks didn't even communicate."

Unable to sleep for hours after retiring, Kilmer awoke unusually early for him, about 6 A.M., both on Sunday, the eve of the game, and Monday. "I went down to the coffee shop both mornings," he said. "I read the papers. There was tension in my stomach. There was no way I could get rid of it.

"Sometimes I walked down to the water with a couple of the guys. On Sunday afternoon, I visited my family in Azusa. Everybody was there and all they were talking about was the game, too. Who's injured? Who's not injured? From there, my father drove me over to the Coliseum, where we worked out at six o'clock.

"Howard Cosell was out on the field joking around with the players. You know how he talks, 'Billy Kilmer, UCLA, throws an interception to Jimmy Nettles . . .' I laughed, but it stuck in my mind.

"The afternoon of the game I thought maybe I could go to sleep, but I couldn't. I was too tense. I remember riding up on the bus to the stadium. Roy Jefferson was stretched out on the seat across from me and he was sound asleep. 'Well,' I said to myself, 'Jefferson seems to be relaxed.' Boy, he was something that night. I threw him eight balls and he caught all eight. If that's what it takes, he ought to go to sleep on every bus."

Even before the Redskin buses arrived, fans, including many without tickets, were already swarming on the Coliseum grounds. Three hours before the game, they began climbing the fence topped with barbed wire ringing the arena. One, two, three, a dozen. Each had his own distinctive style of getting over the wire, but they all made it and disappeared inside for the long wait.

Outside the gates, the less daring pleaded to buy tickets. From automobile radios, George Allen himself could be heard talking about his long-awaited return. "Never before have so many players returned to play their former team," he was saying.

In town at the Ambassador Hotel, many of the Rams had paced the lobby most of the afternoon, prompting a Ram official to observe, "I've never seen our guys so excited for a game."

Waiting anxiously for a close-up glimpse of Allen, about fifty fans greeted the Redskins' first bus as it pulled in through the Coliseum gates, Allen alighting, looking intense, and walking quickly down the tunnel to the Redskins dressing room to polite applause.

Emerging at the other end two and a half hours later, the Redskins were greeted by boos and such banners as "Jack Snows Allen." Seemingly oblivious to it all, shouting and jumping up and down in front of their bench, the Redskins circled around Allen seconds before the kickoff.

"Even in high school," said Kilmer, "I had never been a part of anything like it. We all started screaming. It was like Texas, or something. For one moment, there was mass hysteria, we were letting all our emotions go.

"I was in there hollering and screaming. I looked over at the Rams and they looked at us like 'What's going on?' It lasted just for a moment. I've never experienced anything like it."

If Kilmer was ready, so were the other Redskins, and they drove from the opening kickoff to scoring position when, suddenly, all of Kilmer's preparation seemed wasted. Aiming a pass for tight end Jerry Smith, Kilmer instead saw Smith knocked off stride by a linebacker and his pass float directly into the arms of Kermit Alexander, who ran eighty-two yards to score.

An exciting way to start the game for the record Monday-night television audience of 66 million, the interception proved a shocking development in most of the 450,000 homes around Washington, fully half the TV sets in the metropolitan area being tuned in. For Kilmer himself, the sight of Alexander running for a touchdown was simply horrifying.

Though Howard Cosell's prediction was forgotten at the time, Kilmer's mind staggered as he made it to the sideline.

"If I held it for a second longer . . . All that work for this . . . Don't get excited, don't force your hand . . ."

Seconds later, he was back on the field, sending Larry Brown on two end sweeps and Charley Harraway on a trap up the middle before calling just what the game plan ordered, the bomb to Jefferson. At the Ram twenty-seven, the wide receiver made the catch between two Rams and artfully pivoted into the end zone to complete a seventy-yard play.

After the teams traded field goals, Kilmer struck for another touchdown pass, a thirty-two-yarder to Clifton McNeil, for a 17-10 Redskins lead only 2:37 before the half.

On the ensuing kickoff, one of the Ram rookies, Roger Williams, fumbled, the Redskins recovering at the Ram eight-yard line. On a penalty, the Redskins got a first down at the two with 1:13 left in the half.

Calling Brown's number, Kilmer sent the fullback into the line three straight times, once to the left and twice to the right, straight at Deacon Jones.

"Deacon has a tendency to stand up near the goal line," Kilmer said. "If he has a weakness, that's it. His biggest asset is pursuit. He can catch up to any quarterback. But I know George used to talk to him about standing up near the goal line and he knew we'd go for him in that situation. I think that's why he did so well."

On fourth down, a foot short of the goal line, with thirty-six seconds remaining, Kilmer conferred with Allen. "George decided to go for it," Kilmer said. "We decided on an outside play, twenty-nine-M Boss.

"I remember Mike McCormack was standing next to George and he emphasized that Charley Harraway was supposed to block Kermit Alexander and told me to emphasize that in the huddle. I called the play and then I said, 'Now look, Charley, if we're going to score you've got to get Kermit. Charley, you must get him.' "

Responding nobly, Harraway briskly upended Alexander as Brown moved forward, then cut to the outside to score. Leading 24-10 at the half, then 31-10 early in the third period on Kilmer's third touchdown pass, a five-yarder to Jefferson, the Redskins opened too much of a lead for the Rams to overcome. While they rallied to make it 31-24, Speedy Duncan intercepted a Gabriel pass and ran forty-six yards for a touchdown in the last thirty-five seconds.

Though the scoreboard read 38-24, Redskins, their highest point total of the season, and with the crowd, chilled by the falling temperature, hastening to file out, Allen's worried expression remained fixed until the gun sounded, signaling the start of a celebration befitting the game's significance.

Before the Redskins' dressing-room doors swung shut, all the players having tumbled inside shouting the customary war whoops, two reporters in the front rank of the growing army of press simultaneously took two steps forward and found themselves in the sanctuary of the locker room, the doors closed behind them.

Standing in front of his players, Allen said, "We have a lot to be thankful for," and the team then knelt in prayer led by Tom Skinner, the man responsible for Charley Harraway's turning to Christ. When it was over, they all got to their feet and cheered.

Appearing on the verge of passing out, one hyperexcited equipment boy swayed back and forth until the team doctor inquired, "Are you all right?"

"This is a great, great victory," said Allen, addressing the players. "It's the best win of our lives. Men, let's just go on from here."

Given the first of many game balls, Allen positively beamed, cradling the thing as if it meant existence itself, which, to him, it probably did. Other game balls were tossed to Kilmer, Jefferson, Duncan, even the chaplain, Skinner. As Kilmer accepted his, he shouted in unrestrained joy, "Toddle House breakfast."

At that moment, Kilmer's comeback from a nearly fatal automobile accident nine years before was complete. Having fallen asleep while driving on San Francisco's Bayshore Freeway, he almost had his right foot severed in the ensuing crackup. Not only would he miss the 1963 season, doctors said he would never play football again, might not even walk. He went to work in his father's dry-cleaning establishment, pressing suits.

Fourteen for nineteen, 246 yards, three touchdowns, a hug from his proud father, adulation from Allen — "Mr. Kilmer, what a job Billy's done for us" — and the Associated Press offensive-player-of-the-week honor that was to come the next day, Kilmer could barely contain himself. "This is the biggest thrill of my life to date," he said. "But I don't want it to stop now."

Equally emotional, Allen, surrounded by tens of newsmen, said, "This is the best one ever. It was a complete team victory, which is the way most of our victories are."

Jack Kent Cooke, part owner of the Redskins, reached through the mob to congratulate Allen.

"A great win, a great win," Allen told him with childlike exuberance. "I even got a game ball."

Then it was back to the press, repeating again, "It's our biggest win ever to date. You should know what I mean," the coach said, smiling. Meaning it was even better than the famous 1963 NFL title game when as assistant coach he was presented the game ball by the champion Chicago Bears, a game ball that had helped him get a job with the team he'd just defeated.

"There were other circumstances this time," he explained, referring to the internecine nature of the rivalry. "We were definitely the underdog. We've overcome adversity all year long. When it looked like we might fold we pulled together and won."

In a splurge of generosity as he finished dressing, Allen even offered a reporter an orange — "Here's a good California orange; don't you want one?" — and allowed as how there would be champagne aboard the Redskins' charter home and more of the same for reporters at the next day's press conference. "Make sure we have enough," he told Joe Blair.

Though he felt perfectly fine at that time, the frenzy had been almost too much for him, Jim Snowden, in fact, thinking for a moment the coach was having a heart attack in the locker room before the game.

"I was going back to the bathroom," Snowden said, "and he was holding his hand to his left side; he had a pain there. I asked him, 'You all right, Coach?' The doctor was right there with him. It was just the excitement getting to him."

On the plane ride home, John Wilbur, who sat for a while next to Mrs. Allen, recalled, "I've never seen anybody so happy. All those words put out by the L.A. management had to be eaten.

"No question, that was the biggest victory of my life."

While some men open themselves in defeat, in Allen's case there is nothing like crushing victory to make him expansive and at ease, to allow him to revel in the spoils and reveal parts of his character hitherto hidden by x's and o's.

It was to be expected then, that the day following the Los Angeles triumph, a victory he reiterated "you'd have to say was the biggest of my career," Allen would be at least friendly. In fact, the postgame conference turned out to be his most charming and affable performance of the entire year, as the coach, alternating anecdotes, laughter, and philosophy, seemed to actually relax and open up for the first time in memory.

The highlight of the day was the champagne, two full bottles out of New York State, incredibly labeled "Chateau de George" — "My own company," said the coach, with one of many laughs.

Unaccustomed as they were to serving that beverage, the Redskins chose to dispense it in Styrofoam cups, the bottles being wrapped in rather gauche towels with a single orange stripe, towels usually employed wiping the sweat off dedicated brows. To Allen, it mattered little.

"It isn't often you can celebrate a victory that gets you into the play-offs," he said as he pushed and poked and pulled without success at the metal foil that covered the plastic cork. Archetypally, the trouble he was having made him work all the harder, and he went so far as to say, quite seriously, "If I can't get this cork off, the champagne's defeated me." Finally he cracked, "This thing is tougher than the Los Angeles Rams."

At last it was open, and the habitual milk drinker who had

put his team in its first postseason competition since 1945 answered the smattering of applause by pouring some champagne for assembled reporters, photographers, and office staff, taking "just a little bit" for himself.

"By gosh, that tastes good," he said. "It isn't often you get champagne for breakfast." And a few minutes later, "My gosh, that's pretty good. I'm going to have some more." And some minutes later still, "Let's have a little more champagne." To the victor, etc.

"I don't open these very much," he said, accentuating the obvious. "But we had nine bottles on the plane; each guy got a little swig. Richie Petitbon accused me of being a bartender he knew in New Orleans. He said I didn't pour a big enough drink."

In the wake of what Allen emphasized was his ultimate victory because "we overcame so many adversities, nobody gave us a chance," the coach had been forced to take his phone off the hook once he made it back to Washington.

"It was just ringing so much. I took a sleeping pill and slept for about two and a half hours. President Nixon hasn't called yet — he's in the Azores," Allen reminded the folks. "I'm sure he's elated, though. We've made his predictions come true."

Playing before that massive television audience seemed to please Allen as much as playing well, and he said he had requested a print of the ABC telecast for the team to view, "so that our squad can see the entire game just as it went across the nation. Maybe we could have a special showing at a downtown theater." Cost, as usual, was to be hardly an object.

"Imagine playing that game on TV," he went on as he poured more champagne. "Pete Rozelle came up to me before the game, he was just thrilled about this being the final Monday-night game, and I told him, 'Even Cecil B. De Mille couldn't upstage you on this one.' Imagine, the thirteenth game on December thirteen and both teams having to win it."

Allen was so full of praise for everyone and everything about the team that some bubbled over onto its song, "Hail to the Redskins."

"I love that song," he said with genuine fervor. "When the Rams band played it I was kind of humming it to myself. I've got some trouble with the 'whompum, stompum' part, I kind of stumble through that, but I guess everyone does."

Allen was equally candid about his superstitions, which he seemed to credit with playing as big a part in the victory as his players.

"It was kind of windy, and I came out in a jacket," Allen said. "After Kermit Alexander intercepted for a touchdown, I said, 'Take this jacket and throw it over there.'

"I put it on again at the start of the second half and it felt nice and comfy. I kept it on when the score was thirty-one-seventeen, but when they got that second touchdown to make it thirty-one-twenty-four I said, 'Get this jacket out of here.' "

Even his family, the coach revealed, tended to doubt the team's omnipotence at times, especially early in the game. "When the Rams were moving well on the ground after the Alexander score, my fifteen-year-old son, Bruce, told Mrs. Allen, 'Mommy, it looks like the Rams are going to rout us.' "

It didn't happen, though, and the buoyant Allen, reaching the crest of his first year in Washington, took the occasion to give an unusual, unsolicited glimpse into the deeper motivations of an obviously driven man.

"I think it's a good thing for kids to go through experiences like this," he said. "Before the games it's torture; you don't want to eat, you can't sleep. But this is what you need to succeed. When you get things given to you, you don't appreciate it.

"After it's over, it's so rewarding. Overcoming obstacles, getting torn up inside, then winning — that's what life is all about."

CHAPTER XIV

An End and a Beginning

IF EVER A FOOTBALL GAME had a meaningless look about it, Washington's home season finale was the one, involving as it did two teams, the Redskins and the Cleveland Browns, that had already clinched spots in the play-offs. Yet if there was one person who could be counted on to see things otherwise, it had to be George Allen.

"I don't think this team will look past this week to the play-offs or take Cleveland lightly," said cornerback Mike Bass. "I don't think George will allow us to be that way."

That proved to be true. While local newsmen just about ignored a Browns publicity man who happened to arrive at the Dulles complex the same day the Redskins returned triumphant from Los Angeles, Allen refused to down-play the coming game when it was brought up at the champagne press conference.

"We will play to win," he said with emphasis. "We've got to keep up our momentum; we can't afford to let up at all now. Our immediate thought is to win the division and have a home field advantage in the final play-off game," an eventuality that, unfortunately for psychology, depended as much on the unlikely possibility of St. Louis beating Dallas that Saturday as on the Redskins' efforts the following day.

Allen also strongly nixed the possibility of using the game as a trial run for some people who hadn't seen much action to date. "We will use the people who have won for us all season," he said. "As soon as you change things it backfires on you.

"I remember in nineteen sixty-nine with the Rams, we won eleven games in a row, had the division title clinched, began using different player combinations, and it cost us three losses in a row before losing to Minnesota in the play-offs."

The tack Allen was to use to make even this game appear vital was revealed by Bass when he told a reporter, "There's also this thing about one team dominating another. When was the last time the Redskins beat the Browns?"

The reporter didn't know, but Bass had it at his finger tips: November 11, 1962. The Browns had won eleven in a row from Washington and enjoyed an overall 30-5-1 advantage. In addition, a victory would give Allen his predicted ten for the season, which would be the most for any Washington club since the world championship team of twenty-nine years before.

The 8-5 Browns, who had surprised everyone by not finishing last in the AFC's weak "Pink and Blue" Central Division, still did not look overwhelming. Though currently on a four-game winning streak, they had earlier suffered four straight losses, the worst slide in the club's history, and were made six-point underdogs against Washington.

In addition to everything else, the Redskins felt their pride was once again at stake. "I still don't think it's believed by the country that we're as good a team as our record indicates," Bass said. "But we're sold on ourselves. I don't care what anybody else thinks of us. We don't mind being the sleeper. I hope we keep being the underdog and that people keep counting us out."

Yet, unavoidably, by the time the game started some of the bloom had been taken off the Redskins' desire, for Dallas trounced St. Louis, 31-12, on Saturday to put a mortal lock on first place in the NFC's Eastern Division.

The game Sunday had been designated Vince Promuto Day at RFK Stadium, to honor the offensive lineman who had toiled eleven years for perennially inept teams before retiring to a career in law. Yet instead of showing him how much things had changed, the Redskins played a game reminiscent of those bad old days.

For although they outgained the Browns by more than 100 yards, Washington turned the ball over four times, botched two field goals, made numberless errors, and saw their offense bog down to the extent of refusing to score at all in the second half. The Browns turned two of those turnovers into ten points and came out the 20-13 victors.

As it ended, Browns guard Gene Hickerson summed things up when he ambled toward Redskins defensive lineman Bill Brundige and said, "Well, we played lousy and, Bill, you played lousy." Or as Ron McDole was to say later on, "We just screwed around and screwed around until we lost it."

The atmosphere in that losing locker room was perhaps the gloomiest of the year, with everyone influenced by their leader's complete disgust with losing. "Allen doesn't even like to lose a practice," was how Jack Pardee put it.

As always after a loss, Allen was too upset to be pleasant with reporters, and curtness was the order of the day.

"We had our chances," was the best he could manage. "We didn't take advantage. We did not play well, we made too many mistakes. I just hate to see us make that many mistakes. This is too negative a game to even think about."

Allen was especially hard on those who asked the obvious question about the team's mental readiness for the game. "I don't have anything to say," he snapped at one point. "You're not up for your job every day. Nobody else is either. You'll have to ask the players."

"Of course we had a letdown," volunteered Charley Harraway. "And it wasn't really a surprise either.

"If you consider the circumstances, you can answer all the questions yourself. We were coming off our biggest game of the year. This game meant nothing. Football players are human like everybody else."

And, as Billy Kilmer pointed out, there was always the chance for redemption in the NFL play-offs the following week, when the Redskins were to meet the San Francisco 49ers, who had eliminated the Rams and clinched the Western Division title with a 31-27 victory over the Detroit Lions in the one hundred and eighty-second and very last league game of the season.

"After I walk out this door, I'm going to forget about this game and think only of winning the next one," Kilmer said. "If we win next week, nobody will be thinking about the Browns or the whole season. We've got to win the next two games and get down to New Orleans."

"Last week in Los Angeles was nothing compared to the way we're going to be next week," promised Speedy Duncan, who had 134 yards in kickoff returns against the Browns, with Larry Brown, stopped 52 yards shy of a 1000-yard season, adding ominously, "Any individual lettin' down is messin' with my money."

While the players may have allowed themselves to think in terms of the $25,000 per man that would go to the eventual winner of the Super Bowl, Allen focused his mind exclusively on that first play-off game, December 26 in San Francisco. For the only blot on his matchless professional coaching record, which included two first-place finishes, three seconds, and a third in six years, was a failure to win any play-off games. In 1967, his Western Division Rams lost 28-7 to the Green Bay Packers, and in 1969 the loss was 23-20 to the Minnestota Vikings. People were starting to talk.

Though Allen had put together a fine 11-3-1 record, including a 5-0 preseason mark against the 49ers when he was in Los Angeles, and though these same 49ers had lost twice in the season just completed to the Ram team that Allen's Redskins had handled so smartly two weeks before, the general consensus was that the 49ers were the best team in the West and would provide a more than ample challenge for the Washingtonians.

This was not to say the Redskins had not improved tremendously under Allen. Speedy Duncan was the conference's top punt returner and Curt Knight its top scorer. Next to last in overall defense in 1970, the Redskins were ranked third in 1971 and second against the rush with an average of 99.7 yards allowed per game, the team's best in fourteen years. They led the league with 29 interceptions and allowed only 190 points, the best the Redskins had done since 1945, and the first time they had given up fewer than 300 points since 1959.

Still, the 49ers looked to be their equal, at least, and it was not surprising to find them five-and-a-half-point favorites, and the Redskins, along with Cleveland, the co–long shot to take the Super Bowl at 15 to 1.

Allen started the psychological campaign early, telling reporters at his first convenience, "We're going to have to play a great game and not make mistakes to win," adding in a characteristic attempt at one-upmanship, "I think our players would rather play the Forty-niners than the Rams. It's difficult to beat a team twice and do it in three weeks."

The Redskins motto for the week was "Hit and No Mistakes," and Allen, the master of detail, was leaving nothing to chance, not even the matter of which surface the team would practice on. Since the game on the coast would be on AstroTurf, one might assume that that was what the team would train on, but Allen as usual was one step ahead of things and had everyone working on grass.

"Natural grass is easier on the legs," he explained. "Maybe we will work out on our Astro-Turf once before leaving, but we do not need to get used to it after having it all year. We get a better workout on the natural grass if it is dry. We have more room on it [100 to 70 yards at the Dulles compound]. There is less pounding on the players' legs."

Also determined precisely was where the team would do its practicing. Dispensing with fears about acclimation and changes in body time, Allen said the team would practice in

Washington through Friday afternoon, work out briefly in Candlestick Park on Saturday, Christmas Day, and presumably be ready for the game on Sunday.

"I prefer to keep our players in the same environment, on the same practice field, using the same meeting rooms, and with their families," he said. "We will stay here as long as possible.

"At Los Angeles," he added, turning amateur meteorologist, "we left on a Monday for the game at Minnestota [which the Rams lost], but that was because of the radical weather changes from Los Angeles to there. Washington's weather and San Francisco's are not that much different."

Not even the approach of Christmas was enough to stay Allen from his appointed rounds. Like everything else in the known world, it would have to wait its turn while he was planning football strategy.

"I haven't even had the time to buy a Christmas card or presents for the kids," he admitted. "But I tell the players they'll have lots of Christmases, all kinds of them. We'll try not to do anything special for Christmas. It just interrupts concentration.

"My family is used to this. In nineteen sixty-eight, I was fired by the Rams the day after Christmas. I'll never forget what Dan Reeves said, 'I didn't want to spoil your Christmas.' I always say I was fired on Christmas and rehired on New Year's Day and I didn't know what to expect on the next big holiday."

In Minneapolis and Kansas City, the scheduling of play-off games on Christmas Day was giving NFL commissioner Pete Rozelle the nickname of "The Grinch Who Stole Christmas," but Allen plainly couldn't identify.

"The Washington fans are so great," he said, "they'd sit out in a snowdrift and eat McDonald's hamburgers if we had a play-off game here on Christmas Day."

Out in San Francisco, where the 49ers were calmly looking

toward their second play-off game in as many years, all was sweetness and placidity, with the conversation turning either to the eternally uncertain weather or to Redskins quarterback Kilmer, no stranger to the team he was to face.

For after leading the collegiate nation in total offense at UCLA in 1960, Kilmer became one of the 49ers' three first-round draft choices for the 1961 season. He lasted five years, long enough to set a team record of four touchdowns in one game that still stands. His nearly fatal automobile accident severely hampered both his mobility and his reputation as a running quarterback, and he was eventually to go to the New Orleans Saints in the expansion draft.

Yet those 49ers who remained from his time remembered Kilmer with a fondness of a strength and sincerity remarkable in a league where phony sentimentalizing often becomes a way of life.

"Do I remember him? Hell, he's one of my closest friends," said 49er quarterback John Brodie when approached on the subject. "Whenever he comes into town he either calls me or Charlie Krueger and we play a little golf. He's a lousy golfer but a great partner."

Krueger was a thirteen-year veteran who played with the Redskins' Jack Pardee under Paul (Bear) Bryant at Texas A. & M. Possessed of gray hair, a courtly manner, and a strong side interest in opera to go along with a reputation as perhaps the league's most intelligent and technically expert defensive tackle, he talked both thoughtfully and extensively about his former teammate.

"Let me tell you about Billy Kilmer," he began. "He has a quality about him. He is not a picture passer, not Greg Landry as a runner, but he's got that thing about him, he is a leader.

"If you give the offensive team just a little edge, he can beat your brains out. Last year in New Orleans, he had a severe shoulder separation in the first half. It was one and a half inches, Christ, that's severe. But they strapped him together and he came out in the second half and beat our brains out.

"He used to love to go to the races, so we called him 'Tout' at first. But J. D. Smith, this old fullback we had, thought we were saying 'Trout,' and that was the name that stuck.

"I used to call him the 'Red Fox' myself. He had the red hair, a crew cut, and with those beady eyes you knew the s.o.b. was always thinking.

"We're great friends. We've been to church together and places other than church together, and I hate like hell to see us arrive at the same time he's arrived. I know we couldn't have a stiffer competitor."

It was this aspect of Kilmer, his enthusiasm and easy spirits, that was remembered best.

"He's just a freewheeling guy, a real hang-loose competitor who would do better when he was behind," said offensive lineman Len Rohde. "I hear he set a record one year for the least volume of milk drunk in a one-year period.

"He's not shy of contact either. If he had the physical ability he could be a good middle backer. He really has the temperament for this game, and he can really ignite people. Even the linemen felt he'd get down there with them if he had to."

"Really, he just enjoys playing football, and that type of thing can be contagious on a team," linebacker Dave Wilcox offered. "You know, he doesn't look right, he's kind of got a screwed-up body, but he gets the job done and that's most important. Until this year, nobody ever said, 'This job's yours, take it.'"

Perhaps the most emotional remembrance came from the club's general manager, Lou Spadia, who began by grinning and saying, "If he wasn't on the other team, I'd say some nice things about him.

"I was the guy who signed him to his contract in nineteen sixty-one. He came out to meet me at the airport in his car, an old jalopy. On the way the fan belt broke, leaving us out in the middle of nowhere. That's where we about came to an agreement.

"Why, he had no business even walking after that automobile accident. He was in the hospital from November to May, and you wouldn't have given him a chance in a million if you'd seen him the first year. His ankle was about as wide around as a chicken's.

"You're tempted to say an average man would have given up, but even superior men would have thrown in the sponge. To do what he did, he had to be unusual."

Back in Washington, this type of *joie de vivre* was noticeably absent. As the Redskins gradually became aware that for the first time in twenty-six years they were actually in a play-off game, every pregame happening became blown into a mini-incident.

First came the matter of all-pro selections. When United Press International picked its all-National Conference team, the Redskins had only two members on the first team, Larry Brown and Jack Pardee, compared to four for San Francisco. And the NFC squad for the Pro Bowl, chosen by the league's coaches, while including four Redskins — Brown, wide receiver Roy Jefferson, and specialists Speedy Duncan and Curt Knight — to seven 49ers, included no one from the nonpareil defense locals considered the best since Troy fell.

Allen declared himself "surprised" at the omissions, some of his charges used stronger language, and the usually staid *Evening Star* ran an editorial headlined "Where's Pat?" bemoaning the absence from laurels of cornerback Fischer.

"Oh I used to get excited about those things, but not anymore," the missing man said, while admitting that he was more than pleased by the editorial comment.

"They had me right up there under the editorial about the new Secretary General of the United Nations and above the one about offshore oil leases," the off-season stockbroker said, adding, "I'm making money from those leases."

The next crisis to rear its morale-boosting head had to do with the staying power of the Over the Hill Gang. Tom Quinn of the *Daily News* pointed out to Allen after practice one afternoon that the Redskins had scored 180 points in the first halves of their regular season games and only 96 in the final thirty minutes. Similarly, the opposition scored 68 points in the first halves against Washington only to explode for nearly twice as many, 122, in the second. The fourth quarter was the worst, with Washington being outscored 83-60.

Allen began explaining that there were so many factors involved it was hard to make a general statement. "We were a second-half club over the years in Los Angeles," he said, "but we have been having difficulty in the second half this year."

Quinn persisted, explaining, "Some fans may think it is because of the old players in the Over the Hill Gang."

Hearing this, Allen could barely remain civil. "That has nothing to do with it," he fired back. "Anybody who says that does not know what he is talking about."

Allen got some unexpected support from one Alex Karras, the same former Detroit defensive tackle who refused a chance to be a Redskin himself when the Lions dropped him in September and was now passing his time writing a column for the Detroit *Free Press*.

"For years the Redskins were the laughingstock of all football, a doormat for everyone," Karras wrote. "But George Allen goes in there this year with a new coaching staff and he brings in 21 new players and there he is shooting for the championship.

"If any team was going to lack 'dedication,' it should have been the Redskins, who are a collection of castoff buys, the oldest guys in the league. But George Allen did a tremendous job with them and that was a perfect example of coaches motivating a team."

Contacted by phone, however, Karras refused to disavow his earlier prediction that the Redskins were going nowhere. "I still say the Redskins are very fortunate to go as far as they have," he said. "Any other coach would not have been able to do it. The odds were one hundred to one the Redskins would not be where they are.

"This kid Kilmer has done a tremendous job. I have never seen him play like this before, although he had always been a great competitor. But credit again goes to George Allen. He stuck with Kilmer when everybody was hollering for Jurgensen."

Despite noting, "Anything the Redskins do now is fantastic," Karras predicted a 49er victory, adding, "People may hate me, but I don't care who hates me."

The third and final pregame brouhaha had its start, ironically, in placid San Francisco. It began on Tuesday, but word of it did not reach Washington until Wednesday afternoon and Thursday morning, when the backlash it created made front-page sports publicity in all the cities in between.

Dave Newhouse of the Oakland *Tribune* had the idea of asking 49ers place kicker Bruce Gossett, traded from Los Angeles to San Francisco before the 1970 season and the only ex-Ram on the team, if he had any thoughts on his former coach. He turned out to have plenty, becoming in fact the most vitriolic of the rapidly lengthening list of ex-Rams in cities all throughout the league who seemingly hungered for an opportunity to denounce their old leader. For every man who stood with him, there seemed to be another on the other side.

"There isn't anything good I can say about Allen," Gossett told Newhouse. "I just don't think he's a first-class guy. He lies to you and he's out for himself. There's no question about it."

One of the players absent when the Rams came to Allen's defense after he was canned the first time by Dan Reeves, Gossett said, "I felt if the man was fired there was nothing I could do to get him his job back. Who's to say someone else couldn't have come in and made us a championship team, which he hadn't done?

"We always won a lot of games, but we never got over the hump. And we had the players."

The kicker claimed, "Allen is just dishonest with people when there is no need to be. He told me face to face, in front of my wife, that I would be with the Rams as long as he was. A couple of weeks later, I was traded. What do you think if a guy does that?"

Gossett's retaliation was to call in some handy newspapermen and tell them "the whole story."

"Allen called me in after I was traded to the 49ers because of the stuff I'd been putting in the paper. He said we shouldn't talk like that about each other. I told him he should have thought about that before.

"He said he hoped that we could remain friends, and I said, 'I guess so, but I don't want to play for you again.'

"As I was walking out the door I said, 'George, if you were half the guy people think you are, you'd be one helluva guy.' "

Gossett also felt that Allen "just didn't think I was part of the football team because I was a kicker, and I resented that. I was the only one who was blamed when things went wrong, but I didn't get credit for the ones I won.

"Allen always said that it takes forty men to win and forty to lose, and that he would never mention anyone's name in the paper after a loss.

"Well, I missed a thirty-nine-yard field goal in the third quarter against Chicago and the Bears beat us, seventeen to sixteen. The next day there was this headline in the paper with this quote from Allen: 'Gossett Blows Field Goal, Costs Us A Game.' Tommy Mason fumbled the ball away on first down at their four, but there was no mention of that by Allen in the article. I still have the paper with Allen's quotes. I look at it from time to time."

Once a loner in his dislike of Allen, Gossett claimed other Rams were starting to see it his way.

"My dad saw the Rams play in Pittsburgh Sunday and got a chance to talk with [offensive lineman] Tom Mack. Tom told him that all the stuff I had said in the paper about the defense being the only people Allen ever gave credit to after a win was exactly right.

"It took them a year to realize that I'm not dumb. I can see through people too. I just saw through George Allen. I don't like the man very much."

If the bitterness of the attack surprised even Gossett's 49er teammates, Allen himself was even more taken aback when the first question in a usually routine Wednesday afternoon telephone press conference with the Bay Area press appraised him of Gossett's feelings and asked for his reaction.

After a slight and understandable pause, Allen would say no more than, "It will be a pleasure to play against Gossett and the Forty-niners. I don't want to get into a long discussion about Bruce, but I did vote for him for two Pro Bowls when I didn't have to. He can say what he wants."

Sought out after Allen hung up and surrounded by a swarm of reporters, Gossett responded with a fresh set of charges against his former coach.

"Allen plays favorites," the kicker claimed. "He invites certain players to his house for dinner. A coach can't do that.

"The long practices and the other stuff wears thin when you don't win a title. Allen only thinks about football. When you play for him football is your life. That's wrong. He knows nothing else. He only sees his family on Sunday during the season. Of course, some of the older players are loyal to George because he gives them a chance to stay in the game.

"You wonder why players like Tommy Mason and Maxie Baughan support George Allen? Because without him they would not be in football. They are not good enough to be working for anyone else but George Allen."

The next morning at the Redskins practice, Gossett's quote was brought to the attention of Baughan, who had spent the season on the injured reserve list. Normally a temperate member of the Fellowship of Christian Athletes, Baughan's face colored noticeably when he read what his former teammate said.

"He [Gossett] is not a player, he's not even an athlete," Baughan managed to say after some initial sputtering. "Ask him how many tackles he has made.

"How many times has he been to the Pro Bowl? Check the record. I'm going to talk to him."

The record showed that while Allen might have voted for him, not enough other coaches had and Gossett had never been to the game in question. Mason had gone three times while with Minnesota and Baughan himself nine times, five with Philadelphia and four with the Rams. For want of further controversy, Mason preferring to say of Gossett's feelings, "I wouldn't dignify them with a comment," that is where the matter rested until game time. If nothing else, the controversy further inhibited some already none-too-talkative Redskins, with quarterback Jurgensen refusing to comment at all on the merits of San Francisco's Brodie, claiming, "I don't think I should talk about things like that. They get Washington papers out there, you know."

Always a searcher after omens, Allen was pleased to discover on the day of his departure for San Francisco that he had been selected as the National Conference's Coach of the Year by United Press International, getting nineteen of the thirty-nine votes cast compared to ten for the closest runner-up, Tommy Prothro, his successor in Los Angeles.

Before his players marched through a Dulles Airport that played "Hail to the Redskins" over the intercom in their honor and boarded their charter plane, appropriately festooned with burgundy and gold bunting and large Redskins decals, Allen issued a Christmas message as his final act of the season on the East Coast.

"This is what it's all about," he said, referring to the long-awaited play-off game. "Anybody who is not ready now never will be. But I think we are ready.

"The nicest Christmas present we could give the city of Washington is a win."

After spending Friday night in a San Mateo motel about thirty miles from the game site, the team bused up to Candlestick Park for a brief workout on Christmas Day. Allen, who had spent part of the morning watching Dallas beat Minnesota, 20-12, in another play-off game, made sure to tell reporters, "I've been talking all week about mistakes. See what happened to the Vikings when they made mistakes."

Still searching for some sign of good fortune, Allen was pleased to look out the bus window and spot a rainbow, noting, "That's good luck," as soon as he saw it.

After the workout, Allen, who had played down observance of Christmas all week to keep the team's mind on football, announced that there would be a team Christmas dinner that night in San Mateo, with favors for all the players and bulky 6-foot-5, 265-pound tackle Manny Sistrunk getting the nod as Santa Claus.

It would take more than sleight of hand to win Sunday's game, and both teams knew it. "Allen's style is just not to give up the football," said San Francisco's Dave Wilcox. "Our style is to get it."

"It's going to come down to one basic thing," said Kilmer, up early the day of the game. "Fumbles, interceptions, and penalties. The team that has the least is going to win." Both prophecies would prove highly accurate.

On the bus up to San Francisco on game day, only Kilmer was loose enough to break the pregame tension. When Pat Palumbo, the team doctor, seemingly could not find a seat, Kilmer called out, "We've got one for you back here, Doc," pointing to the rest-room door.

The bus's destination, Candlestick Park, had until that very year existed for the exclusive use of the San Francisco Giants baseball team. But after Kezar Stadium was deemed too decrepit for further use, the 49ers moved in too, and extensive and still incomplete remodeling and the addition of seats behind the right field fence where kids used to wait for Willie McCovey's home runs made the place barely recognizable.

The Redskins, working in a nasty wind and rain that Brodie was to call "the worst conditions I've ever played in," seemed to be their old selves, taking a 7-0 first-quarter lead when Jon

Jaqua's block of a Steve Spurrier punt was followed a minute and a half later by a five-yard touchdown pass from Kilmer to tight end Jerry Smith.

The teams could do no more than exchange field goals for most of the second quarter. Then, in the half's final minute, Speedy Duncan, who would have a phenomenal 181 yards in returns before the day was over, returned a 49er punt 47 yards to the San Francisco twelve, leaving his team thirty seconds to come up with what looked like sure points. None materialized, and after the game, Allen was to say, "The game's big, big play was right at the end of the half, when we came away without any points."

A four-yard flat pass to Charley Harraway at the eight-yard line used up four seconds and then Kilmer called an end around to wide receiver Roy Jefferson. Unfooled was 49er defensive end Cedrick Hardman, who caught Jefferson one-on-one before he ever left the backfield for a thirteen-yard loss.

A third-and-nineteen pass went awry, and with only six seconds left in the half the Redskins were down to trying to get at least three points. But Len Hauss' snap was inept and enabled the 49ers to block Curt Knight's field goal attempt. Instead of getting a last-second lift, the Redskins went into the locker room mentally down despite their 10-3 advantage.

Ironically, that play to Jefferson was to become perhaps the most remembered of the whole season, much utilized by political cartoonists and the like. For Redskins lineman Bill Brundige revealed on television the following night that the nation's number one Redskin fan had called coach Allen the night before the game with an executive request.

"President Nixon told Coach Allen, 'I'd like to see you run a flanker reverse with Roy Jefferson against the 49ers,'" Brundige said. So much for presidential prerogative.

In the opening minutes of the second half, there was to be a further surprise. Duncan took the opening kickoff from his own end zone all the way to the San Francisco thirty-four, and seven plays later the Redskins were faced with a fourth and inches on the San Francisco eleven.

Normally a bulwark of football conservatism, Allen, possibly because of the two Curt Knight misses of the week before, passed up the seemingly sure field goal that would have given his team a 13-3 advantage and chose instead to go for the inches. The Redskins didn't make it, and the San Francisco *Examiner* was to run a front-page bannerline the next day referring to that call and asking in rather large type, "Did Redskins Coach Allen Goof?"

"It amazed the hell out of me," defensive tackle Charlie Krueger said later. "That's not the George Allen I know. If he makes the field goal, he's ahead thirteen to three and maybe — who knows? — psychologically it would have done us in."

"It was just inches," Allen explained wearily afterward. "We made it the first time [on the way to the Redskins' first touchdown]. The percentages were in our favor to pick it up. It was just a few inches."

The play itself came from Kilmer, who asked for a sweep to the left by Larry Brown, with Harraway blocking, the same play that scored a key touchdown against Los Angeles. "It's one of our basic short-yardage plays, where Larry picks a hole and usually goes outside," Kilmer said. "I figured them to play tighter than they did. On another situation they'd left a little gap, and I thought they'd close the thing down. Well, it just didn't work."

The reason it didn't work was that linebacker Frank Nunley, who had earlier blocked Knight's field goal try, had correctly guessed the way Kilmer was guessing, caught Brown for a two-yard loss, and enabled the 49ers to take over on downs. It was the play he and most of his teammates felt, "turned the tide around, made us get going."

"I was anticipating them running off-tackle, so I angled the linemen outside and I took the middle myself. If it's a wide play I have a big hole through the center to shoot into. Sure

I was taking a risk. If they had gone up the middle we would've been in trouble. But when you get into games like this, you've got to take risks. Look at the one they took."

Egged on by this, quarterback Brodie, after first finely faking the ball to fullback Ken Willard, threw "the only spiral I had all day" just three plays later, fooling even the television cameraman in the process. The ball carried thirty-eight yards to the Redskins forty, where wide receiver Gene Washington caught it just behind a lunging Pat Fischer and ran unimpeded into the end zone for a seventy-eight-yard touchdown play that tied the game at 10-10.

"Darn," Fischer said afterward, seemingly about to break up, "I thought that ball was coming right down.

"I don't know what happened, really. I was concentrating on the ball and suddenly it got by me. It came down to the one last step. I wish I had an impression of that last step.

"I wasn't fooled. When the ball was thrown I knew I would either intercept or at least knock it down. It was coming down right on me and I jumped. I guess I jumped prematurely. I don't see how I missed it. I keep seeing the ball.

"I've known this for a long time. You become a bum by one inch. That's how much I missed that ball by."

Receiver Washington had the explanation ready. "The wind got the ball and carried it a little, just enough for me to get under it," he said. "If the wind hadn't carried it, I'm sure Fischer would have gotten his hand on it.

"I never saw Fischer. I never saw his hand. All I saw was about thirty-six lights and finally a BB. All I could think of was how if I dropped it, forty-five thousand people would call me an ass.

"It was a calculated risk, throwing on third and one, but we had to take it. We needed somebody to give us a lift. Up to that point the Redskins had been kicking our ass. Then the defense made a big play, the offense made another right on top of it, and you could feel the game turn around."

Turn around it did. Less than five minutes later, the 49ers, having intercepted a Kilmer pass and profited by a pass interference penalty against Mike Bass that put the ball on the Washington six, were to get the go-ahead touchdown.

With third and two on the two, the Redskins were caught looking for the run by a pass to tight end Bob Windsor that went for the score. An off-season resident of Silver Spring, Maryland, a Washington suburb, Windsor observed, "I guess I won't be too popular when I get home."

There was worse yet to come. With 3:40 to go, after a field goal by Knight had cut the margin to 17-13, the Redskins Mike Bragg lined up near his own end zone to punt, three straight incomplete passes by Kilmer having stalled his team at fourth and ten on its own fourteen.

In to snap the ball, as always, was former Ram George Burman, coaxed out of retirement by Allen for just that purpose. Generally flawless all season, Burman chose this particular snap, his sixty-fifth and last of the season, to have the ball bounce a yard in front of Bragg and squirt between his legs into the end zone. A quartet of 49ers chased after Bragg and the ball, with special teams' member Bob Hoskins submarining under Bragg's lunge to fall on it and record a touchdown.

The Redskins tried to fight back, getting a touchdown of their own ninety-five seconds later on a sixteen-yard pass from Kilmer to Brown, but it was too late. Their last shot came with a first down on their own thirty-seven with forty-nine seconds left in the game. However, Kilmer could only complete one of five passes and was ignominiously buried by San Francisco's Hardman for a thirteen-yard loss as the gun sounded. Final score: 49ers 24, Redskins 20. The future was no longer now.

The walk from the rain-drenched field down a long echoing corridor to their dressing room was a stony-eyed one for the Redskins, the complete silence broken only by the single word "shit" shouted in agony by reserve linebacker Harold McLinton, who had been victimized on the Windsor touchdown. Offensive tackle Water Rock was hyperventilating like a steam engine, Kilmer bled from a cut on his cheek, defensive tackle Diron Talbert looked in an advanced state of glassy-eyed shock. Only the smooth professional Jack Pardee walked in calmly with his head held up.

"You spend six months working for this shot," he said later, "and then we don't get it. It was in our hands."

After all were in, the doors closed, leaving everyone else, including team president Edward Bennett Williams and his companion, Joe DiMaggio, the Yankee Clipper, to wait in the chilled hallway for nearly half an hour. By the time the door reopened, some of the 49ers had already dressed and gone home.

The charging phalanx of reporters literally backed Allen into a corner surrounded by duffel bags containing sweaty gear. As always after a loss, he was testy and in no mood to suffer what he considered foolish or obvious questions.

"I'm only going to say this once," he began. "I'm very proud of our football team. We had a great season, we overcame a great deal of adversity to get this far. We made too many mistakes and they didn't make any, that's why we lost. I said before the team making the fewest mistakes would win.

"I thought we had it, we had the opportunities, excellent field position for the most part, but we didn't take advantage of it. It's a bitter pill to swallow as everyone knows."

When a San Francisco reporter asked what adversities he was referring to, Allen snapped back, "I guess you haven't followed the Redskins this year."

Allen was equally short with the man who asked whether Brodie's long third-and-one touchdown pass to Washington had fooled the Redskins.

"The Forty-niners didn't do anything that fooled us. Brodie's been doing that for ten years," he said. "We had him covered but he misjudged the ball. That's all."

The coach did say that one of the reasons the reporters had been kept waiting was that he had been busy receiving final consolation from the White House.

"The President just called about two minutes ago," Allen

explained. "He said we played a fine game, that all of Washington is proud of the team, and to relay the message to them.

"I just hung up. I haven't had a chance to tell the players yet with all you guys trapping me here," he concluded.

Looking most in need of consolation was center Burman who alternated between tears and a literal state of uncomprehending shock as he sat between minister Tom Skinner and guard John Wilbur, moving only to receive a long embrace from McLinton.

Though speech was difficult, he said the same thing to all the reporters who sought him out, "There was nothing the matter. The ball was fine. Everything was fine. I just made a bad snap. It's the first time in my life that's happened. I can't explain it, I didn't do anything different. George trusted me and I let him down. You know, I never made a bad pass in my life. I blew it, just blew it."

In other areas, the scene was less painful. Charlie Krueger came in to talk to old buddy Kilmer, and Maxie Baughan went over to the 49ers room to see exactly what Bruce Gossett had on his mind.

The two retreated to a far corner to avoid reporters, and seemed to make peace with each other. "It's all settled," Baughan said afterward. "I know that Bruce has some kind of thing against George, that's all. But our differences are settled."

"We cleared the air," added Gossett. "He did not mean what he said and I did not mean what I said. When I made the statement I was being crowded by reporters and things went a little too fast."

Back in the Redskin dressing room, while most of the players were already dressed and gone, Burman still sat naked by his locker. Finally, he put on a towel and, with a similarly clad George Allen, his hand on the center's shoulder, went in to shower and try to forget.

The next day in Washington, after taking a sleeping pill that, like many of the plays of the game, didn't work, Allen agreed to a press conference where he characteristically promised "a better football team next year."

No one in the organization could really believe that the successful season many people had never thought possible in the first place had finally ended. One assistant looked out at the two sun-drenched football fields and said wistfully, "It would have been a great day to be practicing."

Allen, not surprisingly, was already looking ahead, announcing the most extensive off-season training program in Redskins history and moving the future up just one more year.

"I'm glad we could give the Washington area a championship-caliber team," he said. "But I'd like to improve. You have to improve."

There would be no lack of recognition for Allen's efforts that year. In addition to UPI's already awarded accolade as NFC coach of the year, he would be given the same honor for the entire league by the Associated Press, *Pro Football Weekly*, *Gridiron*, the Touchdown Clubs of Washington, Columbus, and Kansas City, and most gratifyingly, the *Sporting News* award, voted by his fellow coaches.

Still, when he was to look back on that first year in Washington some months after the season ended, it was the mistakes that he dwelled on. If he had it to do over again in the 49ers game, Allen admitted, "We would not have run the reverse and we would have kicked a field goal. But it was only inches to go and I felt that if we'd made that play we would have won the game easily. I've looked at the film several times . . .

"I felt we had the game under control and could have won it but we beat ourselves. That's why it was frustrating. We made so many critical mistakes. Like the fumbled punt, the missed field goal at the half, the early fumble in the game, the end around, the fourth and inches, all those goshdanged things.

"Any one of those, if we make any one of those, we might win the game . . ."

He would look back on all of these things, and more. It was the extreme effort of it all from the very beginning, the problems that he kept making believe didn't exist, that, looking back, seemed to have made the biggest impression on him.

"Nobody knows what I went through, from the time I took the Redskin job up to today," he said. "The work, the agony, it hasn't been easy. In fact, my family still hasn't gotten over it. Mrs. Allen still hasn't gotten over it.

"It took so much energy and so many frustrations and I beat myself up physically, flying back and forth, with that biological change, you know, that I wouldn't do it again.

"In fact, I'll tell you what, I wouldn't go through this program again from the start to the finish for anything. I mean I wouldn't go through it for ten million dollars."